Sam Shepard

Twayne's United States Authors Series

Frank Day, Editor
Clemson University

TUSAS 612

SAM SHEPARD
Photograph by Steve Ringman, San Francisco Chronicle

Sam Shepard

David J. DeRose

Yale University

Twayne Publishers • New York
Maxwell Macmillan Canada • Toronto
Maxwell Macmillan International • New York Oxford Singapore Sydney

Sam Shepard
David J. DeRose

Twayne Publishers
Macmillan Publishing Company
866 Third Avenue
New York, New York 10022

Maxwell Macmillan Canada, Inc.
1200 Eglinton Avenue East
Suite 200
Don Mills, Ontario M3C 3N1

Macmillan Publishing Company is a member of the Maxwell Communication Group
of Companies.

Library of Congress Cataloging-in-Publication Data

DeRose, David J.
    Sam Shepard / David J. DeRose.
        p.   cm.—(Twayne's United States authors s   612)
    Includes bibliographical references and index.
    ISBN 0-8057-3964-5 (alk. paper)
    1. Shepard, Sam, 1943–   —Criticism and interpretation.
    I. Title. II. Series.
    PS3569.H394Z67   1992
    812'.54—dc20
                                 92-13511
                                   CIP

10 9 8 7 6 5 4 3 2 1

Printed and bound in the United States of America

For Darlene

Contents

Preface

For over 20 years, Sam Shepard has been considered one of the most talented and important playwrights of his generation. He is the winner of a Pulitzer Prize in drama for his 1978 play *Buried Child* and of nearly a dozen Obie Awards for theatrical achievement in New York's Off-Off-Broadway district. He is the author of more than 40 plays for the stage, three collections of prose, poetry, and memoirs, and six produced screenplays, among them *Paris, Texas,* winner of the Palme D'Or at the 1984 Cannes Film Festival. Shepard's singular vision of the American heartland, especially of the small towns and rural landscape of the American West and Southwest, has gained him the unofficial title of poet laureate of the American West. Theater-goers flock to his family dramas and to the films in which his western maverick persona has made him a minor legend in his own time.

Previous studies of Shepard have focused with dulling repetition on his Americana image, treating Shepard more as a social and literary phenomenon than a theater artist. This study proposes that if Shepard's works are to be fully appreciated, his theatrical intentions as well as his thematic ones must be considered, and a common ground between the two must be established. That common ground is Shepard's preoccupation with heightened or "critical" states of consciousness manifesting themselves in a perception of the self and the world as unfixed. Such states are realized theatrically in the action and stage imagery of Shepard's hallucinatory early plays and again in his jazz-inspired plays of the mid-1970s. They are also articulated by Shepard's characters in plays as different as *Action, Suicide in B-Flat,* and *A Lie of the Mind.*

In order to appreciate this theatrical and thematic current in Shepard's work, it is essential to make a close reading of Shepard's plays and reviews of those plays in production, focusing on Shepard's stage directions, his use of visual imagery, and his physical staging. It is also essential to view his more popular and well-known works in light of his obscure, unpublished, and supposedly "lost" plays. This book is the first published study of Shepard's work to take advantage of personal and archival collections of Shepard's unpublished plays and to include discussions of such "lost" plays as *Cowboys*, *Dog*, *The Rocking Chair*, *Up to Thursday*, and *Blue Bitch*. Thanks to an invaluable interview with composer Catherine Stone, close attention is also paid to Shepard's improvisationally based musical drama, *Inacoma*, and the impact that piece and Shepard's study of jazz music has had on his stagecraft and on his collaborations for voice, music, and percussion with actor/director Joseph Chaikin. In light of these minor works, such Shepard masterworks as *La Turista*, *Tooth of Crime*, *Action*, and the family plays take on new meaning, demonstrating a new commonality, hitherto unexplored, between the various periods of Shepard's career.

Acknowledgments

Grateful acknowledgment is made to Ross Wetzsteon for permission to reprint excerpts from his "Introduction" to *Fool for Love and Other Plays* (New York: Bantam Books, 1984).

I am deeply indebted to Catherine Stone for sharing her insights and her personal materials from the Overtone Theatre and from her work on *Inacoma*, *Superstitions*, and *Pecos Bill*. Special thanks to Margaret Dunn and to John Lion, both formerly of the Magic Theatre, San Francisco, for their insights on Sam Shepard's work at the Magic and for granting me access to production and publicity files, to script storage, and to personal materials. To Ralph Cook, wherever he may be, I am indebted for his Shepard anecdotes and for the Theatre Genesis materials he loaned me from among his personal papers. Many thanks, also, to Robert Goldsby, Angela Paton, and Robert MacDougall, all formerly of the Berkeley Stage Company, and to the late Professor George House, of the University of California. Thanks to Professors Thomas Whitaker and George Ferencz of the Yale Theater Studies Program, to Pam Jordan of the Yale School of Drama Library, and to Patrick Fennell, Leonard Wilcox, David Feiner, Marvin McAllister, and Elizabeth Hackett.

Thanks to the staff and collections of Bancroft Library, U.C. Berkeley; Shields Library, U.C. Davis; Mugar Library, Boston University; and the Yale School of Drama Library.

Portions of this book have appeared in fragments and various early drafts in the following essays:

"*Fool for Love*" [theater review]. *Theatre Journal* 36 (March 1984).

"Heirs of Passion." Program essay for the Teatro Aberto (Lisbon) production of *Loucos por Amor* (*Fool for Love*). Edited by Vera San Payo de Lemos (Lisbon: Novo Grupo, 1990).

"'A Kind of Cavorting': Superpresence and Shepard's Family Dramas." In *Sam Shepard: Contemporary Critical Interpretations*, edited by Leonard Wilcox (London: Macmillan Co., 1992).

Lobster in the Livingroom: The Theatricality of Sam Shepard. Unpublished Ph.D. dissertation, University of California at Berkeley, 1985.

"The 'Realism' of Sam Shepard." Paper presented at the American Theatre Association Conference, San Francisco, August 1984.

"Slouching towards Broadway: Shepard's *A Lie of the Mind.*" *Theater* 17 (Spring 1986).

Chronology

1943   Samuel Shepard Rogers VII, called Steve by family, born 5 November, Fort Sheridan Army Base, Illinois. First of three children (younger sisters Deedee and Sandy) born to Sam Rogers VI and Jane Elaine Schook Rogers. Until 1949, family follows father's military career from base to base in South Dakota, Utah, Florida, and Guam.

1949   Father leaves Army Air Corps. Family moves to South Pasadena, California. Family lives with aunt.

1955   Family buys avocado ranch in Duarte, California, where "Steve" spends his high school years.

1961   Graduates from Duarte High School. Enrolls for three semesters in Mount Saint Antonio Junior College, majoring in agricultural science.

1962   Joins the Bishop's Company, a touring theatrical company, playing for religious communities across America.

1963   Arrives in New York. Shares Lower East Side apartment with Charles Mingus, Jr., former high school acquaintance and son of famous jazz musician.

1964   Changes name to Sam Shepard. First plays, *The Rock Garden* and *Cowboys*, performed 10 October at Theatre Genesis.

1965   *Up to Thursday* performed at Theatre 1965. *The Rocking Chair* and *Dog* at Cafe La Mama. *4-H Club* at Theatre 1965. *Chicago* at Theatre Genesis (Obie Award). *Icarus's Mother* at Caffe Cino (Obie Award).

1966   *Red Cross* at Judson Poets' Theatre (Obie Award). *Fourteen Hundred Thousand* at Firehouse Theatre, Minneapolis.

1967   *La Turista*, first two-act play, at American Place Theatre (Obie Award). *Melodrama Play* at La Mama (Obie Award). *Cowboys #2* at Mark Taper Forum, Los Angeles. *Forensic and the Navigators* at Theatre Genesis (Obie Award). Meets actress O-Lan Johnson.

1968 Works on screenplay for Michelangelo Antonioni's film *Zabriskie Point* (1970).

1969 Marries O-Lan Johnson. *The Holy Ghostly* on tour, La Mama New Troupe. *The Unseen Hand* at La Mama.

1970 *Operation Sidewinder* at Lincoln Center. *Shaved Splits* at La Mama. Birth of son, Jesse Mojo.

1971 *Mad Dog Blues* at Theatre Genesis. *Cowboy Mouth* (with Patti Smith) at Traverse Theatre, Edinburgh, and American premiere at American Place Theatre. *Back Bog Beast Bait* at American Place Theatre. Moves to London with O-Lan and Jesse to become a rock musician.

1972 *The Tooth of Crime* at Open Space Theatre, London, and American premiere at Princeton University.

1973 *Blue Bitch* at Theatre Genesis and on BBC Television, London. *Hawk Moon*, collection of short prose and poetry, published.

1974 *Geography of a Horse Dreamer* at Theatre Upstairs (Royal Court), London. *Little Ocean* at Hampstead Theatre Club, London. *Action* at Theatre Upstairs (Royal Court), London. Returns to California.

1975 *Action* with *Killer's Head* have simultaneous American premieres at Magic Theatre, San Francisco, and American Place Theatre, New York (Obie Award).

1976 *Angel City* at Magic Theatre, San Francisco. *Suicide in B-Flat* at Yale Repertory Theatre, New Haven. *The Sad Lament of Pecos Bill on the Eve of Killing His Wife* at Bay Area Playwrights Festival, San Francisco.

1977 *Inacoma* at the Magic Theatre, San Francisco. *Curse of the Starving Class* at the Royal Court, London. *Rolling Thunder Logbook*, journal of a Bob Dylan tour, published.

1978 *Seduced* at American Place Theatre. *Tongues* (with Joseph Chaikin) at Magic Theatre, San Francisco. *Buried Child* at Magic Theatre. Appears in film *Days of Heaven*.

1979 Awarded Pulitzer Prize for *Buried Child*. *Savage/Love* (with Joseph Chaikin) at Magic Theatre, San Francisco. *Jacaranda* (text to accompany dance by Daniel Nagrin) at Saint Clemment's Church, New York.

1980 *True West* at Magic Theatre. Appears in film *Resurrection*.

1981 *Superstitions* (under name of Walker Hayes) with Overtone Theatre at Intersection Theatre, San Francisco. Appears in film *Raggedy Man*.

1982   *Motel Chronicles*, collection of short prose and poetry, published. Appears in film *Frances* with Jessica Lange.

1983   *Fool for Love* at Magic Theatre, San Francisco; play is moved to Circle Repertory Company in New York (Obie Award). Appears as Chuck Yeager in film *The Right Stuff*; receives Academy Award nomination for Best Supporting Actor.

1984   Screenplay for film *Paris, Texas*, directed by Wim Wenders, wins Palme D'or for Best Film at Cannes Festival. Shepard appears in film *Country* with Jessica Lange. Death of father, Sam Rogers. Divorce from O-Lan Johnson Shepard. Shepard begins living with Jessica Lange.

1985   *A Lie of the Mind* at Promenade Theatre (New York Drama Critics Circle Award for Best Play). *The War in Heaven* (with Joseph Chaikin) on WBAI radio, New York. Appears in Robert Altman's film adaptation of *Fool for Love*.

1986   Appears in film *Crimes of the Heart*. A daughter, Hannah, is born to Shepard and Lange.

1987   Appears in film *Baby Boom*. A son, Samuel, is born to Shepard and Lange.

1988   Writes screenplay for and directs film *Far North*, starring Jessica Lange.

1989   Appears in film *Steel Magnolias.*

1991   *States of Shock* at the American Place Theatre.

Chapter One
Sam Shepard: Self-Made Myth

My name came down through seven generations of men with the same name each naming the first son the same name as the father then the mothers nicknaming the sons so as not to confuse them with the fathers when hearing their names called in the open air while working side by side in the waist-high wheat.

—Sam Shepard[1]

He has been immortalized on screen and in the tabloids as the man with "the right stuff." In some circles, he is even called "the thinking woman's beefcake." He is tall, dark, and ruggedly handsome; his brooding, silent film persona has been compared to Gary Cooper's. His story is the stuff of which American dreams are made. He lives a sequestered family life in the Virginia countryside with two of his children and with their mother, Jessica Lange, one of the most beautiful, talented, and intelligent stars of the film industry. He has been nominated for an academy award; he has appeared in more than 10 films with such notable romantic costars as Brooke Adams, Kim Basinger, Ellen Burstyn, Barbara Hershey, Diane Keaton, Jessica Lange, and Sissy Spacek. He has written more than half a dozen screenplays, including *Paris, Texas* which won the Palme D'Or at the 1984 Cannes Film Festival; and, most recently, he made his film-directing debut with his own screenplay, *Far North.*

He also just happens to be the Pulitzer Prize–winning author of more than 40 plays, and he is generally considered the most talented dramatist in America.

There is no little irony in the fact that Sam Shepard's relatively recent career as a film actor has brought him more fame than has his quarter of a century of writing plays. Like Rabbit Brown, the mystical script-writer of *Angel City* (1976), Shepard has always been both lured and repelled by the film industry. He satirizes it in *Angel City* and regularly harpoons it in print and interview. Much of his work has been an attempt to deconstruct the inflated American myths perpetuated by Hollywood, and his plays are often send-ups of B-movie plots, peopled with ridiculous matinee idols. The last thing Shepard ever wanted was to become one of those idols himself or to be seen as a part of that dream machine.

Yet, like Rabbit Brown, Shepard has been unable to "stay immune." Throughout his career, his work as a dramatist has been subtly influenced by his public image, as though he had to live up to his own press clippings. Sam Shepard has created his own myth, but his life and his art seem to be a constant struggle to retain control of that myth.

The man known to the American public as Sam Shepard was born Samuel Shepard Rogers VII on 5 November 1943 at the Fort Sheridan Military Base in Illinois. As a child, he was known as "Steve" to distinguish him from his father. But when Steve Rogers traveled to New York City in 1963, he reinvented himself. Erasing the identity bestowed upon him by his immediate family and denying seven generations of blood and heritage, he dropped both the given name of Steve and the surname Rogers, which he considered corny (it reminded him of Roy Rogers). Sam Shepard, renegade playwright and overnight genius, was created. "We act ourselves out," one of his characters has said. And in Sam Shepard's career, he has acted out several selves. His artistic identity and public persona have been marked by an endless string of disappearing acts in which the mask we took to be Sam Shepard is shed, and he reinvents himself anew. Yet one of the patterns of Sam Shepard's career has been the gradual acknowledgement of and reacquaintance with the social, geographical, and hereditary elements that made up young Steve, or Samuel Shepard Rogers VII.

For the first several years of his life, Shepard and his family moved from military base to military base, following his father, a serviceman in the Army Air Corps. They lived in Illinois, South Dakota, Utah, Florida, and Guam, where Shepard says Japanese soldiers, hermits from World War II, lived in the caves and stole from the huts of American families. Eventually, Shepard's father withdrew from military service and his family settled in Southern California, first with an aunt in South Pasadena and eventually on an avocado ranch in Duarte, a small rural community about 30 miles due east of Los Angeles.

Shepard is a product of the post–World War II era and the now-romanticized Eisenhower years. America was under the sway of a Hollywood dream machine that was busy generating images of a victorious postwar America, a righteous and innocent Audie Murphy America of heroic proportions and bigger-than-life stars and adventures. As Shepard's work demonstrates, he spent a lot of time in the movie house under the hypnotic spell of matinee cowboys, gangsters, and exotic adventurers. It is likely he frequented the drive-in as well since cars were a prominent feature of life in the teen culture of the time. As Shepard recalls it, hours upon hours were spent "sitting in [your car] at A and W Rootbeer stands. Sitting in it at the school parking lot. Cruising Bob's Big Boy. Racing some chump in a Hudson Hornet on Friday night."[2] But Shepard's generation is marked by the loss of such innocence: like the world of James Dean's "rebel without a cause," the 1950s were a time when the institution of the family began to dissolve; when sons turned to ineffectual and absent fathers for strength and love, and found none; when basically good kids got killed in car crashes; when the society of parents no longer sustained its offspring; and, when the myths of Hollywood's America were found sadly wanting by its youth. This was the advent of the postmodern era in America, when media-generated myths grew to such proportions and with such speed that they lost all connection to the reality from which they once sprang. They became hollow simulacra infiltrating all aspects of America's cultural identity, but no longer capable of sustaining its inhabitants.

The impact of such cultural images and the inability of those images to sustain meaning are evident everywhere in Shepard's work, from the would-be western heroes of *Cowboys* (1964) to the technocratic bumblers of *Operation Sidewinder* (1970) and the syndicate mobsters of *Geography of a Horse Dreamer* (1974). Also evident in Shepard's work is the impact of the postwar population, transportation, and industrial boom on the world as young Steve knew it. Fredric Jameson, in his essay on postmodernism and consumer society, describes a world much like the one in which Shepard grew up.

At some point following World War II a new kind of society began to emerge (variously described as postindustrial society, multinational capitalism, consumer society, media society and so forth). New types of consumption; planned obsolescence; an even more rapid rhythm of fashion and styling changes; the penetration of advertising, television and the media generally to a hitherto unparalleled degree throughout society; the replacement of the old tension between city and country, center and province, by the suburb and the universal standardization; the growth of the great network of superhighways and the arrival of the automobile culture—these are some of the features which would seem to mark a radical break with that older prewar society.[3]

For Shepard, and for Duarte, California, the postwar suburban expansion of Los Angeles broke like a tidal wave over a previously rural life-style. Shepard's description of towns like Duarte reiterates much of what Jameson writes: "They grew out of nothing and nowhere. Originally the valley was covered with citrus groves. The kind you see in Hollywood postcards from the thirties and forties. Rows of neat shining lemon trees and orange trees with smudge pots. . . . Eventually Los Angeles had a population kick back. . . . Weird government industries began to sprout up. Places where they make nose cones and satellite tape recorders. People had work. It was a temporary society that became permanent" ("Azusa," I). This sudden destruction of a traditional, agrarian way of life and of the attachment of farmers to the land appears literally in Shepard's autobiographically based play, *Curse of the Starving Class* (1977), in which developers attempt to hustle a rural family out of their suddenly valuable property. Still, it is not this specific socioeconomic event, but rather the accompanying trauma—the shattering of one's personal and cultural mythology, one's sense of self and the world—that is far more significant to Shepard's work.

Sam Shepard's plays are about a world that has come unfixed. A world in which reality as we know it proves an illusion and we find ourselves at odds with our environment, our beliefs, our heritage, our cultural myths, our sense of personal identity, even our spiritual selves. We find ourselves at odds with, unfixed from, the universe at large. This theme runs through Shepard's plays, in various incarnations, from first to last: from the displaced youths of *Cowboys* (1964), at odds with the urban environment in which they find themselves, to Beth, the battered wife in *A Lie of the Mind* (1985), who must recreate her world and herself from scratch. Shepard's characters exit in heightened or critical states of hyperconsciousness and agitation, and the world around them reflects that agitation. The theatrical implications of such states are the building blocks of Shepard's disturbing theatrical vision. One might say that we, as American theatergoers, have been the fortunate beneficiaries of Shepard's personal postmodern discomfort.

This study examines the entirety of Shepard's dramatic output to date in light of the ways in which his exploded vision of reality, society, and the self are manifest in theme, dramatic structure, and theatrical presentation. Shepard's plays do not fall neatly into categories, but for the sake of this study I have attempted to group them according to some of the dominant chronological, theatrical, and thematic patterns of his career.

Shepard's early plays, climaxing with *La Turista* (1967) and the revised *Cowboys #2* (1967), have less to do with theme or plot than with the pure theatrical expression of acute, and usually highly personal, states of psychic agitation. As Shepard said many years later, "Many of my plays center around a character in a critical state of consciousness. I like to operate off that dynamic."[4] Standing in for Shepard at the center of most of these early plays is a "Young Man," frequently appearing out of place or out of touch with his surroundings. Because the media-fed Shepard drew so heavily on popular culture images in these early plays, critics worked overtime trying to give them meaning. But Shepard himself appeared neither conscious of nor interested in the social ramifications of his plays from this period.

It is not until late in 1967, when Italian filmmaker Michelangelo Antonioni approached Shepard to write the screenplay for a film on America's youthful counterculture, that Shepard's work begins to show the signs of a growing social consciousness. As if others, like Antonioni and the press, had brought his attention to the potential significance of his pastiche creations, Shepard assumes the role they have set forth for him: he attempts to become the chronicler of America's decay, and his work exhibits a greater and greater effort to create a meaningful statement about postmodern America through his surreal juxtaposition of pop culture milieus. Starting with *Forensic and the Navigators* (1967), continuing through *Operation Sidewinder* and the plays of the early 1970s, and culminating in *The Tooth of Crime* (1972), Shepard's plays from this period are peopled with figures from American film and folklore who embody the battle between our spiritual and cultural heritage and the empty, high-tech simulations of life we accept as modern civilization. Gone is the personal agitation, so acute in the earlier plays; it is replaced by the vague social and cultural malaise of the early 1970s, the malaise of an America still at war in Vietnam and only beginning to understand the repercussions of the Watergate scandal.

In the midst of this period, in 1971, Shepard moved to London in the hope of reinventing himself once again and becoming a rock-and-roll star. But in England, Shepard was struck by the same sense of rootlessness and personal agitation that drove him from New York City. Although the trip resulted in two of his most important plays—*The Tooth of Crime* and *Action* (1975)—Shepard returned to the United States late in 1974 and settled in the San Francisco Bay Area.

As early as 1967, with *Melodrama Play*, rock-and-roll music was making inroads into Shepard's writing. In Shepard's plays of the late 1960s and early 1970s, live bands are frequently incorporated in the plots. Possibly Shepard's greatest critical and popular success, *The Tooth of Crime*, is a kind of rock-and-roll tragedy with the characters singing their laments to harsh electronic tones. But when Shepard arrived in San Francisco in 1974, he began to explore the more fluid qualities of jazz.

The experimentations he began at this time with improvised jazz music, percussion, and the human voice, eventually led to his successful artistic collaboration with Joseph Chaikin, actor, director, and founder of the Open Theatre. Improvised jazz was, for Shepard, just one more manifestation of reality coming unfixed. In *Suicide in B-Flat* (1976), the "free-form" music and life-style of jazz musicians are seen as threats to at least one character's grip on reality.

While Shepard was improvising with jazz music, he reinvented himself once more, writing two family dramas—*Curse of The Starving Class* and *Buried Child* (1978)—and taking his career into what was for him entirely uncharted territory. As Samuel G. Freedman has noted, "Whatever else any great American playwright has done . . . the measure of achievement in American drama has been a writer's ability to place a vivid family portrait within a larger, societal frame."[5] In 1979, Shepard—who once said, "I'm not interested in writing a treatise on the American family"[6]—won the Pulitzer Prize in drama for *Buried Child*, thus fulfilling Freedman's maxim and placing himself within the ranks of the American canonical mainstream of drama. While *Buried Child* can be called neither conventional nor naturalistic—it is, as this study demonstrates, "suprarealistic," and thus yet another theatrical incarnation of reality unfixed—it is Shepard's increasingly conventional family plays, appearing side by side with his highly publicized film career, that have brought widespread attention and popular acclaim to this one-time renegade of Off-Off-Broadway.

Shepard's film career has no place in this study; and although he has been canonized by those who see him as a chronicler of America and the American family, that is not my intent. While Shepard's vision of the American people cannot be ignored, and while his family histories touch an archetypal chord in us all, the demons that drive him to write for the stage are extremely personal. His is a world unfixed: a world in which we have lost or rejected those things that make us whole; a world where sons reject, and must rediscover, their heritage; a world in which a multimillion-dollar computer is created to achieve the ends once accomplished through communal ritual; a world in which we are suddenly strangers, even when we return to the place we once called home; a world in which artists have lost the roots of their inspiration and heroes don't remember what heroism is; a world that remains seemingly unchanged but that has actually turned into a foreign planet before our eyes.

Shepard's accomplishment as a dramatist has been to share his personal trauma through a highly physical and disturbing theatrical vocabulary of words, theatrical images, and physical staging that manifest the strangeness of his characters' world (and ours), not just in spoken language and dramatic events but in time, space, sound, and sight before us on the stage.

Chapter Two
Cowboys and Indian Country

With the exception of *The Rock Garden* (1964), none of Shepard's earliest plays has survived in performance past its first production. Shepard has never wanted to publish these plays nor to circulate them for further production. Despite the claim by most Shepard scholars that *Cowboys* (1964), *Up to Thursday* (1964), *Dog* (1965), and *The Rocking Chair* (1965) are "lost" plays, copies of the typescripts of all these early Shepard works exist in various libraries and personal collections.[1]

For the most part, these plays have earned the obscurity to which they have been relegated. *Cowboys* is survived by the far more tightly crafted *Cowboys #2* (1967), and *Dog, The Rocking Chair,* and *Up to Thursday* are noteworthy, as is Shepard's *Fourteen Hundred Thousand* (1966), primarily for their transparent debt to the theater of the absurd and to such popular playwrights of the early 1960s as Samuel Beckett, Eugene Ionesco, and Edward Albee. Yet, however awkward or derivative in style and presentation these plays may be, their presence in this study helps to shed additional light on Shepard's early experimentations with hallucinatory language and his obsession with altered states of consciousness and awareness.

Up to Thursday, Dog, and *The Rocking Chair* all radiate the anxiety of a hapless young man at painful odds with his hostile environment. In this respect, they foreshadow *Chicago* (1965), *Icarus's Mother* (1965), and *La Turista* (1967). The earliest of the "lost" plays, *Cowboys* also creates a palpable friction between its young heroes and their environs. It offers too the unique opportunity to glance back at an early draft of Shepard's *Cowboys #2*, giving one a far richer understanding of the maturing of Shepard's style and aims in that revised version of his first play.

The Rock Garden and *Cowboys*

The Rock Garden and *Cowboys* were first produced under the direction of Ralph Cook at the Theatre Genesis in October 1964. In both thematic concern and theatrical technique these two plays embody the spirit of many of Shepard's more mature writings. *The Rock Garden* foreshadows

8

Shepard's family plays, addressing issues of domestic life, heredity, the alienation of youth, and the dissolution of the family unit. *Cowboys* prefigures another major trend in Shepard's writing: the deification and the decline of American pop culture icons—in this case, cowboys of the old West. As a double bill, the two plays serve as a dramatic prologue to Shepard's work in the theater.

The Rock Garden has been viewed as a triptych of family tedium:[2] three short scenes, each reflecting the barren landscape of the title, address various aspects of the generational and sexual void between members of a small family. The scenes are short and uncomplicated, yet each is dominated by a startling visual image. In the first scene (absent from the original production),[3] a man, a teenage boy, and a girl sit at a dinner table. The man (the father, one presumes) reads a magazine, while the boy and girl sit across the table from each other, passing a glass of milk back and forth in silence and occasionally exchanging glances. The extended silence is broken only when the girl suddenly drops and spills the glass of milk. A blackout follows.

In the second scene, a woman lies in bed, her body hidden under several layers of blankets. Beside her, the teenage boy sits in a rocking chair, wearing only his underpants. The woman talks incessantly, mentioning family camping trips, burnt marshmallows, snake bites, poisonous mushrooms, and catching cold. The boy's contributions to the conversation are virtually monosyllabic. Three times the woman compares the boy's features to his father's or grandfather's; each time, the boy leaves the room and returns with the inherited feature covered by clothing, finally wrapping himself in an overcoat. When the man appears, also in an overcoat, the boy exits hurriedly. The man then strips to his underwear and sits in the rocking chair. The woman is now silent, staring at the ceiling.

The final scene of *The Rock Garden* was included in Kenneth Tynan's stage manifesto of sexual liberation, *Oh! Calcutta* (1969). In this scene, the man and boy both appear again in their underwear. As in the previous scene, a rambling monologue is accompanied by a nearly static stage image. The man, sitting on a couch, sermonizes on the proper maintenance of his yard and, in particular, of the rock garden he has started by the driveway. The boy, sitting in a chair facing upstage, his back to the man, adds a question or comment only occasionally. More frequently, he nods off, falling from his chair. The man punctuates his speech with "You know?" and "You know what I mean?" The boy never responds. After a final "You know?" and a long pause, the boy suddenly explodes into a graphic cataloging of sexual pleasures. He, too, punctuates his

speech with "You know?", but now the refrain takes on a calculated
edge. Eventually, the man falls off the couch.

In an interview much later in his career, Shepard described his search
for a symbolic gestural language that would "take the impulse that was
behind [a moment on stage] to its absolute extreme," while still keeping
it "intrinsic to itself" (Lippman, 45). Certain actions in *The Rock Garden*,
such as the spilling of the milk or the man's fall from the couch, appear
to fulfill precisely this function. One recognizes almost immediately that
the dropped glass of milk is no accident but rather the extreme, physical
extension of the tension lurking unspoken between the family members.
Likewise, the play's finale not only illustrates the total lack of common
ground between father and son—neither responds to "You know?"
because neither does know, neither has any point of reference to the
other's world—but climaxes with the man being toppled from his seat
(both figuratively and literally) by the boy's revelation of his inner world.
Shepard invests the son's shocking imagination with a palpable physical
impact that transcends the otherwise static staging of the scene to give
the audience a heightened appreciation of the man's suddenly precarious
condition. What his son has to say to him literally blows him out of his
chair.

However striking these simple gestural images from *The Rock Garden*
might be, it was not Shepard's visual imagery but rather his extraordi-
nary use of idiomatic language that first brought attention to his work
and that, in the play itself, tumbles the father from his couch. Each of the
three speaking characters in the play possesses an idiolect of specific
imagery. The woman talks of childhood and of "angels on horseback," a
snack her father used to make from saltine crackers and toasted marshmallows. The man speaks of sprinkler heads, irrigation pipes, different
shades of white paint, and finding the right rocks for his rock garden,
rocks of "the right size and shape and color and everything."[4] Each
character's specific parlance reflects the nature of his or her personal
reality. The woman lives in a world of childhood and youthful memories;
the man is preoccupied with domestic gadgetry and housework. When
the boy finally ends his silence, his language reveals an inner world
completely foreign to that of his parents: "When I come it's like a river.
It's all over the bed and the sheets and everything. You know? I mean a
short vagina gives me security. I can't help it. I like to feel like I'm really
turning a girl on. It's a much better screw is what it amounts to. I mean
if a girl has a really small vagina it's really better to go in from behind.
You know?" (*RG*, 226). Each of the characters expresses, through his or

her language, a personal mythology of the events, people, and things that make up "the world" as he knows it. The final image of the play, with the father tumbling from his couch, physically manifests the enormous distance between the personal experience of two people occupying the same house. The revelation of the boy's dark and sexual world has the power to topple the man from the comfort of his personal mythology, to shake the world he has built around himself.

Cowboys also deals with the shattering of a worldview and the failure of personal mythology. The phrase *Indian country* referred, in the old West, to those areas of the frontier under the control of the various Indian nations: they were areas of danger, unsecured by the white man's "civilization" or his firepower. During the Vietnam War, "Indian country" again came to represent hostile, unsecured territory: the Indians now being replaced by the Vietcong or North Vietnamese. Eventually, the use of the phrase by Vietnam veterans was expanded to refer to any situation in which one felt threatened, whether physically, mentally, or emotionally. "Indian country" was a state of personal anxiety that could happen anywhere, anytime. When young Sam Shepard—then Steve Rogers—arrived in New York City's Lower East Side, straight off a cross-country bus trip from the tiny farming community of Duarte, California, he found himself in "Indian country." He was, in his friend Joseph Chaikin's words, "like a refugee."[5] Shepard might as well have landed on a foreign planet, or traveled through time, for the world in which he found himself contradicted everything he had known of life to that point. *Cowboys* is unquestionably the work of the young man from Duarte whose previous sense of reality was subtly unfixed by his new environs. Something of a *Waiting for Godot* gone western, the one-act play depicts two young men, surrounded by an apparently hostile urban environment, who try to escape the imposition of that reality by playing at being cowboys, thus creating an alternative world to the one in which they find themselves. But their games do not sustain them, and they are eventually failed by their mythological models. Stu and Chet (thinly disguised versions of Steve and his roommate, Charles) engage in a series of cowboy games and "occupations," meant to fill time and distract them from the surroundings with which they seem constantly at odds. They invent a number of fantasy roles and situations: playing father and son as they practice baseball; pretending to be two old cowboys fighting off Indians, thirst, and death in the desert; splashing in the mud of a sudden cloudburst; and, eventually, fighting to the death over an imaginary canteen.

Stu and Chet have no trouble simulating the outward appearance, behavior, and language of matinee cowboys; and yet neither of them seems to grasp the origins of such romanticized myths. Stu, for instance, easily assumes the role of an old cowhand scanning the ominous black clouds in the distance. But he does not understand the importance of the clouds or his actions. Does he need to find shelter from a storm? Is this the long-awaited end to a drought? Neither Stu nor Chet seems to locate the significance of the narratives they enact. Later, when imaginary rain has covered the stage with mud, the two young men roll about in it, laughing and pounding each other joyfully on the back. But after a few moments of this playfulness, they roll over onto their backs and stare at the ceiling. Again, the outward form of their occupation sustains them momentarily, but it eventually leaves them stranded because they have no first-hand experience or understanding of the lives they simulate.

The play's ambiguous environment is crucial to the antics of the characters. While the action appears to take place in an urban setting, Shepard offers no objective reality, no concrete details about the location or situation within which the two young men find themselves. The only piece of scenery is a "sawhorse" with two blinking yellow lights, placed against the back wall of the stage. One might seek this wooden structure as a kind of visual pun—a sawhorse being the only horse these urbanized cowboys will find in their present surroundings. But the use of the term *sawhorse* on Shepard's part further suggests the distance between his own experience and the city in which he arrived in 1964. For what Shepard describes is not a sawhorse, per se, because it is not used for sawing wood: it is a traffic barrier, painted yellow with flashing caution lights on it. The two wooden structures are in most ways identical, but Shepard, the country boy from Duarte, would never call this object a traffic barrier, and no New Yorker would ever call it a sawhorse.

In contrast to the traffic barrier, which is intrinsically urban, there is another reality, this one rural, suggested by the relentless chirping of an offstage cricket. This chirping, accompanied by the continuous blinking of the yellow lights on the traffic barrier, permanently strands the action of the play between two realities, creating a constant contradiction in setting. The presence of offstage sounds and voices during the opening moments of the play further complicates the relationship between the characters and their environment. The lights come up on Chet and Stu, both dressed entirely in black and apparently sleeping, propped against the back wall of the stage. The cricket is the only sound for several moments, then it is suddenly interrupted by construction noises: the sounds of a saw, a hammer, and a shovel. The first words of the play come from an unidentified voice offstage, which comments that it is going to rain. Stu asks the voice if he thinks so, and Chet, thinking Stu is talking to him, responds. Thus the dialogue begins.[6] However one reads the scene, the identity of the offstage voice remains ambiguous. It could be interpreted as an offstage prompter, giving Chet his first line. Or, if one were to literalize the setting of the play, it might be a worker at a construction site who makes a comment that Stu overhears in his daze and takes for Chet's. In either case, the presence of an offstage character and Stu's response to his comment contradict the stage reality of the two men sleeping by the sawhorse. If the voice is a prompter, the stage's conventional "fourth wall" has ben unceremoniously demolished; if it is a construction worker, Chet's response to Stu's question makes no sense. Like the traffic barrier and the cricket, both possibilities exist simultaneously, but neither excludes the other as it rationally should.

As the play continues, the relationship between the two young men and the offstage sounds becomes increasingly complicated, creating juxtaposed and contradictory planes of reality. City noises such as car horns and the roar of passing buses dominate the earliest portion of the play. Later, as Stu and Chet are drawn into their cowboy fantasies, one hears, as they must, the sounds of approaching rain, of galloping horses, and, finally, of attacking Indians. No distinction is made between the "real" sounds of the city and the "fantasized" sounds of the old West. The rain, for instance, is mentioned by the offstage voice at the beginning of the play and is also incorporated by Stu and Chet into their western scenario, thus suggesting it exists outside their "fantasies." But the rain also disappears when Chet and Stu shift from their old man personas into their normal voices. They start talking about the stars in a sky that, seconds before, was full of rain clouds. Only a few minutes later the harsh sun threatens the cowboys' lives.

In building to the climactic moment of the play, Shepard combines the sounds of the city with those of attacking Indians. Stu and Chet's animosity toward the Indians is transposed into a hatred of the modern urban environment within which their heroic western models have no meaning. Their battle with Indian marauders becomes a battle against urban America and its sprawling suburban masses. When the two characters fire their imaginary guns into the audience, presumably fighting off another Indian attack, it is evident that their real foes are the city dwellers seated in the theater. Two long speeches prepare the audience for this assault. The first, given by Chet, is an account of the rape of the land in which he berates suburbanites who, with their peacocks, swimming pools, and air conditioners, have overrun what was once fertile farmland. Later, Stu undertakes a much more direct attack upon the live audience in the theater, saying they make him sick. What are they whispering about, he wants to know, the size of their air conditioners?

Like the boy's speech at the end of *The Rock Garden*, these speeches are an apparent assault on the status quo of what Shepard must have perceived to be mainstream America. But, whereas the boy's attack was aimed primarily at his father, these characters turn directly upon the audience, expressing a panicked response to a postmodern America in which their personal myths have no meaning and in which they cannot function. These heavy-handed assaults upon the audience did not go over well with Jerry Tallmer of the *New York Post*, who commented that "Mr. Shepard is angry at (a) everybody who must watch his play, (b) everybody in crowded, ugly New York City, (c) everybody."[7] Tallmer's negative review almost brought an early end to Shepard's career. But *Village Voice* critic Michael Smith saw *The Rock Garden* and *Cowboys* a week later and joyfully announced in his column that the Theatre Genesis had "actually found a new playwright" who had written a pair of "provocative and genuinely original plays."[8] The overnight genius of Off-Off-Broadway was born.

When Shepard returned to *Cowboys* in 1967, revising it and renaming it *Cowboys #2*, the adolescent rebelliousness and the audience confrontations were gone.

Up to Thursday

Shepard's next play, *Up to Thursday*, received national attention as one of three works on the premiere bill of Theatre 1965's New American Playwrights Series. Shepard, with fellow playwrights Lanford Wilson and Paul Foster, was pictured in *Newsweek* magazine as a spokesman for "that already tiresome new breed, the pop existentialists."[9] Seeming to accept this judgment of his play, Shepard later referred to *Up to Thursday* as "a bad exercise in absurdity": "This kid is sleeping in an American flag, he's only wearing a jockstrap or something, and there's [*sic*] four people on stage who keep shifting their legs and talking."[10]

The play occurs in two scenes. The first, extremely short, is reminiscent of Samuel Beckett's *Act without Words* (1958), a curtain raiser with a hapless hero manipulated by unseen forces. In *Up to Thursday*, a young man in jeans, a T-shirt, and bare feet sits centerstage on a chair.

Downstage is a large rock. As in *Cowboys*, the play opens with offstage noises and voices. A threatening crane descends from the flies above the rock and two men dressed in orange construction hats and work clothes enter from the wings. They argue briefly with the young man, who does not want them to move the rock. Eventually, they hold him down while a third man, the unseen crane operator, removes the rock from the stage.

The next scene reminds one not of Beckett but of Ionesco. Again the young man is present; this time he lies (presumably naked) in a bed covered by an American flag. As the lights come up, he is humming. Seated downstage are four young people in evening attire—two boys to the left, two girls to the right—named Larry, Harry, Terry, and Sherry. As though at a concert, these four break into applause each time the young man finishes humming.

The dialogue is a malt-shop rendition of Ionesco's *The Bald Soprano* (1950). The girls are shy, giggly, and monosyllabic. The boys try to act unruffled. Sherry wants to ask Larry a question, but she is too bashful. Terry urges her on while Harry tries to get in on the conversation as well. Sherry's giggling becomes contagious and all four end up laughing at anything and everything. Eventually, nobody can speak without a spasm of laughter. This sort of teenage banter is punctuated by the young man's humming, the accompanying applause, and the synchronized crossing and uncrossing of legs by the four seated teenagers. At one point, their laughter is interrupted by the young man who jumps up on the bed to inquire whether the woman with his clean underwear has returned. Receiving no response from the four others, who stare across the stage at each other, he lies back down under the flag.

Gradually, the sexual game playing increases in intensity. Petty competition starts as the girls vie for attention and status by whispering secrets to the boys. When Terry turns her back on the other three, feeling an outcast, Sherry approaches each of the boys in turn, kissing them passionately on the mouth. Acceptance and rejection both by the group and by the opposite sex takes a number of metaphorical guises, including a back rub that starts as a subtle sexual approach and ends in an outbreak of repressed hostility. The play concludes with one couple making increasingly passionate love under the flag while the other crawls off-stage, having been permanently crippled by their attempted communication. The young man stands downstage center, waving at the audience until two construction workers drag him forcefully offstage.

Up to Thursday is interesting not because of what it succeeds in doing but because of what it attempts: namely, a purely immediate, nonreferential stage reality. As in *Cowboys*, the stage image is often irrational; no conventional plane of reality could contain the boy in the bed, the four applauding youths in their chairs, and the two construction workers who burst in at the end. The events on stage do not "hold the mirror up to nature" through the representation of any quotidian reality; the only reality here is the created stage reality, made concrete by its occupation of the physical theatrical space.

As to the play's meaning, it has been suggested that it is about a boy facing the draft,[11] but other than the open-ended symbolism of the young man wrapped in the American flag, there is no suggestion in the text of any such political intent. Still, the young man does appear, as in most of Shepard's earliest work, to be inhabiting a different conscious plane than the rest of the characters. If he were to be seen as one facing the draft and the Vietnam war, the typically carefree teenage rituals of the courting couples might assume an even more absurd quality in light of his far more serious concerns.

The Rocking Chair and *Dog*

The Rocking Chair and *Dog* premiered at the Cafe La Mama on 10 February 1965, the same night that *Up to Thursday* opened at the Cherry Lane Theatre.[12] Like *Up to Thursday*, both *Dog* and *The Rocking Chair* revolve around an innocent and bewildered young man seemingly at odds with his environment.

Shepard once said that many of his plays started as a single image: "I would have like a picture, and just start from there" (Chubb et al., 6). This certainly seems to be the case in *The Rocking Chair*, for the play works on one level only: as a single image, a fascinating, almost surreal painting for the stage. At the compositional center of the play and the stage image is a quiet young man in a rocking chair, apparently there for us to watch, but sitting with his back to us. He is both at the center of the play and yet completely out of tune with his surroundings. He converses with a young girl about a recent train trip, but the nature of that trip is left undisclosed, as is everything else in the play. The play does not move linearly toward a dramatic goal but spirals outward from the young man at its hub. Each action or bit of dialogue presents a further clue to deciphering the image before us, but by the end of the play, the clues add up to an even larger mystery, asking more questions than they answer and revealing more canvas, rather than filling in the details of the existing sketch.

"If there is no meaning hidden here," a reviewer once said of Shepard's early work, "then the author is a skillful illusionist indeed."[13] *The Rocking Chair* leaves one with the sense of having been deceived by a series of mysterious images that, while captivating, add up to nothing. Nevertheless, the presence of the young man as a guiding consciousness on the stage is riveting in this play, and it foreshadows the central figures of *Chicago* and *Red Cross*.

Dog is a relatively realistic confrontation between yet another young man (this time in a sport coat and tie) and an old black drunk— "a sort of *Zoo Story*–type play," according to Shepard (Chubb et al., 8). The drunk embodies the threat of urban street life to which the young man is unaccustomed. His straightforward declaration that the young man is a dog forms the nucleus of the play. The young man asks the drunk if he means that he is an animal, like any other animal. The old man repeats that the young man is a dog. Pressed further, the old man asks if the young man has a girlfriend and if he loves her. When the young man responds affirmatively to both questions, the old man repeats his statement of fact: the young man is a dog and his girlfriend is one too. If the old man is suggesting that the young man is a dog because he accepts all of the bourgeois values represented by his conventional relationship with the girl, he never makes this point explicit. His single-minded declaration serves only to raise serious questions in the young man's mind about the state of his life. Despite the irrationality of the old man's declaration, his words effectively rob the young man of his sense of self. He must either dismiss the old man as crazy, which he does not wish to do, or he must accept an interpretation of the stranger's declaration that undermines his existence, leaving him unable to act without self-doubt.

Although Shepard is clearly under the influence of Edward Albee's *The Zoo Story* (1958) here, he is also, whether consciously or not, reflecting the concerns of Italian dramatist Luigi Pirandello. In Pirandello's play *Henry IV* (1922), the Italian dramatist describes a disruptive revelation much like that experienced by the young man in *Dog*: "Do you know what it means to find yourselves face to face with a madman—with one who shakes the foundations of all you have built up in yourselves, your logic, the logic of all your constructions? . . . You feel that this dismay of yours can become terror too—something to dash away the ground from under your feet and deprive you of the air you breathe!"[14] Like Pirandello, Shepard is attempting in his own primitive fashion to dramatize the disintegration of a character's fixed perception of himself and of reality. In a final monologue, the young man faces the terror of complete disorientation as described by Pirandello.

Dog begins with the young man strolling in a self-absorbed manner, experimenting with different types of walks. However, after his encounter with the old man, he undergoes a frightening change. He finds himself unable to place one foot in front of the other. In an effort to ignore his immobility, he sings. But there again he fails, his voice silent. Next, attempting to laugh at his own predicament, he utters only a loud braying noise. The lights fade as the young man stares at the audience, unable to move or speak, his mouth open wide in a petrified silent scream.

In this single theatrical image, which makes no reference to the preceding expository scene, Shepard physically manifests the revelatory and destructive impact of the old black man's vision on the young man's consciousness. Clearly New York in general was having this influence on the young, unsophisticated Shepard. He was overwhelmed by an environment entirely foreign to his life's experience, and his acute awareness of that environment as a force with which he was unequipped to deal was reflected in his plays in heightened states of consciousness, crumbling assumptions about reality, and a growing sense of agitation and paranoia.

This sense of life being unfixed, a kind of existential anxiety, is the very fabric of Shepard's work as a dramatist from 1964 until nearly 1970. Critics who have sought to give conventional "meaning" to these early plays have been trapped by the limitations of their own rationalizing approach. For these plays are not thematically "about" a sense of anxiety or a state of consciousness; rather, they materially manifest those conditions on the stage. As Robert Corrigan noted in 1974, "Our contemporary playwrights are not interested in presenting an action in any Aristotelian sense. They are, rather, dramatizing a condition."[15] Such a theatricalized condition, having more to do with the poet than the philosopher, does not open itself to discussions of meaning.

In order to give theatrical life to a heightened sense of consciousness on stage, Shepard had to develop a theatrical form that did not follow conventional ideas of dramatic action but instead, in Eugene Ionesco's words, "progressed not through a predetermined subject and plot, but through an increasingly intense and revealing series of emotional states" (cited in Corrigan, 95). With his next group of plays, Shepard begins to find the theatrical means to shape his images into an effective dramatic structure.

Chapter Three
The Accumulation of Image

In 1965, after a half dozen Off-Off-Broadway productions, Shepard found a theatrical style that, at least temporarily, gave shape to his personal vision. With the notable exception of *Fourteen Hundred Thousand*, which in many ways seems a throwback to the mechanized absurdism of *Up to Thursday*, Shepard's next five plays, leading up to *La Turista* (1967) and the revised *Cowboys #2*, demonstrate a growing comprehension of dramatic form in image and language, as well as a greater continuity of theme, style, and theatrical intent.

4-H Club, *Icarus's Mother*, *Chicago*, and *Red Cross* are all characterized by a palpable sense of paranoia (sometimes seemingly drug-induced) and a hypersensitivity to the fragmentary quality of contemporary existence. They focus on the bizarre minutiae of experience, accumulated in language and images, and exhibit a deeply disturbed view of reality unfixed, tumbling toward apocalypse.[1] The sense of acute discomfort that Shepard manifested variously in his first plays here takes control of his work and becomes the guiding structural and perceptual force of the worlds he represents.

4-H Club and *Icarus's Mother*

4-H Club and *Icarus's Mother* take the long monologues introduced in Shepard's first plays and launch them, spiraling out of control, into deep space. Progressing dramatically by means of long hallucinatory speeches, the plays steadily mount to the point where imagery spills beyond the confines of conventional perception and manifests a landscape of apocalypse and destruction. These plays are more like communally induced and experienced psychedelic trips than dramatic narratives, and it is no secret that Shepard's use of drugs at this time in his life heightened his already acutely tuned sense of reality's fragmentation. Joyce Aaron, Shepard's constant companion at the time these plays were written, has said that *Icarus's Mother* was the result of a shared acid trip (Oumano, 46). Shepard himself once said that the drug Methadrine gave life "more of an edge; when you walked down the street, your heels sparked" (Goldberg,

193). That electrically charged hyperawareness appropriately describes the language and action of *4-H Club*.

Originally produced at Theatre 1965, *4-H Club* gives further evidence of Shepard's acute dis-ease with his urban surroundings. Set in a tenement apartment, not unlike the one Shepard shared with Charles Mingus, Jr. in 1965, the play depicts three young men in a ragged and aimless existence of poverty, near-starvation, and pest infestation, all masquerading as youthful independence. Shepard has never glorified the youthful alternative life-style of the 1960s. Reflecting on his days in New York's Lower East Side, he has declared, "I wasn't celebrating back then, I was surviving," (Goldberg, 193). *4-H Club*, the title making ironic comment on the unwholesome activities of the young men in the play, attempts to recreate Shepard's heightened consciousness of the squalor of that time, place, and mind-set.

Language and staging work independently in *4-H Club*, but they share the common goal of creating an overwhelming sense of mental and physical disorientation. At any point in the play, the dialogue can develop into bizarre and frightening dreamscapes, as it does, for instance, when a character sweeping broken glass from the floor suddenly launches into a jazzlike riff on the importance of maintaining a clean kitchen:

As far as clean goes, if I was thinking of clean we could get a fire hose in here and blast the walls and the floors and the stove. Just a great huge blast of hot water. That would do it . . . You'd need permission, I guess. How much would it cost to hire a fireman for one day to blast this place? I don't think he'd do it. It would knock down the walls, anyway. It would probably wash the stove out into the audience. It'd take a week to dry anyway. There'd be puddles of water all over the floor . . . If a fire starts, all they do is knock down the walls with blasts of water . . . Hunks of wet wood and pieces of cement all broken to pieces . . . Then all the firemen stand around in puddles of water and grin.[2]

The accumulation of such images, here progressing well beyond a rational discussion of housekeeping and into a fantasized world of fire hoses, crumbling walls, and grinning firemen, is typical of the language throughout the play. Elsewhere, a suggestion to clean the floor leads to images of trash cans tossed out windows, innocent bystanders killed on the sidewalk below, gathering crowds, and battles with the National Guard. The possibility of attracting mice turns into a battle cry against rodents in which furless baby mice are stomped beneath boots before they grow into man-eating mandrills. Each new image is explored "almost as if, since they [the images] have been mentioned, they have triggered a need to fantasize."[3] Such paroxysmal narratives do not discuss particular thematic issues as much as they create an acute awareness on the spectator's part of the possibility for apocalyptic turns behind each moment of existence, of an unseen terror pressing in upon the seemingly mundane world and insignificant actions of the characters. The result is a dramaturgical model that undertakes the impossible task of sharing an intense emotional state of psychic discomfort with the audience, not by describing it but by evoking it on the stage in a manner that causes the audience to experience it as well.

A more tangible source of discomfort in *4-H Club* is Shepard's juxtaposition of stage space and real space in the ground plan of the play: "An empty stage except for a small kitchen extreme upstage left. Three flats compose the walls of the kitchen with a swinging door in the upstage wall. On the floor downstage left of the kitchen is a hot plate with a coffee pot on it. The floor of the kitchen is littered with paper, cans and various trash. There is a garbage can in the upstage right corner. The walls are very dirty. The lighting should be equal for the whole stage with no attempt to focus light on the kitchen" (*4H*, 203). This unorthodox use of the performance space draws attention to the limited realm of mimetic reality represented by the kitchen and the containment of that plane of reality within the more physically immediate reality of the theater space. Thus, Shepard's use of the space is "emotional rather than physical,"[4] creating an antagonism between the created performance reality and the underlying reality of the stage itself. Shepard allows his characters to walk in and out of the kitchen and onto the empty stage during the play, shattering the mimetic convention of the kitchen space and potentially creating a sense of psychic discomfort in the spectator akin to that evoked by the verbal imagery in the play.

The same discomfort is evoked in *Icarus's Mother*, both through language and through the ambivalent relationship between actor and character. But rather than blatantly defy conventions of realistic stage space as he does in *4-H Club*, Shepard explores the far subtler unfixing of conventional, psychologically motivated character.

Icarus's Mother begins on a relatively realistic note. Indeed, the opening scene is both comic and familiar to most Americans: five bloated picnickers, having just completed a large holiday meal, lie on their backs in the grass, burping at random while the barbecue pit continues to smoke. In one respect, the play is about nothing more than walks on the beach, low-flying planes, and a fireworks exhibit. But, as in *4-H Club*, every event in *Icarus's Mother* holds the potential for unforeseen terror.

Icarus's Mother is composed of sudden shifts in action and inhabited by characters whose motives remain inapproachable. One of the most disturbing actions of the play is a repeated sequence in which two characters use the barbecue pit to send smoke signals when all other characters have left the stage:

Bill and *Howard* look at each other for a second, then they both get up and cross to the barbecue. *Howard* picks up the tablecloth and drapes it over the barbecue, *Bill* holds one side of the tablecloth while *Howard* holds the other, they look up at the sky, then they lift the tablecloth off the barbecue and allow some smoke to rise; they replace the tablecloth over the barbecue and follow the same procedure, glancing up at the sky; they do this three or four times, then *Frank* enters from the left in bare feet and carrying his shoes . . . *Howard* and *Bill* turn suddenly to *Frank* and drop the tablecloth on the ground.[5]

This action, carried on almost ritually, is one of the most powerful disrupters of the play. The sense of an unspoken conspiracy, enhanced when the two men suddenly drop the tablecloth, creates in Howard and Bill a surreal quality. Their action takes on an air of danger and threat. However, the possibility of a conspiracy between the two men is never confirmed in the play. Shepard, not unlike fellow postabsurdist Harold Pinter, allows his characters' actions to remain "unverified" (Pinter's term),[6] thus denying simple rationalization of the isolated stage images.

When *Icarus's Mother* was first produced, this type of irrational sequence created great frustration for conventionally trained Method actors. Directors have repeatedly found the overall imagery and movement of the play explosively theatrical, but they have been tormented in rehearsal by actors who do not understand the motivations behind their characters' actions. Michael Smith and Kenneth Chubb—who directed the American and British premieres, respectively, of the play—both address this point in essays. Smith found his actors especially distraught over the smoke signal sequence: "Our nexus of anxiety was the smoke signals. . . . 'Why?' Don't think about that, just do it. 'What is the motivation?' I could make things up, but they seemed irrelevant. I figured out how to make smoke, I showed the actors how to hold the blanket, gave them gestures and rhythms and sounds. Not enough. They were confused, uncomfortable, floundering. How could I get them simply to *do* it, not *act* it? They felt foolish just going through the motions, and the results were self-conscious and hollow."[7] Although Shepard offers virtually no information on the characters, Smith and his cast found it necessary to postulate characterizations and relationships based on the individual patterns of response specific to each of the characters in the play. It was decided that two characters were married, another depressed, while still another was an outsider to the group. The smoke signals were determined to be a retreat into boyhood by two male characters who need to shut out the women. This explanation of motives, standard to ensemble Method acting, assumes that the author wished to rationalize the actions of the characters. By "verifying" the relationships and motivations of the characters in the play, Smith condemned the play to realism, denying expression of the surreal aspects of the script. Chubb, learning from Smith's mistakes, attempted to address the need of the actor to approach Shepard's work as situational rather than psychological: "*Icarus's Mother* exemplifies a problem that puzzles directors and actors—the way the flow of the imagery seems to overpower and negate character and structure. As Michael Smith points out, the characters in the play are distinct, but we are given almost no information about them and, for an actor to 'assume' certain facts about them, to define them as characters, is to limit them and eventually the play itself. The lack of information demands that an actor call on his own resources, more than he usually needs to. He must concentrate on the *situation* as it is stated in the play." (Chubb, 18; italics added) Creating a rational chain of events and/or justifying character choices means sacrificing intentionally irrational events for the sake of continuity. It follows that if the actors rationalize, denying the fragmented texture of Shepard's created world, the audience will experience the play as a comprehensible series of events, not a fragmented one.

Shepard's approach to character in *Icarus's Mother* suggests the influence of the Open Theatre, a New York–based acting collective with which Shepard had contact in the mid-1960s. Under the direction of Joseph Chaikin, the Open Theatre sought to reject psychological realism and redefine character not in terms of "the social and psychological influences on his past, but by his visible acts."[8] This type of characterization was approached by means of improvisational acting techniques such as "the Transformation" in which "the established realities or 'given circumstances' (the Method phrase) of the scene change several times during the course of the action."[9] Whatever motivational realities or "truths" were established at the outset of an action could be changed without warning either by altering a character, that character's objective, or the situation, time, or given circumstances within which that character is acting. The Transformation, as an acting exercise, was meant to "break the grip of the Method and the dependence on psychological motivation and logical transition between situations."[10]

Beyond its function as exercise, the Transformation was intended, in performance, to throw into doubt the spectators' conception of stable reality and character. It was a means of "questioning our notion of 'reality'" and "raising certain questions about the nature of identity and the finitude of character" (Feldman, 201). This disruptive quality of the Transformation in performance, as employed by Shepard, sought effectively to unfix the reality of his plays and their characters.

Shepard's kinship with the Open Theatre is reflected not only in the characterization of *Icarus's Mother* but also in the greater psychic impact to which character contributes in the play. That impact represents the creation of theatrical images which, in Shepard's words, "penetrate into another world. A world behind the form."[11] Shepard saw precisely this type of event in the works of the Open Theatre: "Where most other groups were running around screaming and purging themselves of sexual energy the Open Theatre was making clear, distinct theatrical pictures that carried you beyond its form into another kind of understanding."[12] While Shepard identifies artistic intent as the key which separates himself and the Open Theatre from other ensembles of the period, critics have seen the difference as one of theatrical form. Shepard has been hailed frequently as a sort of messiah: "He has brought the word back into the theatre where, since the canonization of Artaud, the word and all that it implies—literacy, literature, imaginative connection—has been silted up with non-verbal, sensory overloads."[13] This lopsided approach to Shepard's work ignored the theatrical intentions behind his use of language. What separated Shepard from his contemporaries was not his refusal of the Artaudian influences around him but rather his appreciation of Artaud as theatrical spirit and not as a series of self-indulgent techniques. Whether or not Shepard was ever consciously aware of the influence of Artaud, "or, more likely, the influence of Artaud's influence,"[14] his own work, and his keen appraisal of the Open Theatre's intent to carry its audience to another level of understanding, demonstrate a consciousness of the stage as a means of arresting the spectator's rational perception of events.

Discussing the original impulse behind the creation of *Icarus's Mother*,

Shepard describes a vague experience of terror that inspired him and that
he intended to evoke through the presentation of the play: "You've got
this emotional thing that goes a long way back, which creates a certain
kind of chaos, a kind of terror, you don't know what the fuck's going on.
It's really hard to grab the whole of the experience . . . There's a vague
kind of terror going on, the people not really knowing what is happening" (Chubb et al., 9). In action and in language, Shepard attempts to
recreate in the audience the sense of unseen terror that led him to the
composition of *Icarus's Mother*. In Artaud's words, he is approaching
the "great metaphysical fear which is at the root of all ancient theater."[15]
The smoke signals, which Shepard employs three times during the play,
are evocative of this type of terror because they have no rational context
in the play. They are also an application of Artaud's principle of the
"objective unforeseen," an object or event that is "entirely invented,
corresponding to nothing, yet disquieting by nature" (Artaud, 44). This
same metaphysical intent can be witnessed in Shepard's use of speech,
heralded by critics as an escape from Artaudian esthetics, but, in actuality, remarkably similar to the French theorist's intentions. Like the
"objective unforeseen" in images, language can, according to Shepard,
"explode from the tiniest impulse": "In these lightning-like eruptions
words are not thought, they're felt. They cut through space and make
perfect sense without having to hesitate for the 'meaning'" ("Inner
Library," 54). Both Artaud and Shepard speak of language as a tangible
object to be used in a "concrete and spatial sense." Artaud calls for
language that "overturns and disturbs things, in the air first of all, then
in an infinitely more mysterious and secret domain" (Artaud, 72).
Shepard, likewise, proposes that "the organization of living breathing
words as they hit the air between the actor and the audience actually
possesses the power to change our chemistry" ("Inner Library," 53).
Language becomes physical "incantation" and words are used not in the
utilitarian sense of rational communication but to produce a physical and
emotional shock capable of "making leaps into the unknown."

In *Icarus's Mother*, as in *4-H Club*, language is used to transport the
audience into "moments of heightened perception" ("Inner Library", 53)
by the escalation of verbal images in the shape of long monologues. Early
in *Icarus's Mother*, a discussion of air travel leads to a long monologue on
the sense of disorientation from which pilots occasionally suffer: "Then
you get kind of dizzy and sick to the tum tum and your head starts to spin
so you clutch the seat with both hands and close your eyes. But even
inside your closed eyes you can see the same things as before . . . So you

quick open your eyes and try to fix them on the control panel. You
concentrate on the controls and the dials and the numbers . . . You're
straight in front straining not to see with peripheral vision" (*IM*, 43).
Anyone having seen film footage of pilots flying upside down or aerial
stunts filmed from inside the cockpit cannot help but suffer acute
discomfort during such a speech. Once that discomfort arises, the spectator views everything in the play with a certain physical dis-ease that
mounts as new images and verbal accounts add to the play's equivocal
mood. The unexplained intrusion of a low-flying jet overhead, the
mysterious smoke signals, the conspiratorial undertones, the disruption
of cause and effect by Bill and Howard who predict the crash of the plane
before it happens—these events accumulate so that the audience's sense
of equilibrium, both physical and mental, is finally pushed to its limits.

The play climaxes, not traditionally through plot, character, or theme,
but through the accumulation of language and image. Bill and Howard,
discovered sending smoke signals, inform their female companions that
according to a third man, Frank, the plane has crashed. Frank was
onstage moments before and said no such thing. As the two women run
off to see the crash, Frank enters in a daze. The plane, he announces, has
crashed. His chillingly detailed account of the crash is accompanied by
offstage explosions and the showering of the darkened stage by the
colored lights of fireworks. Frank's description of the plane's impact
upon the surface of the ocean evolves from a small watery plunge into an
eruption of cataclysmic proportions, "exploding the water for a hundred
miles in diameter around itself. Sending a wake to Japan" (*IM*, 59). The
flickering fireworks and the offstage sounds escalate simultaneously with
the spoken imagery. The lights fluctuate in color, overloading one's
visual sense, while the offstage booms follow in rapid succession, accompanied by the rising noise of a vast crowd of people. The speech climaxes
with Frank totally enraptured by his own frenzied images of catastrophe
while Bill and Howard look on in horror:

The water goes up to fifteen hundred feet and smashes the trees, and the firemen
come. The beach sinks below the surface. The seagulls drown in flocks of ten
thousand. There's a line of people two hundred deep. Standing in line to watch
the display. And the pilot bobbing in the very center of a ring of fire that's
closing in. His white helmet bobbing up and bobbing down. His hand reaching
for his other hand and the fire moves in and covers him up and the line of two
hundred bow their heads and moan together with the light in their faces. Oh you
guys should have come! You guys should have been there! (*IM*, 59–60)

Shepard uses the intensification of language, stage action, light, and noise to sweep the spectator away in their great physical dynamism, creating not just an understanding but an experience of the metaphysical terror that led to the writing of the play.[16]

Chicago and *Red Cross*

With *Chicago* and *Red Cross*, Shepard continues to explore theatrical images of a fragmented reality, but in these plays the perceptual force behind those images has been narrowed to a single consciousness. Like *Dog*, *Up to Thursday*, and *The Rocking Chair*, these pieces revolve around a single individual—a young man—at odds with his surroundings. But, even more than in those earlier plays, Shepard now allows that young man to shape experience on behalf of the audience.

Chicago is Shepard's first truly hallucinatory play in the sense that the reality of the play seems to emanate from the subjective mind of its hero, Stu. This rather expressionistic theatricalization of Stu's perception works both for and against Shepard's development as a playwright. It demonstrates, on the one hand, his increasing freedom from realistic restraints. Yet, at the same time, it contradicts the metaphysical repercussions of that freedom by rationalizing the imagery of the play as hallucination on the part of the central character.

If *Cowboys* was Shepard's early *Waiting for Godot*, then *Chicago* is his *Endgame*. Like Beckett's Hamm, Shepard's Stu sits immobile, attempting to dictate reality around himself through an elaborate spoken narrative. And, as Stu is to Hamm, so is Stu's companion Joy to Beckett's Clov, passing in and out of the kitchen, threatening to leave and thus cut short the only form of sustenance, both physical and emotional, that the central character enjoys. *Chicago* opens on a light note with Stu sitting centerstage in a bathtub—naked, one assumes—talking to himself in a singsong manner. Offstage, Joy bakes biscuits. When Stu stands up, he reveals that the tub is empty and that he is wearing pants. If spectators have assumed that this is a play about a man in his bath in his bathroom, that image is suddenly transformed into the rather incongruous presence of a half-clothed actor in an empty tub on a bare stage. He becomes, as is so often the case in Shepard's work, a man at odds with his environment.

Stu employs the tub metaphorically in his various narratives. It becomes an island, a womb, a boat adrift in hostile water. But always, in the shifting subjective reality, it is a bathtub on a stage, "the only continuously real"[17] element of the play. Stu is trapped in the tub by an overwhelming fear of action and perhaps of life itself. His self-engrossing fantasies are a retreat into nonaction and/or nonbeing. When Joy attempts to draw Stu out of the tub and back into life, he creates an imaginary environment—a great beach—which becomes a source of anxiety and a justification of his retreat from life: "You just lie there and the sun dries you and the sand gets all stuck to you. It sticks all over. In your toes. In your ears. Up your crotch. Aaah! Sand between your legs! Aaah! Sticking in your pores. Goddam! (He sits back down in the tub and puts the towel over his head . . .)."[18] Rather than leave the tub, Stu manipulates and subjectifies reality throughout the play to meet his own ends. Faced with Joy's romantic approaches, he changes the tub from a lovers' boat adrift in the moonlight (as Joy imagines it) into a raft afloat in a sea of man-eating barracudas.

Stu's subjective vision and his manipulation of reality begin to manifest themselves physically in the stage action when Joy's friends arrive and the audience sees them as Stu must. Myra, for instance, enters dressed in a fur coat and dark glasses, carrying a suitcase. She stands at the back of the stage while Stu and Joy fight, then kiss. Without looking up, Stu announces that "Myra's here," as though she did not exist until he gave her recognition. Seemingly identical in Stu's mind, each of Joy's friends enter wearing a suit (men) or fur coat (women), carrying a suitcase, and wearing sunglasses. When Stu talks about the symbiotic relationship between fish and fishermen, the other characters enter and exit with fishing poles in their hands. By the end of the play, the action is almost entirely the product of Stu's imagination. His obsessive fear of losing Joy eventually assumes a permanent physical reality: the play ends with Joy repeatedly walking back and forth across the stage, pulling a wagon filled with suitcases, as if forever fixed in the act of leaving Stu.

Long, escalating monologues play an important role in *Chicago* as in earlier plays. Stu's manipulation of reality regularly takes the form of a manipulation of language. Important to note, however, is the difference between a speech that appears to be consciously manipulated by a character and a speech that, in Robert Pasolli's words, shows "the story taking control of the storyteller."[19] In the first instance, the spectator becomes conscious of one character manipulating language to affect another character, as the boy uses language to shock the man in *The Rock Garden*. Likewise, Stu's description of barracudas is unquestionably directed at Joy: "Them's barracuda, lady. They eat people when they feel like it. . . . They'd eat you like nobody's business. . . . See the way

they flash around. That's 'cause they're hungry. . . . Starvin' to
death. . . . Just lookin' fer a nice young virgin. . . . Just lookin' fer
somethin' to bite. (He grabs her and tries to push her out of the tub)"
(*Chicago*, 10–11). Because Stu's language has a natural target, the audience is not threatened. We are able objectively to remove ourselves from
his line of fire by recognizing and observing the intended target.

In contrast, a speech that seems to possess the speaker is much more
horrifying because it is unmotivated. Watching an unseen force at work
upon the mind of the character, the audience is drawn into an empathetic
relationship. The long, hypnotic monologue at the end of *Chicago*, like
that at the end of *Icarus's Mother,* appears to possess the speaker; the
character becomes a shaman who carries the audience with him into
the unknown and unseen root of his anxiety. Stu's immediate, physical,
and apparently uncontrolled involvement in the building frenzy of his
speech should have a direct physical impact upon the audience. He
envisions mankind copulating in masses on the beach, smothering itself
in the security of domesticity, breaking free and returning to the beach
only to walk straight into the water and finally be reborn. Humanity
learns to sense and breathe all over again:

Good! In and out! Ladies and gentlemen, the air is fine! All this neat air is
gathered before us! It's too much! (The other actors start to breathe slowly,
gradually, making sounds as they inhale and exhale.) The place is teeming with
air. All you do is breathe. Easy. One, two. One, two. In. Out. Out, in. I learned
this in fourth grade. Breathing, ladies and gentlemen! Before your very eyes.
Outstanding air. All you need to last a day. Two days. A week. Month after
month of breathing until you can't stop. Once you get the taste of it. The hang
of it. What a gas. In your mouth and out your nose. Ladies and gentlemen, it's
fantastic! (They all breathe in unison.) (*Chicago*, 24)

Stu's speech climaxes in a state of acute physical self-awareness. Like the
young man's paralysis at the end of *Dog,* the words spoken here draw
attention to each and every passing breath. At the play's conclusion,
Shepard leaves the audience in this state, slowly becoming conscious that
we have begun to breathe in sync with the actors.

Shepard's next play, *Red Cross,* further heightens the spectator's sense
of physical self-consciousness in an increasingly discomforting fashion.
In *Red Cross,* empathetic breathing is only the beginning; it soon gives
way to crawling flesh, vicarious drowning, and an exploding head. In a
world where microscopic insects and undiagnosed skin diseases are

confined to the rarefied atmosphere of an all-white set, a single trickle of blood can bring gasps from the audience.

The action of *Red Cross* occurs in the rented room of a woodlands cabin, where Jim and his girlfriend Carol are afflicted by a mysterious malady that causes a tingling of the skin under Carol's eyes and acute physical discomfort on Jim's part. Shepard has converted the cabin into an emotional "vivisectory" by removing every color but white; like "looking at snow in the sun."[20] The beds, the floor, the walls, the lighting, even the clothes worn by the characters are white. The result is an intensification of consciousness, a magnification of every sound and action, to the point where, in the words of director Jacques Levy, "startling things occurring in such a climate become magnified" and even the smallest of explosions can be felt "a mile away" (Levy, 96).

With the exception of the actors' flesh tones, the only color introduced during the entire play comes in the final moment when a single drop of bright red blood trickles down Jim's forehead. Within the heightened dramatic conditions created by the characters' actions, Shepard's language, and the blinding white stage setting, this tiny red spot suggests an oncoming apocalypse of proportion equal to that which concluded *Icarus's Mother*. According to director Levy, the effect had a great enough impact that "the ending, followed by a sharp blackout, made a lot of people gasp, and there was always dead silence in the house until the lights came up for bows" (Levy, 96).

Shepard prepares us for this final image early in the play when Carol gives a long speech about snow skiing, which increases in intensity as, standing in a tucked position on her bed, she imagines herself moving faster and faster down a snow-covered hill. Reaching peak speed, her head starts to throb as if it will "break clear open":

Then it'll come. It'll start like a twitch in my left ear. Then I'll start to feel a throb in the bridge of my nose. Then a thump in the base of my neck. Then a crash right through my skull. Then I'll be down. Rolling! Yelling! All these people will see it . . . Then my head will blow up. The top will come right off. My hair will blow down the hill full of guts and blood . . . My nose will come off and my whole face will peel away. Then it will snap. My whole head will snap off and roll down the hill and become a huge snowball and roll into the city and kill a million people.[21]

Like the plane crash at the end of *Icarus's Mother*, Carol's story travels beyond all realm of human possibility to reach unforeseen catastrophic proportions. Her speech prepares the audience, at the very top of the play, for an inevitable catastrophe. She creates a prophecy that Jim will fulfill at the play's conclusion. She predicts: "All you'll see is this little red splotch of blood and a whole blanket of white snow" (*RC*, 102).

During the play, Jim intensifies the audience's sense of agitation by revealing the source of his own physical discomfort: pubic crabs. Jim's crabs take on the same status as the offstage plane in *Icarus's Mother* or the unseen mice in *4-H Club*. They contribute to the audience's discomfort by their palpable yet unseen presence, and they symbolize an intangible source of anxiety from which Jim cannot escape. He scratches his legs, jumps on the bed, climbs trees, goes swimming, runs—all to distract himself from his physical discomfort. For Jim, the simple act of existence has become unbearably painful. The actor's frantic behavior, accompanied by the continual mention of microscopic crabs, of their hatching eggs lost in the sheets of the bed, and of Jim's crawling skin, should certainly be enough to make the audience begin to squirm in their seats. Where *Icarus's Mother* or *4-H Club* worked on the audience psychologically, *Red Cross* evokes a physical rather than a metaphysical discomfort.

During a sequence in which Jim teaches an intrusive maid how to swim, Shepard expands upon the effect of the synchronized breathing at the end of *Chicago*. Part of Jim's malady is his inability to *be* without *doing*, and during the maid's visit, he distracts himself by attempting to transfer some of his own sense of physical discomfort onto her. She is required to lie on a bed while repeating the basic underwater breathing and rhythmic movements of swimming. This private tutorial is to a great extent an act of domination. As the maid tires and her back and sides cramp, Jim forces her to keep swimming—"Move it! Work it out! Keep it up!"—actually picking up the pace and warning her that if she stops she will drown. But the maid turns the tables on Jim by transforming the image of her own drowning into a fantasy about turning into a fish. Rather than submit to Jim's verbal domination, the maid wrestles control of his own images away from him, leaving him in an even more heightened state of agitation.

When Carol returns, announcing that she too has discovered crabs on her body, Jim's condition has, quite literally, reached the bursting point. As Jim turns to face the audience, a stream of blood runs down his forehead. Shepard has captured Jim's inner state in what Ross Wetzsteon calls a "metaphoric crystallization" (Wetzsteon, 7): his psychic agitation is physically manifest in the oncoming explosion of his head.

La Turista

Acute agitation, confining rented rooms, and an eruptive final image all figure again in Shepard's next play, La Turista. Once more, drawing from his own life, Shepard wrote La Turista in Mexico "under the influence of amphetamines and dysentery."[22] Perhaps the ultimate stage expression of Shepard's sense of personal estrangement from reality, La Turista juxtaposes mock-Mayan ritual, the transformation of character, the fragmentation of spatial and temporal realities, live animal sacrifice, and long, stylized monologues to create a frequently funny but ultimately devastating frenzy of images illuminating the malaise of the modern American male.

La Turista is Shepard's first full-length play. The first act is set in a gaudy Mexican hotel room, the second (which chronologically precedes the first) takes place in another hotel, this one somewhere in the United States. Throughout both acts, Kent, an American tourist accompanied by his wife, Salem (both of whom are named after cigarette brands), suffers from debilitating maladies: severe sunburn and "la turista" (dysentery) in the first act and sleeping sickness in the second. In each act, local doctors are called upon to treat Kent's condition.

Thematically, Kent's malaise echoes the central metaphors of the plays that immediately precede La Turista. Like Jim in Red Cross, Kent finds himself stranded in a hotel room with a bodily infestation demanding immediate attention and causing extreme physical discomfort. In the second act, Kent has fallen victim to sleeping sickness as the result, it appears, of the tedium of his life. Like Stu in Chicago, he is in a state of nonbeing, although unlike Stu he does not appear to have induced it voluntarily. In Salem's words, he has simply "gone away," disappeared.

The same sense of estrangement and personal alienation that led Shepard to write Dog and Cowboys shortly after his arrival in New York City is again apparent in La Turista. Here, though, Shepard's tourists are at odds not with an urban environment but with the mythic subculture and lethal bacteria of a foreign land. As Elizabeth Hardwick points out in her introduction to the play, "Kent dies, a sacrifice to 'la turista'—his lack of resistance to the germs of the country he arrogantly patronizes with his presence."[23] Like the characters in Jean Cocteau's The Wedding on the Eiffel Tower (1924), eaten by the lion whose presence they refuse to acknowledge as rationally possible, Kent dies by ignoring primitive forces to which he thinks he is superior. The embodiment of modern

America, Kent is complacently out of touch with the mythic and metaphysical roots of his existence. When he comes into contact with such metaphysics by way of powerful forces in a primitive (read "irrational") land, he is unable to fight them with the conventional (read "rational") means at his disposal.

This self-consciously "American" theme, unusual at this point in Shepard's career, is accompanied by a change in the playwright's use of transformational characterization. *La Turista* is a pastiche of visual, verbal, and theatrical images that suggest a heightened, perhaps shattered, state of consciousness. While the play's thematic exposition touches upon this shattered state, the play relies predominantly on theatrical imagery and techniques to manifest it physically. The transformation of character, space, and time, the accumulation of language and stage action, the manifestation of physical impossibilities, and the breakdown of rational cause and effect serve to dramatize "the force of an unconscious which constantly threatens to break through the conventional fabric of personal and social existence."[24]

The first act, for instance, reads like a poisonous nightmare brought on by the dysentery from which Kent suffers. When confronted by a Mexican shoeshine boy, both Kent and Salem overreact, breaking into appropriated patterns of stereotypical behavior. Salem tries to distract the boy by throwing money at him the way a camper might throw food at a foraging bear. Kent, adopting the jargon of an animal trainer or safari guide, describes the deadly habits of some untamed beast to a group of tourists. When the boy rips the phone from the wall and spits in Kent's face, Kent rushes from the room. The phone, no longer connected, rings, and the boy, now acting and speaking like an American teenager, answers it in perfect English. He takes off his pants and climbs into Kent's bed, calling Salem "Mom." When Kent returns, having fought off a bout of "la turista," he has been transformed. Wearing a cowboy hat, pistol, hand-tooled boots, a linen shirt, and underpants, he struts across the stage like a matinee idol. He brags that there is nothing "like a little amoebic dysentery to build up a man's immunity to his environment."[25] But Kent's pop culture heroics are no match for the primitive force of the boy's Oedipal threat. Seeing the boy in his bed, Kent faints dead away.

The witch doctor and his son, who arrive to treat Kent, constitute a reality in complete contradiction to that already established on the stage. They behave "as though they have nothing to do with the play and just happen to be there" (*LT*, 23). As the witch doctor initiates a sacred ritual over Kent's prostrate body using live chickens, the Mexican boy jumps from his bed to address the audience directly. He identifies the witch doctor as a local Mayan tribesman and explains the significance of his ritual action. The witch doctor and his son also acknowledge the audience's presence, but not in the same manner as the boy: "They should now and then look at the audience and wonder why it's there" (*LT*, 25). Thus, halfway through the first act, Shepard has disrupted his characters' rational, psychological core; juxtaposed various temporal/spatial realities; produced physically impossible events; and shattered the invisible "fourth wall" between the actors and the audience. The play operates in a kind of dream structure; but, unlike *Chicago*, which offers Stu as dreamer and psychic originator of the aberrations on stage, *La Turista* has no dreamer. These irrational events must be judged on their own merit, neither rationalized nor dismissed as the hallucinations of any one character.

In the second act, a country doctor and his son are introduced. Dressed in Civil War costumes, they represent an American totemism as native to the American South as is the witch doctor to central Mexico. The live chickens of the first act are replaced by medical charts and diagrams. Rather than chanted ritual, "Doc" offers a scientific exposition on the history, causes, symptoms, and treatment of chronic *"Encephalitis Lethargica"* (i.e., sleeping sickness). Doc's treatment, however, has as little impact as does the witch doctor's; it seems that the doctor's scientific theses are ineffectual in treating Kent's metaphysical malady, just as Kent's refined American immune system is ineffectual in combating the dysentery. Kent is as much a foreigner to the empty myths and totems of civilized America as he is to the living mythic subculture of Mexico. He represents a modern American everyman who, through the "civilizing" process, has lost touch with the origins of his primitive self and who has also outgrown the tired, empty myths of his civilization.

The visual and verbal images of the second act of *La Turista* are less startling than those of the first, focusing on subtle shifts of character marked by escalating speeches. The final sequence of the play, climaxing with Kent's leap through the upstage wall of the set, takes the form of a drawn-out gunfight between Kent and Doc, with words as ammunition. Kent, with nothing but a finger to point, and Doc, with his pistol aimed at Kent's face, back each other around the stage, the verbal advantage shifting back and forth. Through a hypnotic narrative, Doc attempts to transform Kent into a gentle Frankenstein creature and become his paternal creator. He describes how he and his faithful son stay up all night, working patiently on the creature's torso and arms, creating "beautiful womanly hands that look like they've never been outside of goatskin gloves until this very moment" (*LT*, 65). But before Doc can complete his image, Kent seizes the narrative and the creature breaks its leather straps and storms out of the laboratory. The two men struggle to manipulate the narration, each reshaping reality as he goes. As Kent pumps himself up with mounting animal images, Doc fires his pistol. But Kent keeps advancing: language now dominates reality, transporting both the story and the stage action onto a new plane. Kent leaps from the stage into the auditorium. Doc tries to lure him back onto the stage while Salem and Doc's son make a lunge for him. Kent grabs a rope and swings over their heads, running straight upstage and leaping through the stage wall, "leaving a cut-out silhouette of his body in the wall" (*LT*, 72).

When asked to comment on the theme of *La Turista*, Shepard has stated flatly that "it doesn't correlate to any thesis that I had and worked out afterward. I mean it to be a theatrical event, that's all."[26] Ross Wetzsteon, in his introduction to Shepard's *Fool for Love and Other Plays*, relates his first experience with Shepard's stagecraft, noting how the final image of *La Turista* expresses the play's theme more intrinsically and immediately than could any speech:

I can still recall the first moment I was stunned by Shepard's stagecraft—the final image of *La Turista,* the American Place Theater, 1967. . . . [J]ust as when we awaken we try to reduce our dreams to their meanings, so in the theater we instinctively ask "what is the playwright trying to *say?*" and, in spite of my increasing enchantment, I didn't have the vaguest idea what it was. Then, at the end of the play, at the very moment that Shepard's fragmentary glimpses seemed about to come into focus, providing some sort of illumination at last, the flash of lightning came instead—the hero, in a panicked flight for freedom, turned his back to the audience, reached full speed toward the rear of the stage, and crashed through the wall, leaving only the outline of his body before our straddled eyes. And staring at that image, an image that dramatized the themes of the play far more precisely than could any words, an image that communicated the emotional texture of the characters' lives far more vividly than could any speech, at that instant I realized that Sam Shepard was more than just another promising young playwright, he was the most instinctive, the most purely theatrical playwright of his generation. (Wetzsteon, 1–2)

Rather than use the stage as a spatial or a narrative entity, Shepard has here transformed it into an emotional landscape. Like Jim's head about to burst open in *Red Cross* or the young man paralyzed at the end of *Dog*, this final image from *La Turista* becomes the rarefied theatrical expression of a personal state of extreme psychic agitation.

Cowboys #2

By the time *La Turista* was produced in 1967, Shepard's originally feverish artistic output had begun to slow. After producing eleven plays between October of 1964 and March of 1967, Shepard wrote only one new script following *La Turista* in 1967—*Forensic and the Navigators*, which he created on a day to day basis during rehearsals at Theatre Genesis. Although Shepard had two other plays produced during 1967—*Melodrama Play* and *Cowboys #2*—these were not new scripts. *Melodrama Play* was written sometime in 1966 before the production of *La Turista* and before the publication of Shepard's first collection of plays, *Five Plays*.[27] *Cowboys #2* was not an original script but a rewrite of Shepard's first play, *Cowboys*.

Cowboys #2 offers a rare opportunity to examine a completely reworked version of a playwright's early work. It also, significantly, brings to a close the first major creative period of Shepard's writing, ending, as he had begun, with his tale of young men playing at being cowboys. Although written only three years apart, *Cowboys* and *Cowboys #2* are separated by nearly a dozen other plays, not to mention the pages upon pages of Shepard's unpublished and unproduced work from this period.[28] The original *Cowboys* is the first fruit of the "overnight genius" of New York's Off-Off-Broadway scene. *Cowboys #2*, however, is the work of a widely recognized American playwright, solicited by a major regional theater in Los Angeles. As in the original *Cowboys*, two young men, Chet and Stu, jump in and out of cowboy characterizations with lightning speed. But Shepard's revisions have created a more consistently threatening and theatrical experience, demonstrating a mastery of the disruptive techniques that, by this point in his career, had become his trademark.

The first change one notices in the new script is that many of the recorded sound effects have disappeared. Originally, the script included several recorded effects intended to create an urban backdrop for the action: a dog barking, a woman calling her son, a crying baby, buses, sirens, an explosion. These have been streamlined, and all offstage dialogue has now been assigned to one of two actors, who are referred to only as Man Number One and Man Number Two in the text. The live presence of these two offstage characters creates a far greater threat to the world of the cowboys than did the original taped soundtrack. While taped sounds can be easily dismissed as a theatrical convention by most audiences, the presence of actors, speaking from just out of the audience's sight and drawing attention to the space beyond and behind the set, cannot. Whereas many of the urban sounds of the original soundtrack seemed incidental to the action onstage, the scraps of dialogue, the live sound effects, and especially the live offstage whistling of the two live actors in *Cowboys #2* creates a far more disturbing quality, an effect at greater physical odds with the actors on stage.

On several occasions in the script, for instance, one or both of the offstage men whistles in a manner that appears to disrupt the flow of action on the stage, yet which is somehow tied to it at the same time. In each case, Chet and Stu wait for or listen to the whistling before continuing their dialogue. In one instance, both Chet and Stu "look in the direction of whistling, then at each other."[29] Although the whistling does not seem to change the nature of their dialogue or appear to mean anything, Chet and Stu are both conscious of it and uncomfortable with it. They both acknowledge an intrusive offstage presence and make sure that the audience acknowledges it as well. The next time there is whistling, Chet and Stu anticipate it. Their dialogue comes to a sudden stop and they turn and stare at each other as if waiting for the whistling to begin (*C#2*, 233). This time the sound comes from both sides of the stage, as the two men whistle back and forth to each other. Chet and Stu remain silent until the whistling has stopped. When they do speak, they have been transformed, without warning, into the characters of the old cowhands. This type of juxtaposition between onstage reality and off-stage reality, especially at moments of sudden transition within the fragmented flow of the play, suggests a relationship between the two realities that the text of the play leaves unresolved.

The play's new conclusion, far from reconciling the contradictory realities inhabiting the play, crystallizes them into a state of permanent antagonism. The original *Cowboys* climaxed with a somewhat adolescent harangue of the audience and ended weakly with Chet and Stu fighting to the death over a canteen.[30] In *Cowboys #2*, the western fantasies enacted by Chet and Stu turn fatal when Stu falls unconscious and apparently dies. As Chet drags Stu's inert body across the stage, struggling to treat his friend's sudden stillness as just another western adventure, the lights, which have been dim throughout the play, come up slowly, reaching "full brightness at the end of the play" (*C#2*, 240). The sounds offstage, which have been building during the final sequence

of the play, also intensify as car horns and then horses and Indians reach
a deafening roar. As Chet chases away imagined vultures, the two
offstage men enter from opposite sides of the stage. They are of the same
age as Chet and Stu but are dressed in suits and carry scripts in their
hands. "They read from the scripts in monotone, starting from the
beginning of the play" (*C#2*, 240). Chet stares in front of him as the
harsh, white lights fade to black.

With this final image, Shepard shatters any possibility of a mimetic
stage reality, creating instead a self-contradicting reality that is purely
theatrical. While Shepard has employed contradictory realities in earlier
plays such as *Chicago* and *La Turista* and will use them again in later
plays such as *Geography of a Horse Dreamer* (1974) and *Curse of the Starving
Class* (1977), his theatrical imagery is never more intrinsically surreal
than at the conclusion of this play. The two suited men are entirely
irrational within the context of the stated action of the play, yet their live
presence on the stage gives them a physical credibility that calls out for
rational explanation. Even more disturbing are the scripts in their hands
that place them in some sort of parallel or mirror universe to the one
already inhabiting the stage. By projecting a comparatively anemic and
civilized universe of coats and ties, while reading the lines of cowboys,
these men suggest the ultimate threat to Stu and Chet's existence: the
appropriation of the cowboy myth by those who have no understanding
of it and who are antithetical to it by their very nature. In a universe that
could hold these two business-suited men, the cowboy myths from
which Chet and Stu seek sustenance lose all power and meaning. Far
more than the diatribes from the original *Cowboys* on the creeping
infiltration of the frontier by urban expansion, this theatrical image
expresses the devastating loss of personal and cultural self that drove
Shepard to write and rewrite this play. Such a growing consciousness on
Shepard's part of the broader social ramifications of this type of personal
imagery may well have led him to the next major period of his writing.
During that period, mythic icons like the cowhands in *Cowboys #2* begin
to speak not only for Shepard's personal experience but also for the
condition of contemporary America as a social and cultural entity.

Chapter Four
Pop American Pastiche

From the very beginning of Shepard's career, his work drew both critical and popular attention for no other reason more than his startling use of language—in particular, his use of eccentric and undeniably American idiolects and idiomatic vernaculars. From the Gabby Hayes westernisms of *Cowboys* and the porno magazine graphics of *The Rock Garden*, to "Dr. Frankenstein" in *La Turista*, Shepard's early characters are defined largely through the outrageous stereotypical voices they adopt. For the most part, these various voices and idiolects hold no ulterior significance: they are unself-consciously adopted by characters as needed to express a particular moment or sensation, then just as quickly and unceremoniously dropped. There is no symbolic significance to be found behind a particular character's adoption of a particular voice. That Jim in *Red Cross*, for instance, should sound like a swimming coach certainly is no reflection on the coaching profession.

But with political and social disillusionment escalating all around him as the 1960s wore on, Shepard's use of adopted voices became more and more the self-conscious manipulation of popular cultural images into commentary on modern America. In *La Turista*, when Kent struts onto the stage, having assumed both the voice and the accessories of a matinee idol cowboy, Shepard is calling forth the image of a mythic hero who must stand for the spirit of American manhood. That Kent, in such a guise, is easily defeated by the vision of the Mexican boy in his bed, symbolizes the devaluation of such iconographic American idols. The boy, embodying both primal psychological (Oedipal) and mystical (Mayan Indian) forces, renders the mock-mythic force of a media-generated image such as the matinee cowboy meaningless.

Seeming to sense that his own lost investment in myths which no longer sustained him was indicative of America at large, Shepard began to see character and reality in terms of images and narratives assembled from his nation's collective cultural consciousness. *Forensic and the Navigators* (1967), for instance, is the first of Shepard's plays that could be said to contain a consciously sociopolitical statement: young ineffectual revolutionaries, dressed in the costumes of traditional American

"outlaws"—cowboys and Indians—are pitted against an unseen technological authority that, careless of human life, gasses its own agents along
with the nest of revolutionaries. More and more during this period in
Shepard's career, cowboys and Indians inhabit his plays, as do pirates and
lumberjacks, revolutionaries and cheerleaders, rock stars and movie stars,
even sci-fi monsters, space invaders, and faceless exterminators. For the
first time in his career, Shepard seems to be consciously attempting to
voice the experience of the American people. In Robert Brustein's words,
Shepard "mingle[s] past, present and future into a pastiche of legend and
actuality which describes prole America more effectively than the most
fastidious documentary."[1]

Noticeably lacking in the majority of these pastiche plays are the
menace and agitation that were vital to Shepard's early work. His highly
personal sense of terror is traded in for a vague sociopolitical malaise.
During this period, a new force seems to be working on Shepard as
playwright and on his characters: a force that no longer manifests itself in
the shattering of one's personal reality, but rather a force that extends to
the disintegration of the cultural heritage and mythic fabric that hold
America together. As Shepard later wrote, "you could hear the sound of
America cracking open and crashing into the sea."[2] To further mark the
shift in Shepard's work, the insubstantial sources of menace in the earlier
plays are here given physical form in the various manifestations of a
technocratic authoritarian government. Just as the menace to the young
men in Cowboys was literalized by the appearance of the two corporate
figures, absently reading from scripts in Cowboys #2, so the literalized
threat of military apocalypse in Shepard's next series of plays, including
the above-mentioned Forensic and the Navigators as well as The Unseen
Hand (1969) and Operation Sidewinder (1970), takes the shape of authoritarian governments, out of touch with the people and the land, who gas
revolutionaries, wage war on Indian tribes, and implant mind control
devices in the heads of their slaves.

Shepard's new thematic concerns are accompanied by a new theatrical
agenda and a redirection of many aspects of his old aesthetic. The
paroxysmal escalation of imagery and language is, for the most part, gone
from everything written after Cowboys #2. However, the radical juxtaposition of contradictory realities remains intact, but with a new dramatic
function. No longer intending to unfix reality, Shepard juxtaposes
various pop culture realities or milieus in an attempt to express the
media-fed consciousness of the American public. He gathers archetypal
characters and master narratives not from classical or mythical sources

but from such American pop culture sources as the B-movie (the western, the sci-fi thriller, and the gangster film), and he freely mixes them with characters and images from American folklore, rock-and-roll, comic books, television, and car racing. The result is a postmodern, intertextual pastiche of American popular culture in which Shepard is torn between declaring the official death of the old cultural myths and lamenting their loss.

Operation Sidewinder

While working on *Forensic and the Navigators* late in 1967, Shepard was contacted by Italian filmmaker Michelangelo Antonioni, who wanted him to write the screenplay for what would become *Zabriskie Point* (1970). Antonioni was interested in creating a film about the social turbulence in America and particularly about American youth. Shepard, who had been brought to Antonioni's attention as an artistic represen- tative of the American counterculture, left America just after the open- ing of *Forensic and the Navigators* and traveled to Rome where he worked daily for two months with Antonioni on the script. But Shepard was not the radical leftist Antonioni hoped and assumed he would be, and with a first draft of the script barely finished, the relationship was broken off. Against his wishes, Shepard's name remained in the screen credits.

It is difficult to say which came first: Shepard's growing consciousness of political and social content in his plays, or his election by the popular media (and by fashionably ignorant image makers like Antonioni) to the office of American mythmaker. In either case, one seems to have fed the other, and Shepard began to explore the implication of being an Amer- ican.

The influence of the *Zabriskie Point* experience is evident in Shepard's next play, *Operation Sidewinder*, which he calls "a movie for the stage."[3] Thematically, both *Zabriskie Point* and *Operation Sidewinder* "attempt to paint the current condition of the American spirit in its true pathological colors."[4] Both are set in the American Southwest and both revolve around a young armed revolutionary and a girl whom he finds in the desert. The similarities in plot end there, but the expansive, cinematic structure of Shepard's play demonstrates the apparent influence of his scriptwriting experience; with 12 scenes over two acts, 36 speaking characters (plus crowds of Indians), 11 songs, and a UFO landing, *Operation Sidewinder* was far more narratively complicated and technically demanding than anything Shepard had written before.

Operation Sidewinder pits a power-hungry, technology-crazed military against a group of black radicals planning to use drugs to take control of the country. When a state-of-the-art Air Force computer, disguised as a giant sidewinder and programmed to track UFOs, escapes into the desert, an Indian tribe mistakes it for the long-awaited snake god that will reunite them with their spiritual selves. Tying these various subplots together are the pseudorevolutionary, known only as "the young man," and his new girlfriend, a "very sexy chick" named Honey.

In a *New York Times* interview from November 1969, Shepard acknowledged the change in his direction as a playwright. He claimed to be taking more pains with the structure of his plays, writing more slowly, and leaving behind the "spontaneous freaky thing [you get] if you write real fast" in order to focus on the creation of "mythic characters." He also announced that he now saw his quickly written, early plays as "kind of facile" (Gussow 1969, 42).

Facile, however, is a term more properly applied to Shepard's treatment of character and of political issues in *Operation Sidewinder*. Shepard's previous plays were more concerned with creating a theatrical reality than with making a thematic statement, and characters needed to be fleshed out only enough to manifest the intensity of their personal anxiety. But in his first real attempt at writing a political tract, Shepard's characters are even less individuated than before. He relies on broadly drawn, comic book stereotypes. Even their names reflect their media-nurtured, one-dimensionality: the ridiculous military villains are Capt. Bovine and Dr. Vector (a Dr. Strangelove look-alike), and the black revolutionaries are Dude, Blood, and Blade. But rather than assume the stature of modern American archetypes, these characters come across as poorly thought-out clichés. Burdened with the complexities of a broad-reaching sociopolitical statement and situated in a conventional dramatic formula, neither Shepard nor his characters offer much in the way of profound political or social criticism. The play's structure, while far more intricate than anything Shepard had previously written, suffers from the loss of his earlier artistic spontaneity. In his attempt to write within a more conventional formula, Shepard's work itself becomes tediously conventional.

The play's trek to production was no less problematic than the script itself. Black students at Yale University, where *Operation Sidewinder* was originally to be performed, found Shepard's stereotypical portrayal of black revolutionaries offensive.[5] The Yale production was blocked in December 1968, and the play was not produced until March 1970 when it appeared as part of Lincoln Center's American Playwrights Season. In that production, the offensive scenes involving black revolutionaries were rewritten, with the blacks now silently superior to an idiotic white carhop who patronizingly expresses her support of their militancy while she waits on cars at a drive-in restaurant.[6] But, even in its revised version, Shepard's first "uptown" production met with considerable disfavor and was attacked for its lack of originality and its simplistic treatment of character. Reviewer Brendan Gill neatly summed up the play's lack of substance when he called it a "Disney version of damnation."[7]

While *Operation Sidewinder* was a disappointment artistically, in the course of Shepard's career as a dramatist it marks an important development. In the figure of the young man, Shepard once again places himself (however well disguised) at the center of his work. But the agitation the young man feels is no longer metaphysical; it is cultural. Ambiguously drawn, he expresses Shepard's consciousness of his country's maladies, while at the same time embodying the personal and political qualities that Shepard found so frustrating in the hippies and yippies. Shepard distrusted the radical Left as much as the establishment, and so the young man, while a voice for Shepard's own anxieties, is also a killer and a junkie. With little or no motivation, he shoots the first two people he meets in the play and is involved in the yippielike doping of a military base's water supply in return for drugs. Yet, in one of the play's finer speeches, the young man speaks on behalf of a generation of young Americans in despair:

I was all set to watch "Mission: Impossible" when Humphrey's flabby face shows up for another hour's alienation session. Oh please say something kind to us, something soft, something human, something different, something real, something—so we can believe again. His squirmy little voice answers me, "You can't always have everything your way." And the oppression of my fellow students becoming depressed. Depressed. Despaired. Running out of gas. "We're not going to win. There's nothing we can do to win." This is how it begins, I see. We become so depressed we don't fight anymore. We're only losing a little, we say. It could be so much worse. The soldiers are dying, the Blacks are dying, the children are dying. It could be so much worse.[8]

Later, the young man's loathing of his country is turned on himself: "I am truly an American. I was made in America. Born, bred and raised. I have American scars on my brain. Red, white and blue. I bleed American blood. I dream American dreams. I fuck American girls. I devour the planet. I'm an earth eater" (*OS*, 67). A similarly confused young revolutionary, again wielding a gun and paired with a beautiful young nymphomaniac, appears in *Shaved Splits* (1970), victimizing innocent bystanders while he preaches about a lost America.

Shepard has no political or social solutions to offer in *Operation Sidewinder*: he can redeem neither his confused protagonist nor his failing country. Instead, he offers a far-fetched spiritual solution in the shape of a kitschy, folkloric deus ex machina. The play ends with an elaborate Hopi snake dance in which Indian folklore meets science fiction and the sidewinder computer communicates with extraterrestrials hovering overhead in a flying saucer. When troops arrive on the scene and open fire on the ceremony, the Indians, along with the young man and Honey who have joined them, disappear into the beams of light emanating from the UFO. No resolution is offered: instead, like Kent leaping through the wall of the stage in *La Turista*, the young man's only solution is physical escape, here in the form of a contrived spiritual transcendence. But whereas the ending of *La Turista* so precisely articulates Kent's condition, the ending of *Operation Sidewinder* explains nothing.

The only redeeming characters in *Operation Sidewinder* are the Indians, seen by Shepard as inherently noble and spiritually whole because of their personal and religious ties to the land they inhabit and to the spirit world. That Shepard would place his young man's fate in the hand of Indian shamans is indicative of his belief in the great powers of ancient or primitive religions and mythologies, those which tie humanity to the earth and the spirits rather than isolating us from our spiritual selves and our environment through technology. This type of ancient tribal spiritualism also appears in the Mayan rituals of the witch doctors of *La Turista*. Shepard seems to see these ancient power structures as somehow authentic, as transcending the technological power of a civilization that has grown out of touch with the world. Kent's matinee cowboy has no real power because it is based on a glorified Hollywood image. In contrast, the witch doctors receive their power from their intimate interaction with their world. In *Shaved Splits*, a similarly exotic and "authentic" spiritual wholeness is embodied in a sketchily drawn Chinese servant who, sensing the nearness of his own death, performs an ancient and elaborate masked dance before jumping from a window. He is, at least according to the young revolutionary in that play, the only character whose death will have any meaning, for he is the only character in contact with his true self.

The Unseen Hand

With *The Unseen Hand*, Shepard again mines the rich mythic terrain of America's old West, introducing the Morphan brothers, a wild trio of gunfighters whom he pits against the futuristic forces of extraterrestrial tyrants. Also geared for battle are Willie the mutant space freak and a male high school cheerleader, sans pants, who has been beaten and humiliated by crosstown rivals. But Shepard never gives the Morphans the opportunity to prove their mettle in battle. Instead, they seem to disappear in the junkyard of American pop culture, becoming folkloric relics that lie discarded in the play's contemporary American setting.

The Unseen Hand opens on a stripped-out '51 Chevrolet convertible, deserted beneath a freeway off-ramp and surrounded by cans, bottles, cartons, and other detritus of consumer America. These discardables lie abandoned by the roadside while overhead on the freeway America races recklessly into the future. The cultural significance of the setting is reinforced by the name of the town in which the play takes place, Azusa, whose slogan is "Everything from A to Z in the USA."

From among these cultural artifacts appears Blue Morphan, a 120-year-old cowboy. He lives in the abandoned car and is himself little more than a discard of the American West. Blue's long opening monologue, delivered to an imagined companion, is all about the West of long ago, of a time when things were simpler, when he and his gang were loved by the people—"The real people I'm talkin' about. The people people"—and when justice was served with a six-gun. Today, he feels, is full of menace: "It's all silent, secret. . . . Don't know when they'll cut ya' down and when they do ya' don't know who done it."[9]

As if summoned by Blue's misgivings, in runs Willie; dressed in futuristic clothes, he is half man, half baboon, with a black handprint burned into the top of his head. He has traveled through two galaxies to meet with Blue and his two resurrected brothers, Cisco and Sycamore, in order to plot the overthrow of the High Commission of his native planet, Nogoland. The handprint on his head, he explains to Blue, is the result of "the unseen hand," a mind control device that effectively enslaves him to the High Commission by keeping him from conceptualizing "beyond a certain circumference." As in earlier plays, Shepard is again dealing with an unseen force at work upon the consciousness of his characters; but here the source of that force is identified as an authoritarian government.

Whereas Kent, posing as a cowboy in *La Turista*, is relegated to the position of empty media image, Shepard somehow sees the Morphan brothers as an authentic and potentially formidable force within his personal "mythosystem." It is Willie's belief that the Morphan brothers, with their blazing six-guns, represent a reality too primal and too authentic for the synthesized technology of his civilization. In his words, "All their technology and magic would be at a total loss. You would be too real for their experience" (*UH*, 11).

This proposed encounter between dead and dying cowboys and futuristic aliens is yet another manifestation of Shepard's thematic struggle between the discarded ways and means of the primitive (read "authentic") past and the impersonal technology of the civilized (read "unauthentic") present. The Morphan brothers stand beside the Indians of *Operation Sidewinder* and the cowboy and Indian figures in *Forensic and the Navigators* in facing a dehumanized technocracy. Here, as in those earlier plays, the battle never materializes. Instead, Willie is freed from the tyranny of the unseen hand by another character from American pop culture, a high school cheerleader. The Morphan brothers, having been resurrected and rejuvenated for their greatest shoot-out ever, are set adrift in the twentieth century. But with no trains to rob, no battles to fight, they have no identity or purpose. As Cisco laments at one point, "Here we are stuck in some other century in some hick town called Azusa somewheres" (*UH*, 46). Sycamore, deciding to stay behind in Blue's abandoned car, is immediately aged and withered when he stares into the face of the cheerleader and into a future where he has no place.

The intruding cheerleader, a comic stereotype of the unpopular, unathletic high schooler who resorts to the cheering squad, preaches an apple pie patriotism and devotion to his beloved home town, Azusa (i.e., to everything in the U.S.A.). His pop culture pledge of allegiance is like a rallying cry: "I love Azusa! I love the foothills and the drive in movies and the bowling alleys and the football games and the drag races and the girls and the donut shop and the High School . . . and the Laundromat and the liquor store and the miniature golf course and Lookout Point and the YMCA . . . and fixing up my car and my Mom, I love my Mom most of all. And you creeps aren't going to take that away from me. You're not going to take that way from me because I'll kill you first!" (*UH*, 42). Although satirized by Shepard and beaten in the play by students from a rival high school, this American innocent from the romantic era of Eisenhower and Kennedy offers Willie a rhetoric of patriotic fervor rooted in unimpeachable faith. Willie then falls into a trance, translating the cheerleader's words into the ancient tongue of

Nogo. As he speaks the sacred words, his people back on the planet of Nogo are miraculously freed.

As in the plays that immediately precede this one, Shepard's social comment suffers from nostalgic simplification. Not unlike Dorothy in *The Wizard of Oz*, Willie learns that the ancient language of Nogo has been in his head all along but that he has been kept from seeing it by the unseen hand. So the power to transcend outside forces has always been with him, if only he could have seen that there was "no place like home." As in *Operation Sidewinder*, it is a sense of faith and spiritualism that transcends the forces of contemporary technology, but unfortunately, as in that earlier play, the manner in which Shepard's theme is dramatized reduces it to the ethical or political complexity of a comic book.

Despite Shepard's inability to bring this play to a gratifying thematic resolution, *The Unseen Hand* represents a state of affairs far more complex than its comic book resolution would allow. If Shepard cannot be said to offer feasible or sophisticated social solutions to his characters' problems, he still excels, as in his early plays, in theatrically manifesting their experiential condition—in this case the postmodern condition of media-fed consumer America. Shepard's failure in these plays is not in creating this condition but in attempting to suggest a remedy to it. As though feeling the weight that goes along with being declared the artistic voice of his generation, Shepard tries to assume the responsibility of resolving the problems of the society he so masterfully depicts.

Failing to offer plausible solutions to America's postmodern malaise, Shepard is nevertheless a master at creating the theatrical essence of our fragmented reality. Shepard juxtaposes contrary and antagonistic pop culture images and characters on stage as they exist in the American consciousness: characters are isolated from their traditional elements or genres. Old West cowboys meet with a 1950s-era cheerleader and a futuristic space freak beneath a Southern California freeway off-ramp. They are not only juxtaposed to each other (each representing a radically different world) but their individual realities are juxtaposed to the situation at hand, for they are forced to deal with events entirely foreign to those of their original milieus. The cowboys must face the twentieth century as well as Willie's futuristic powers. The cheerleader must decide what to make of these apparent outlaws and their alien leader. Willie the space freak is from a slave culture that never appears on stage but that is clearly and radically different from anything beneath the freeway off-ramp. Each is stranded without a cultural or social frame-work, a master narrative, that would give meaning to their lives. So, like

the consciousness of the culture they represent, they remain unintegrated, a collection of discordant images.

Mad Dog Blues

Early in Shepard's next play, *Mad Dog Blues* (1971), a character leaps into
a customarily apocalyptic flight of Shepardesque language, describing an
American bald eagle flying into a smoke-filled sky, then dropping the
world from its taloned grip. The world, plunging into the ocean, sends
out a huge tidal wave. As though to undercut the potential political
significance of this image and bring a hasty conclusion to Shepard's
descent into the underworld of American political commentary, one of
the characters quickly and angrily remarks, "I'm getting fucking tired of
apocalypses. All I ever hear anymore is apocalypse, apocalypse. What
about something with some hope?"[10]

Mad Dog Blues leaves behind the apocalyptic political contrivances of
Operation Sidewinder, *Shaved Splits*, and *The Unseen Hand*. In many ways, it
is about the search for, if not the discovery of, hope: about a return to
one's roots and the defeat of one's personal demons. In 1971, when *Mad
Dog Blues* first appeared, Shepard's demons were many. His marriage of
less than two years was faltering. Having left his wife, O-Lan, and their
infant son, Jesse, Shepard was living in the Chelsea Hotel with rock poet
Patti Smith, whom he had met at a reading of her work in 1970 at the
Theatre Genesis. When *Mad Dog Blues* opened at the Theatre Genesis in
March, Shepard performed offstage with the band while onstage his
estranged wife performed the role of Mae West. The backstage scene was
tense. The following month, things were even worse: *Back Bog Beast Bait*
(1971) and *Cowboy Mouth* (1971) opened as a double bill at the American
Place Theatre. O-Lan starred in the first play, while Shepard (at least for
the opening night) played opposite his lover and coauthor, Smith, in the
second play. Shepard was also struggling at this time with increasing
drug dependency, as well as a growing hatred of the New York theater
scene, the focus of which, as Shepard saw it, had turned to competition,
money, and fame.

Mad Dog Blues is laced with autobiographical passages about the mad-
dening effects of the city, drug addiction, separation from one's home
and family, and the menace of money-hungry treasure seekers who place
fame and fortune before friendship. As if to combat these forces, Shepard
brought the script to his oldest family of theatrical friends and collaborators at the Theatre Genesis, where his first plays had been produced.

Like Shepard's earlier Theatre Genesis plays, *Mad Dog Blues* has no political ax to grind but instead attempts to recreate theatrically a particularly personal state of consciousness. The sense of rootless anxiety and restlessness with which the play opens is reminiscent of *Cowboys* in particular and of Shepard's early experiential plays in general. But in *Mad Dog Blues*, Shepard has relinquished the personal imagery of his earliest plays and chosen instead to continue dreaming and speaking in the vocabulary of American pop culture. Like the young protagonists in *Cowboys*, the two young heroes of *Mad Dog Blues* seek to escape their oppressive urban environment through a journey into their own fantasized adventures. But the rather vacuous characterizations of Chet and Stu have been given a hip stylistic reincarnation in Yahoodi and Kosmo, whose hallucinatory landscape is not the parched desert of the old West but the exotic back lots of Hollywood's classic adventure films. Their companions on this journey are idols from film and folklore. Mae West and Marlene Dietrich, Captain Kidd and Paul Bunyan, Jesse James and Waco Texas, all join Kosmo and Yahoodi on an adventure that is a cross between *The Treasure of the Sierra Madre*, *Treasure Island*, and an LSD trip.

As he will do again years later in *True West*, Shepard seems to split himself into two protagonists here, with Kosmo and Yahoodi representing contradictory factions within his consciousness: Yahoodi, the drug addict who prefers isolation but hates to be lonely, is lost in despair and violent self-destruction; Kosmo, the tall, lean cowboy, is struggling to overcome such darker forces and find a way home. At one point, the mortal debate between these two goes so far as to bring the play to a stop. Yahoodi, having committed suicide, is called back to life by Kosmo who accuses him of abandoning their story before it is finished. Yahoodi responds, "I'm struggling with something in me that wants to die!" Kosmo counters, "And I'm struggling with something that wants to live" (*MDB*, 189). On this unresolved note, the two part company and the play is taken over by the fictional characters of film and folklore for whom narrative resolution is both possible and mandatory.

Cowboy Mouth

The supporting cast of famous characterizations in *Mad Dog Blues*, lifted from film, folklore, and Shepard's own imagination, exemplify the playwright's continued search for an American genealogy of myth. In *Cowboy Mouth*, this exploration turns to one of America's most powerful modern cult heroes: the rock-and-roll star. Music plays a progressively more important role in Shepard's work at this time. *The Unseen Hand, Operation Sidewinder, Mad Dog Blues*, and *Back Bog Beast Bait* were all performed to the accompaniment of live bands. In the latter three, musical numbers were written into the text of the plays, and in *Mad Dog Blues* those numbers are sung, in character, by the cast. To a greater or lesser extent, Shepard was actively involved in the production of this music, occasionally sitting in on drums with the Moray Eels during *Operation Sidewinder*, again drumming with Lothar and the Hand People during *The Unseen Hand*, and actually leading the band, playing electric guitar, for *Mad Dog Blues*. With *Cowboy Mouth*, both Shepard and his music step out of the backstage shadows and move to centerstage as Shepard continues to tap a vein of autobiographical images he had begun to draw from in 1967 with *Melodrama Play*.

Melodrama Play was the first instance in which Shepard introduced music into the text of the play and the first time he focused thematically on the entrapment of the artist by work, producers, and the public. Until this play, Shepard had dealt with personal entrapment and escape only in existential terms. In *Melodrama Play*, Shepard presents a more literal (and semiautobiographical) form of entrapment, translating his own confining experience as a public figure of growing acclaim into a subject for his play.

Melodrama Play's Duke Durgens is a rock star who has produced only one great hit, a song that he actually stole from his brother, Drake. His manager is now demanding a new hit, and Duke is being held prisoner until he can deliver. Like Shepard himself, Duke is a young talent who scored early and must now continue to live up to his own public image. In *Cowboy Mouth*, the image of the artist as prisoner of his own talents and of his own public persona is repeated, but here the portraiture is more transparently autobiographical. *Cowboy Mouth*, written collaboratively by Shepard and Patti Smith, is based on their relationship during the period that they lived together in 1971. Shepard and Smith allegedly created *Cowboy Mouth* by pushing a typewriter back and forth across a table.[11] They later performed it together at the American Place Theatre for a single preview audience before Shepard, like Slim in the play, disappeared.

Judging from the first two pages of the script, one might offer the hypothesis that Shepard wrote Cavale's (Smith's) lines and Smith wrote Slim's (Shepard's). The dialogue during the opening beat of the play rings of mimicry as though Shepard and Smith were satirizing their perceptions of each other. Cavale spews forth obscenities at Slim—"Fuck

you. Fuck you. Fuck, fuck"[12]—while she hunts with a little too much
desperation for her dead crow, Raymond. The portrait of Slim is just as
extreme: the first words out of his mouth are a parody of the incantatory
speeches of Shepard's plays: "Wolves, serpents, lizards, gizzards, bad
bladders, typhoons, tarantulas, whip-snakes, bad karma, Rio Bravo,
Sister Morphine, go fuck yourself!" (*CM*, 199). When this poetic pretense is dropped, one discovers what is really important to Slim: "My
little family. My little baby," he whimpers, too mournfully. Within a
few pages this mutual ravaging of weaknesses and habits burns itself out,
and the characterizations become more sympathetic and consistent (perhaps taken over completely by Shepard's hand).[13]

Although Shepard has constantly downplayed the influence of any
literary figures upon his work, *Cowboy Mouth* resounds with famous
literary names, themes, and images, including references to Jean Genêt,
François Villon, Charles Baudelaire, Gérard de Nerval, and William
Butler Yeats. Structurally, the play appears to be modeled after Beckett's
Waiting for Godot, with each round of game playing punctuated by an
inevitable lapse in activity and the familiar refrain, "What're we gonna
do now?" No unseen Godot for these two hipsters, however: they wait
upon the new cult savior, "a rock-and-roll Jesus with a cowboy mouth,"
who, in Yeatsean fashion, will come "rocking to Bethlehem to be born"
(*CM*, 208).[14] Their rock messiah eventually appears in the form of the
"Lobster Man," a delivery boy, dressed like a giant lobster, who arrives
with take-out seafood.

Cowboy Mouth is about the quest for a new messiah who can speak to
and for contemporary American culture. "The old God is just too far
away. He don't represent our pain no more," Cavale laments (*CM*, 208).
Believing that she can transform Slim into a rock-and-roll god, "created
from our own image," Cavale has kidnapped him. When Slim inquires
how he can fulfill the role she has set for him, Cavale describes the process
through which great myth is created, the formation of a national hero
based on the collective consciousness of his people: "You gotta collect it.
You gotta reach out and grab all the little broken, busted-up pieces of
people's frustration. That stuff in them that's lookin' for a way out or a
way in. You know what I mean? The stuff in them that makes them
wanna see God's face. And then you gotta take all that into yourself and
pour it back out. Give it back to them bigger than life. . . . You gotta
be like a rock-and-roll Jesus with a cowboy mouth" (*CM*, 208).

Cavale accurately describes the task that Shepard has set for himself as
playwright: to climb inside America's collective consciousness and

evolve a theatrical language and a mythological genealogy that speaks to America about America. As the play ends, Slim slips away, suggesting that perhaps at this point in his life Shepard was not ready or willing to assume the role of "rock-and-roll messiah" himself. But in his next play, *The Tooth of Crime* (1972), Shepard demonstrates that the time had come to put a rock-and-roll savior—in the guise of a modern-day tragic hero—on the stage.

The Tooth of Crime

The Tooth of Crime marks the culmination of Shepard's second major period as a playwright. If Shepard's first period of writing could be characterized by a myopic obsession with altered or heightened states of awareness, his second period is marked by a spectrum of interests as wide-reaching and eclectic as the various pop culture milieus his characters inhabit. Yet, in *The Tooth of Crime*, the themes and images of this second period crystallize into a multi-faceted work of singular impact. The imprisoned rock stars of *Melodrama Play* and *Cowboy Mouth;* the father/son Oedipal pairing of old and young in *Back Bog Beast Bait* and *The Holy Ghostly*; the battle between the authentic old and the menacing new in *Operation Sidewinder;* the juxtaposing of pop culture idiolects in *The Unseen Hand* and *Mad Dog Blues;* and, at the center of it all, the rock-and-roll music that appeared more and more frequently in the texts of Shepard's plays: all these elements are dramatically united in *The Tooth of Crime.* Rather than employing legendary American figures from film and folklore as he had done in *Mad Dog Blues*, or juxtaposing B-movie stereotypes and genres as in *The Unseen Hand*, Shepard devised his own hybrid pop culture milieu for *The Tooth of Crime*, one born not of the juxtaposition but of the creative synthesis of several pop culture environments, populations, and vernaculars.

The Tooth of Crime was written in 1972 in England, where Shepard had fled after a series of personal disasters that began with the Lincoln Center production of *Operation Sidewinder* and almost ended in the breakup of his marriage. He would later tell interviewers, "I was into a lot of drugs then—it became very difficult, you know, everything seemed to be shattering" (Chubb et al., 12). With his wife and son, Shepard headed for London. It was not London's world-famous theater scene that attracted Shepard, but another of the city's great artistic industries: rock-and-roll. Shepard moved to London because he wanted to become a rock star: "London was notorious for its rock'n'roll bands, and my favorite bands are The Who, groups like that, so I had this fantasy that I'd come over here and somehow fall into a rock'n'roll band. It didn't work . . ." (Chubb et al., 12). While Shepard's aspirations may have been more than a bit naive (even for the overnight sensation of Off-Off-Broadway), he was not totally inexperienced in the music scene. He had been a drummer since childhood, and even before Patti Smith pegged him as "a rock-and-roll Jesus with a cowboy mouth," he had played drums on and off for three years (and two albums) with the Holy Modal Rounders, and with two Rounder spin-off bands, the Moray Eels and Lothar and the Hand People. But while Shepard's heart was in rock-and-roll—"I much prefer playing music to theatre," he has said—his true gift was for the stage. Failing to find musical stardom waiting for him in London, Shepard wrote a rock-and-roll tragedy about the outlaw spirit of America.

Shepard's rock-and-roll hero, Hoss, is the ultimate American outlaw: dressed in black leather, he is a combination rock star, gangster, drug addict, and gunfighter whose nebulous livelihood, "the Game," is populated with hit men, astrologers, disc jockeys, souped-up cars, and rock-and-roll music. Hoss surrounds himself with an entourage of advisers and followers from the various milieus he encompasses. Becky, his beautiful girlfriend, is part gangland moll, part backstage groupie. His private physician and personal adviser, Doc, is derived from TV westerns, except that Shepard's Doc supplies Hoss with illicit drugs, not just sound cowboy advice. Hoss's driver, Cheyenne, likewise combines the attributes of a TV western sidekick with the expertise of a race car mechanic: he is both loyal companion and resourceful technician.

Hoss and his entourage have their classically tragic side as well;[15] like some modern-day Oedipus, Hoss is advised by two Teiresian seers: Star-Man, who reads the astrological signs like ancient oracles, and Galactic Jack, a disc jockey, who dresses like a "white pimp" and "studies pop charts like the entrails of animals."[16] The first act of the play is even structured after classical Greek tragedy with clearly defined episodes in which Hoss meets individually with the various members of his household. These episodes are divided by monologues, much like the choral "stasima" of ancient tragedy, during which Hoss sings or speaks his innermost thoughts.

Like Oedipus, Hoss chooses to ignore the oracles and the warnings of his seers. The equilibrium of his reign is disturbed when he goes "against the charts," defying their prophetic powers. Hoss's position as master of the Game is threatened by Crow, a young "gypsy" renegade who ignores "the code" and depends on his own ruthlessness and bravado to stay alive. The style and substance of Crow's run for the crown serves as example of the synthesized, multigenre quality of the world Shepard creates in *The Tooth of Crime*. Like a mobster, Crow has "hit" several of Hoss's territories, including the capital of both crime and entertainment, Las Vegas. Having "marked" Hoss, Crow now rides into town to meet Hoss in personal battle like some young gun ready for a shoot-out with a legendary older lawman. And, like a James Dean street racer, Crow is identified by the car he drives—a "'58 black Impala, fuel injected, bored and stroked, full blown Vet underneath."[17] When he finally appears at Hoss's hideout, his style is that of a 1960s rock star, "just like Keith Richards."

Just as language serves as the primary means of weaving the various subgenres of the play into a single fantastic tapestry of pop culture idiom, so it becomes the ultimate weapon in the duel between the old master and the young upstart. The stylistic battle between Hoss and Crow successfully encompasses the various cultural and thematic polarities that Shepard had struggled to express in plays such as *Operation Sidewinder*, *The Unseen Hand*, *Mad Dog Blues*, and *Back Bog Beast Bait*. In a variety of guises, these plays juxtapose the old with the new, the authentic with the synthesized, the emotional and spiritual with the technological and mass-produced, the cowboy with the city hipster, and the past with the future.

In *The Tooth of Crime*, Hoss is the genuine article: the gifted artist of the old school of heartfelt rock-and-roll, whose vision arises out of a connectedness to heartland America and a sense of his roots there. His style is personal; it is his alone, arising out of the experiences and emotions that have shaped his being. Crow, on the other hand, is the cold, self-created stylist: his craft means nothing to him. He can adopt any mask, master any style. He is without personal identity or substance: "I believe in my mask," he sings. "The man I made up is me" (*TC*, 232). But, beneath the mask of adopted style, Crow does not exist; rather than "be" himself, he "performs" himself. His mask is, in his words, his "survival kit."

As always in Shepard, language plays a key role in creating character. Shepard has said of *The Tooth of Crime* that "it started with language—it started with hearing a certain sound which is coming from the voice of this character, Hoss" (Chubb et al., 11). In the battle of language between Hoss and Crow that dominates the second act of the play, Hoss draws his various "voices" from within himself. The images of American jazz, the Delta blues, Creole, the old West, gangsters, are all variations of Hoss's own experience, his connection to the styles of the American heartland that gave birth to his own way of talking and singing. Crow's language is rootless; it does not come out of himself but out of the moment's need: he can jump anywhere and everywhere, adopt whatever style he needs to make his kill. Like his adopted persona, his language is cold and hard-edged: "Very razor. Polished. A gleam to the movements. Weighs out in the eighties from first to third. Keen on the left side even though he's born on the right. Maybe forced his hand to change. Butchered some instincts down. Work them through his high range. Cut at the gait. Heel-toe action rhythms of New Orleans. Can't suss that particular. That's well covered. Meshing patterns. Easy mistake here. Suss the bounce" (*TC*, 228). When Hoss suggests that Crow might have something to learn from getting in touch with his own origins, Crow responds, "I'm a Rocker, not a hick!"

For Crow, the Game is just that, a game: he does not play out of necessity, as does Hoss; he plays only to win. At the play's conclusion, Hoss demonstrates for Crow that he is born to play the Game with all his being, that he is "a Born Marker" who can perform one last authentic act, an act of bravery that is far beyond anything of which Crow, the empty stylist, is capable. With the victorious Crow looking on, Hoss puts a gun to his mouth and pulls the trigger, killing himself. "A genius mark," Crow admits. But Hoss's final performance has no impact on the calculating Crow. Moments later, he tosses away his title as quickly as he has won it and decides to leave the game before it catches up with him. "I'm throwin' the shoes away. I'm runnin' flat out to a new course" (*TC*, 250). The game that means everything to a real player like Hoss means nothing to Crow.

Crow has been seen as the embodiment of postmodern America:[18] the mask without a face, the speaker of a language that has no roots and no meaning beyond its pure intensity of style. He is an inhabitant of the realm of the simulacra where there is no meaning to be found beneath the surface of floating images. Hoss, on the other hand, is a throwback to a time when America saw the presence of something real behind the style. Style was the outward form or expression of the inner being of the American people. Hoss is the artist whose work is an expression of his deepest self; he is the player who believes in the spirit of the system, understands the origins of the system, and plays by its rules. Crow is the stylist, the self-created star whose "art" is a combination of whatever stolen bits of others' work will bring success: he is the parasite who exploits the loopholes in the system to his own end. The two characters together represent both a longed-for America, which Shepard associates with the past and the authentic, and the contemporary, fallen America, which so proficiently mimics the values of the old to its own end and of which Shepard despairs.

Chapter Five
Critical States

In a 1974 interview, Sam Shepard told British stage director Kenneth Chubb that it was not until he lived in England that he really began to discover "what it means to be an American" (Chubb et al. 10). *The Tooth of Crime*, perhaps the most archetypically American of all Shepard's plays, was the first fruit of that discovery. The two plays that follow it, *Blue Bitch* (1973) and *Geography of a Horse Dreamer* (1974), examine not just what it means to be an American but what it means to be an American living in a foreign land. Both plays articulate the peculiar disorientation of Americans abroad in a land where the people speak their language but are nevertheless foreign to their personal experience.

Several of Shepard's earliest plays dealt with the plight of the individual at odds with a threatening new environment, and Shepard first focused on the theme of Americans abroad in *La Turista*. In that play, Kent and Salem fall victim to the unseen influences of Mexico's microscopic bacteria and primitive mythic roots; their physiological immunities and social amenities are broken down in a foreign environment that seems to affect their personal beings on an unconscious level. Shepard seems to be saying that the "otherness" of foreigners, their customs, and their lands—people and places that are "like" the people and places one has always known, yet are at the same time inexplicably different—create a sort of psychic distress. This distress was theatrically manifested in *La Turista* through the fragmented structure of reality and the sudden shifts in character and situation.

In *Blue Bitch* and *Geography of a Horse Dreamer*, the characters' distress is even more acute, for the differences between the Americans in these plays and their foreign counterparts is far less obvious but equally real. In England, an American might assume that because the citizens speak his language, their customs and behavior will be similar to his. But, as one of the characters in *Blue Bitch* notes, just because people speak your language does not mean they are like you. In *Geography of a Horse Dreamer*, the titular dreamer, Cody, does not know where he is. He has been drugged and transported overseas without his knowledge, yet he senses that he has left his native soil. His psyche somehow detects different atmospheric vibrations than those of his homeland, Wyoming. Both *Geography of a Horse Dreamer* and *Blue Bitch* suggest that the awareness of such dislocation is the source of great personal agitation and that the place in which one is raised and lives invisibly shapes the way one thinks, perceives reality, and relates to the environment. When removed from one's native environment, the psyche is mysteriously at odds.

Blue Bitch

Shepard wrote *Blue Bitch* in 1972. It was produced on stage only once in January of 1973 at the Theatre Genesis in New York City.[1] That production received a favorable review from the *Village Voice*,[2] yet Shepard has never allowed the play to be published or produced again. *Blue Bitch* is a clever, funny (albeit gimmicky) play about an American's paranoia when faced with foreigners whose intentions he cannot judge based on his personal cultural standards. Cody and Dixie, an American couple living in England, have placed an ad in *Sporting Life* in order to sell their greyhound racing dog, a "blue bitch" named Breeze. Cody receives a series of mysterious phone calls from Scotland. A growling voice on the other end of the line offers Cody outrageous sums of money for the dog if he will ship it by train immediately. Cody and Dixie are suspicious. Being new to the dog racing circuit and never having shipped a dog by train, they are unable to judge the legitimacy of the deal. Their anxieties over the possible intentions of the caller and the repercussions if they sell the dog spiral toward paranoia.

Cody follows in the anxiety-ridden footsteps of Jim in *Red Cross* and Stu in *Chicago*. Like *Chicago*, *Blue Bitch* seems to operate in an expressionist manner; the audience experiences reality through the eyes of the central character—in this case, Cody. Throughout the play, Cody is strangely unable to place himself. He and Dixie are recently returned from a visit to America. During their trip, Cody apparently sought to reorient himself by reestablishing contact with his geographical roots. But back in England, he is as much at a loss as ever to establish a sense of self. All memory of America, as well as Cody's personal sense of identity, vanish upon his return to England. He feels as though he has left something behind in America, perhaps a notebook with all the dates, places, and facts of their trip.

Cody's "notebook" is the combined formative experiences of his American roots: the events and determinants that make him an American. Shocked into objectivity by his contact with "an alien world as authentic as his own, he is left poised uncomfortably somewhere in between" his personal (and unavoidably American) conditioning of reality and the equally valid, yet quietly unnerving environment within which he finds himself (Washburn, 69).

Cody asks Dixie to aid him in recreating a personal reality for himself by reliving the trip through America. Like an amnesia victim, he attempts to find himself, to recreate "Cody" by recalling the experiences that comprise that person's existence. Cody begins to rediscover himself as Dixie describes the sights and people in several of the stops along their trip—Reno, Winnemuca, Salt Lake City. But Cody's reprieve is temporary. By the conclusion of the play, he faces a realization more frightening than his earlier disorientation: having assimilated aspects of British culture into his person, he recognizes that he would now feel just as rootless if he were to return to Wyoming. Set adrift, Cody will feel a sense of rootlessness wherever he goes, for he is basically at odds with the world, with reality.

Cody is one of Shepard's most self-consciously ontological beings. He not only perceives reality in a heightened fashion but also is personally aware of the peculiarities of his perception. When faced with suspicions about the motives and demeanor of the Scottish buyer, Cody attempts to place his paranoia in check by calling his own interpretation of events into question, suggesting that it is he and not the Scotsman who is acting strangely. None of Shepard's earlier characters has been so conscious of the inner origins of his particular anxieties. None has so objectively faced and systematically attempted to overcome the unseen forces at work on his perception of reality.

As in *La Turista*, Cody's heightened perception of his environment is theatrically manifest in a surreal and fragmented stage reality. One hears, for instance, the mysterious caller from Scotland as he must sound to Cody: his voice is not human but rather that of a growling dog, likened by one of the characters to the Hound of the Baskervilles. When a milkman is dragged onstage to offer an outsider's point of view, he has the look of another world. Dressed in spotless white clothes, hat, and shoes, he represents a wholesome, healthy reality, which Cody mistakes for objectivity. Cody tells the milkman to be strong and to not let himself be persuaded by demons. But as the milkman hears Cody's tales of the sordid underworld of crime, betting, and greyhound racing— introducing disturbing new aspects of reality into his consciousness— the milkman is physically transformed into a monster. Like Jim in *Red Cross* teaching the maid to swim, Cody takes a sadistic pleasure in watching the shattering of the milkman's wholesome perception of the world. Eventually, the milkman converses by phone with the potential buyer in a series of growls and snarls. Then, suddenly returning to his old self, he assures Cody that the offer on the dog is legitimate.

Blue Bitch is autobiographical in that Shepard, upon his arrival in England, had quickly become involved in dog racing. A great fan of horses and horse racing in the United States when younger, Shepard had always wanted to own or breed horses but found it too expensive. The dog racing scene—so similar to horse racing in the excitement of the track, the animals, the crowds of owners, trainers, and betters—was far more accessible to someone of Shepard's limited means. In his next play, *Geography of a Horse Dreamer*, Shepard takes full dramatic advantage of the similarities between these two racing scenes.

Geography of a Horse Dreamer

Geography of a Horse Dreamer, like *Blue Bitch*, is set within dog racing circles and deals with an American miserably out of his own element. Shepard's central character, again named Cody, is a gifted "horse dreamer" who predicts the outcome of horse races. He is being held prisoner by a syndicate boss, Fingers, in a hotel room somewhere in England.[3] It is Fingers's hope that Cody will be able to turn his horse dreaming talents to the dog circuits.

On one level, *Geography of a Horse Dreamer* is a transparent stage allegory: Cody represents Shepard, the artistic cowboy genius who wishes to return to his old home and ways but who has been kidnapped by commercial entrepreneurship and forced into creative slavery. In this respect, he is yet another incarnation of the captive artist of *Melodrama Play*.[4] But approaching the play on a more metaphysical plane, it is Cody's condition—that is, his gift of horse dreaming, and the loss of that gift in the face of intangible environmental forces—that is the central metaphor of the play. Like so many of Shepard's plays, *Geography of a Horse Dreamer* examines the influences of a disruptive force upon a character's consciousness. In Cody's case, that force is the insubstantial "local frequency" of a particular geographical location.

"I have a feeling," Shepard once wrote, "that the cultural environment one is raised in predetermines a rhythmical relationship to the use of words" ("Inner Library," 52). That environment, the cultural and geographical soil from which one springs, also determines the way in which one thinks, perceives, and experiences reality, even the way in which a dreamer envisions winning horses. Shepard calls the stored images of this personal predisposition the "inner library." He once noted, in reference to his own inner library, that he "can't be anything other than an American writer" ("Inner Library," 52). Cody, the gifted "horse dreamer," is likewise inherently linked to the American soil from which he springs. His gift of dreaming winning horses, his inspiration, "springs from an attachment to his natural roots."[5]

In *Geography of a Horse Dreamer*, Cody's natural talent as a dreamer has faded because his native roots, what he calls his "geography," have been destroyed by isolation and relocation. Fingers locks Cody away in a hotel room, assuming that if he is held in a state of suspension from the outside world, his mind will be free to dream. But Fingers does not understand that Cody's gift arises from his particular sensitivity to his environment. It is only when Cody's inner library, his "geography," becomes attuned to his environment, that he is able to "dream" that environment. As Cody explains: "He don't understand the area I have to dream in. . . . The inside one. The space inside where the dream comes. It's gotta be created. That's what Fingers don't understand. He thinks it's just like it was when I started. . . . He's blocked up my senses. Everything forces itself on the space I need. There's too much chaos now. He'll never get a winner out of me till the space comes back."[6] The deterioration of Cody's gift at the outset of the play is the result of isolation not only from his native environment but also from any sense of environment whatsoever. His "inner space," the world of images within which he dreams, has faded because he has been removed from any source of fresh images. Lacking the reinforcement of daily exposure to his surroundings, his predispositions, his views of the world, vanish.

Cody's situation is complicated by the fact that, despite Fingers's attempts to keep him isolated, he senses that he is no longer in America: "We're on a whole different continent here aren't we? I can feel it" (*GHD*, 92). Under conditions of captivity, stranded in a foreign environment, at odds with his own inner "geography," Cody can do little more than rehash old victories by dreaming the winners of races 10 years past.

Eventually, his inner space becomes attuned to the "local frequency." Dog racing being the local sport, Cody begins to dream greyhound winners. Unfortunately, the strain of this foreign system, with its own rules and assumptions, is too much for Cody. He loses his personal equilibrium: seemingly insane, he is possessed by the spirit of the local dream frequency. Speaking in assumed tongues, he is transformed into a dog breeder and then an Irish trainer. By the time Fingers arrives in the second act, Cody has been transformed once again—this time into a dog, whimpering and scurrying away from the other characters, "crashing into things like a frightened animal" (*GHD*, 118).

Adrift in England, Shepard must have felt much of the same psychic disorientation that the heroes of *Blue Bitch* and *Geography of a Horse Dreamer* feel. The impact of England's culture is apparent not only in the theme of *Geography* but in the subtle changes in Shepard's characterizations and language as well. In 1977, he noted that his new environment had forced him to "Anglicize" his work: "I noticed . . . after living in England for three straight years, that certain subtle changes occurred in this rhythmic construction [of language]. In order to accommodate these new configurations in the way a sentence would overblow itself (as is the English tendency), I found myself adding English characters to my plays" ("Inner Library," 52). Fingers is one such character. He typifies Shepard's blending of American characteristics with British. He is a syndicate kingpin who made his fortune in California and who has American strongmen working for him. But he acts and speaks with the mannerisms of a London dandy. "Good God man," Fingers pronounces upon his entrance, "you'd think it was Fort Knox in here the way you carry on with the bloody locks" (*GHD*, 112). Fingers's reference—Fort Knox—is American, but his language—"Good God," "carry on," "bloody"—is British.

Throughout the play such British gangland characters are placed in sharp juxtaposition to Cody, the cowboy. However, the disorienting and fragmentary quality of that juxtaposition (which Shepard surely would have exploited in his early plays) is not fully explored until the last moment of the play when Cody's two brothers burst violently and theatrically onto the scene in order to rescue Cody: "Cody's two brothers, JASPER and JASON enter. They're both about six foot five and weigh 250 lbs. They wear Wyoming cowboy gear, with dust covering them from head to foot. Their costumes should be well used and authentic without looking like some dime store cowboys. They both carry double-barreled twelve-gauge shotguns and wear side guns on their waists. . . . FINGERS whimpers on the floor. JASPER and JASON look at him stony-faced" (*GHD*, 129–30). As Willie said of the Morphan brothers in *The Unseen Hand*, "If you came in . . . blazing your six guns they wouldn't have any idea how to deal with you . . . You would be too real for their experience" (*UH*, 11). Certainly the sudden appearance of Cody's two brothers, an unforeseen deus ex machina, introduces an entirely new and contradictory reality onto the stage. They are "too real" for the anemic hotel room and shallowly drawn gangsters. Only upon seeing these two bigger-than-life outlaws from the American West does one understand how much a foreigner Cody must have felt, trapped in a fancy hotel room, captive of a suave city gangster. Like the two suited men at the end of *Cowboys #2*, Cody's brothers drop in as if from another play, planet, or plane of reality, shattering our preconceptions of the world of the play we have been watching.

Action

With *Action* (1975), Shepard's last play written and originally produced in England,[7] the playwright abandons, once and for all, his extended foray into pseudosocial relevancy and spectacles of Americana pastiche. He returns, instead, to a theatrical exploration of the intense and highly personal psychic agitation that characterized his earliest work. In Shepard's own words, *Action* constitutes a "major breakthrough" in his career.

Although it does not deal with the American abroad as do *Blue Bitch* and *Geography of a Horse Dreamer*, *Action* continues to demonstrate the influence of Europe and European culture on Shepard's writing. In contrast to the postmodern themes and pastiche quality of Shepard's plays from *Operation Sidewinder* to *The Tooth of Crime*, *Action* might better be called *postabsurdist*, reflecting the influence of Samuel Beckett in particular on Shepard's work.[8] The self-conscious performances and the self-reflexive narratives of the characters, along with the seemingly postapocalyptic setting of the play, are especially reminiscent of Beckett's *Endgame*. In theme and dramatic style, the play has been compared to works by Beckett, Harold Pinter, and Peter Handke, among others.[9] The sometimes heavy and self-conscious literary quality of the text is common to plays written by Shepard's European contemporaries but generally foreign to his own work. Like those European models, *Action* thematically examines and exhaustively discusses the acute ontological agitation of its characters. The play demonstrates that, as much as Shepard may have firmly denied any conscious meaning in his earlier plays or any influence from his European contemporaries, he possessed a substantial intellectual grasp of their modernist philosophical and dramatic concerns.

Action is filled with images reminiscent of Shepard's early work. Like Stu in *Chicago*, Shooter attempts to seal himself off from life by retiring to an overstuffed armchair. Jeep smashes furniture with the same unfore-

seen violence and frustration with which the boys of *4-H Club* dashed
their coffee cups to the floor. But more important than the resurrection of
such images is the fact that *Action* dismisses any attempts at social or
cultural relevance and returns to a style of presentation whose sole aim is
to manifest theatrically a state of being or consciousness. Moreover,
Action verbally articulates in a direct and thematic manner the acute
existential/ontological anxiety that Shepard's early plays expressed only
via obscure theatrical imagery and metaphor.

Conventional plot is virtually nonexistent in *Action.* Four young
people, two men and two women, sit at a table drinking coffee and
waiting for their turkey dinner. (As is Shepard's habitual pattern, the
men contemplate existence while the women wait on them.) The lights
on a Christmas tree blink upstage, leading one to assume that this may be
a Christmas dinner. Yet the tree's presence is never acknowledged or
explained. Nor is it clear who these people are, what their relationships
are, where the play takes place, or whether the period is the past, the
present, or the future. As one review noted, "The setting is a cabin in
the middle of nowhere and, as far as I can make out, nowhen."[10] The
characters, as well, are from nowhere and "nowhen." While their literary
and geographical allusions are American, they are entirely free of any of
the American cultural traits or the verbal idiosyncrasies that had marked
Shepard's characters to this point in his career. Their only distinguishing
feature is their perception of their state of being.

The characters speak of a "crisis" they have survived, potentially
placing the action in postapocalyptic America. However, the contradictory evidence of the play leaves the physical reality of the apocalypse
unconfirmed. The men, Shooter and Jeep, are bundled in identical heavy
clothing and overcoats with their heads shaved. They look like postapocalyptic figures from films such as *The Road Warrior* or *A Boy and His Dog.*
The women, Lupe and Liza, on the other hand, are dressed lightly and in
particularly feminine attire; they wear, respectively, a 1940s-style floral
print dress and a Mexican peasant skirt with blouse. These types of
contradiction, carried out in all aspects of the play, create an intentional
obscurity that takes the action out of the realm of conventional reality
and onto a more archetypal plane.

The devastation from which the characters suffer appears to be personal or psychological rather than physical: they are the survivors of a
personal crisis of ontological consciousness. *Action* is concerned with
states of "consciousness"—the consciousness of one's self, of one's identity, of one's physical environment, of unseen forces at work upon one's

life, and even of one's alienation from one's own body—acute consciousness of the self in a body in the world. For Shooter and Jeep, the self can be both a prison and an illusive intangible. On the one hand, the accumulated experience of life and the predetermination of social and genetic influence that one calls the self can be a trap, a social mask through which one interacts with life. But when that mask is removed, does any sense of "self" remain? Is there a self without these trappings? Shepard touched lightly on these types of questions in *The Tooth of Crime*, presenting Hoss as a man trapped in his public image and Crow as one who does not exist without his self-created mask. But in *Action*, he pursues questions of being and identity in a far more rigorous manner.

Action is filled with a complex system of images, revolving around the concept of "being" as something that takes place either "inside" or "outside" of the accumulated self. To be "outside" is to experience being in a fashion that is unsheltered, unpredetermined, face to face with unconditional existence. Being "outside" can also mean being existentially free, unconfined, out "in the world." To be "inside," conversely, is to be protected from the world, to have reality filtered, to rely on a constructed reality. It is also to be trapped by the restraints of that accumulative filtering process, by the restrictive range of perception that such a process or mask allows or provides.

The psychic agitation that Jeep and Shooter experience arises from the fact that neither "inside" nor "outside" is, in the end, a satisfactory mode of existence. The latter offers a frightening freedom, the former offers safety at the price of independence. Jeep searches for a way "out," a way to contact life; Shooter seeks safety. Both eventually conclude that any differentiation between the two modes of existence is an illusion. Jeep will always feel imprisoned, while Shooter will always fearfully face the maelstrom of unfiltered existence.

These two views of being are developed in the play by means of several stories, images, and metaphors that serve to illustrate the impact of each view on the individual. Shooter, for instance, refuses to leave the safety of the group to go upstairs and take a bath. He fears a direct confrontation with his physical self and the objective self-examination that must follow. "When I look at my hand I get terrified. The sight of my feet in the bathtub. The skin covering me. That's all that's covering me."[11] Reality, it seems, will burst through its thin skin if observed too closely. Shooter again expresses a fear of self-awareness when he retreats to the protective womb of a large armchair he drags on stage. Like Stu's bathtub in *Chicago*, the armchair becomes a place "very much at home" where "the world can't touch me." Within a few minutes, however, Shooter regrets his decision. The safety of the chair has become a conceptual prison: "It was short-sighted. I'd give anything just to travel around this space. Just to lick the corners. To get my nose in the dust. To feel my body moving" (*Action*, 140). Having retreated from life, Shooter immediately seeks to reestablish contact. This impulse, too, is short-lived, for he sees the outcome of one move or the other as identical: "Now neither one is any good. The chair doesn't get it on, and neither does the adventure. I'm nowhere" (*Action*, 140). He eventually attempts to halt his consciousness of existence completely. He creates a symbolic nonbeing by turning the chair over on top of himself and disappearing under it. "Am I completely hidden?" he asks Jeep. "Maybe I'm gone" (*Action*, 143). Reminiscent of the old man in Beckett's *Film*, Shooter experiments with the concept that to be is to be perceived and that by being completely hidden from the world, he can cease to be. But like Beckett's old man, he discovers that he perceives, is conscious of, himself. After hiding under the chair for a few minutes, he tells Jeep that "something creeps back in." That something is self-awareness.

Jeep seems to have no desire for safety. "Inside" is for him a conceptual prison, the unseen hand of social, emotional, and psychological restrictions and predeterminants. He refers to his childhood and family life as imprisonment: "Once I was in a family. I had no choice about it. I lived in different houses. I had no choice. I couldn't even choose the wallpaper" (*Action*, 144). The young Jeep's sense of confinement changed only when he "got in trouble" and was arrested. What for almost anyone else would be considered a loss of freedom and of the luxuries of family and home was for Jeep a revelation. "It wasn't until I got in trouble that I found out my true position. . . . I was in the world. I was up for grabs" (*Action*, 144). With the destruction of his domestic life and the exposure to a new mode of existence—what he calls being "in trouble"—Jeep's frame of reference is expanded. He is able to see beyond the limited world of his family and friends to "something bigger." With his changed frame of reference—that is, with the unfixing of Jeep's domesticated worldview—came a flood of consciousness, the objective, unjudgmental consciousness of being alive in the world: "And everywhere I noticed this new interest in my existence. These new details. Every scar was noted down. Every mark. The lines in my fingers. Hair. Eyes. Change in the pocket. Knives. Race. Age. Every detail. . . . I entered a new world" (*Action*, 144).

Shooter's reaction to Jeep's description of freedom is typical of his viewpoint: "Weren't you scared?" he asks. But the only fear Jeep experiences is the awareness that his newfound freedom is not complete. He becomes acutely conscious of the forces that keep him from being in total control of his own destiny:

> I used to have this dream that would come to me while I was on my feet. I'd be on my feet just standing there in these walls, and I'd have this dream come to me that the walls were moving in. It was like a sweeping kind of terror that struck me. Then something in me would panic. I wouldn't make a move. I'd just be standing there very still, but inside something would leap like it was trying to escape. And then the leap would come up against something. It was like an absolutely helpless leap. There was no possible way of getting out. (*Action*, 144–45)

In an interview conducted the same year he wrote *Action*, Shepard used similar terms to describe the unconscious restrictions that combine to create a personality:

> But you have this personality, and somehow you feel locked into it, jailed by all of your cultural influences and your psychological ones from your family, and all that. And somehow I feel that isn't the whole of it, you know, that there's another possibility. . . . [But] [y]ou can't escape, that's the whole thing, you can't. You finally find yourself in a situation where, like, that's the way it is—you can't get out of it. But there is always that impulse towards another kind of world, something that doesn't necessarily confine you in that way. Like I've got a name, I speak English, I have gestures, wear a certain kind of clothes . . . but once upon a time I didn't have all that shit. (Chubb et al., 16)

Shepard's belief in the possibility of "another kind of world," one of unconditional freedom from accumulated and self-created dispositions, is the source of Jeep's revelation of a "bigger" world. Shepard's acknowledgment that such freedom seems unattainable, that total escape from unseen influences is impossible, is reflected in Jeep's final words, the final words of the London production of the play: "No escape. That's it. No escape."[12]

The terms "inside" and "outside" are also used in *Action* to refer to one's consciousness of the self interacting with the physical world. To be "inside" a moment is to be living that moment as an immediate experience. However, the characters in *Action* are more frequently "outside" of their own actions, watching them from a self-objectified distance, as though outside of and alienated from their own bodies and experience. At one point in the play, when Jeep has smashed a chair to the floor, he and Shooter stand over it, examining it like a work of art, "as though seeing it as an event outside themselves" (*Action*, 131). The first line of the play reveals this same self-alienation: "I'm looking forward to my life," Jeep reflects. "I'm looking forward to uh—me. The way I picture me" (*Action*, 125). Jeep has made an object of himself.[13] He speaks as though his own life were a movie he could passively observe.

Shooter offers two stories that illustrate the theme of alienation from life. The first is of a man (Shooter himself?) who was afraid to take a bath—"something about how it distorted his body when he looked down into it" (*Action*, 137). The man becomes completely alienated from his body and begins to fear it. He is afraid to sleep "for fear his body might do something without him knowing" (*Action*, 137). Eventually, the body kills the man but continues to exist without him: "It's still walking around."

Jeep is shaken by this story and feels the need to determine whether the same thing could ever happen to him—perhaps whether it has already happened. "How did it get started?" he asks Shooter. Then, "Can anyone tell? I mean if we ran into this body could we tell it was vacant?" (*Action*, 139). When Shooter is unable to provide a satisfactory answer, Jeep attempts to solve the dilemma himself, but he is unable to determine what comprises the "person" inside the body: "There must be a way. I mean something must be missing. You could tell if he wasn't all there . . . You'd know. I'd know. . . . We know. We hear each other. We hear our voices. We know each other's voice. We can see. We recognize each other. We have a certain—We can tell who's who. We know our names. We respond. We call each other. We sort of—We— We're not completely stranded like that. I mean—It's not—It's not like that. How that would be" (*Action*, 139). Pushed to define that which tells us who we are beyond our appearance, voice, and name, Jeep is at a loss. He further fails to explain how or why his own condition is any different from the man's. Unable to define the man's condition, he vaguely refers to it as "how that would be."

Shooter's second story represents the potentially volatile union of the self with experience. He tells of an ancient Persian fable in which a group of moths are attracted to a candle behind a window. "They longed to be with this candle but none of them understood it or knew what it was" (*Action*, 140). The leader of the moths sends three separate scouts "inside" to investigate the flame. The first reports what he sees but does not understand it. The second touches the flame with the tip of his wings, but the leader is still not satisfied. Finally, a third moth finds his way to the candle and throws himself upon the flame. Seeing that the moth and the flame appear to be one, the leader turns to the others and says: "He's learned what he wanted to know, but he's the only one who understands it" (*Action*, 141). The self is united with experience: action and actor become one. But the result of this embrace is self-immolation. Fearful of such fatal loss of self, the characters in *Action* shrink from contact with life.

The alienation between the self and experience, between actor and action, is theatrically reinforced upon several occasions in *Action* when the characters bring attention to themselves as performers. Jeep notes at one point that Shooter, who is supposedly looking for his place in a book, may be merely flipping through pages: "Not even looking. Not even seeing the paper. Just turning them. Acting it out. Just pretending" (*Action*, 130–31). When Shooter responds that he is really looking for the place, Jeep says he admires his concentration. The conversation sounds like that of actors discussing the level of concentration required to create a convincing performance or to believe in one's own performance. The alienation between the actor and his performance, Shepard suggests, is not unlike that between the self and experience. Just as the bad actor, distracted or unmotivated, will carelessly run through the actions of his performance without uniting himself with his role, so Jeep finds himself a poor performer, unable to unite himself with his life.

The book Shooter reads is itself a self-reflexive allusion within the play, drawing attention to the characters as role players. Throughout the first half of the play, all four characters take turns trying to "find their place" in the text. The few snatches of the book's plot that Shepard supplies suggest that it is about a band of individuals (the characters themselves?) who survive an interplanetary crisis and return to a post-apocalyptic Earth (the setting of the play?). Like Hamm's self-reflexive narrative in Beckett's *Endgame*, the book, along with other allusions in the play, draws attention to the characters as potential performers within a fictional narrative.

Shepard seizes every opportunity in *Action* to highlight the presence of the actors behind their characters by creating moments in which the illusion of rationally motivated characterization is disrupted. These disruptions, unlike those in Shepard's earliest plays, are supported thematically by theoretical discussion that draws attention to them. At one point, Shooter pretends to be a dancing bear, relating what it feels like to be "performing." The bear senses but is not conscious of the act of performance. He "finds himself doing something unusual for him" (*Action*, 127). Having thus drawn attention to himself as performer, Shooter suddenly halts his performance and "looks blankly at the audience" (*Action*, 127). The moment is not unlike an actor suddenly removing his mask—a momentary stasis in which the man behind the performance is laid bare. Elsewhere, Jeep finds himself in similar moments of existential stasis.[14] He asks Shooter to "create some reason for me to move. . . . [s]ome justification for me to find myself somewhere else" (*Action*, 141). He sounds, as he did when discussing the book, like an actor who has lost or forgotten his "motivation." Shooter gives him an "objective" to perform by having him clean a dead fish. As Jeep "gets more involved" in his immediate objective, he feels less anxious: "I'm starting to feel better already. . . . Now I've got something to do" (*Action*, 143). As he loses himself—that is, loses his distance from himself—in the task, his anxiety dissolves.

Other incidents in the play illustrate the same type of existential dilemma. The holiday dinner is a formality at best; Liza snatches the plates away from the others as they have barely begun to eat. The meal becomes an unfulfilled act symbolic of daily routines that have lost their ability to nourish the characters' lives. They perform the task like bad actors, and the entire meal seems a piece of poorly directed stage business. Shooter cannot even remember, later, whether he has eaten or not.

This forgetfulness exemplifies Shooter's inability to collect experience in his consciousness. The past has no relationship to the present for him. He does not gather experience and store it to create the accumulated self that would be, for him, a basis of future action or decision. Instead, he continuously creates himself from scratch, living moment to moment in a purely existential fashion. He repeatedly forgets recent events. When Jeep reminds him of his fear of bathing, Shooter treats the event like a past life. He relates only to the present moment, the present state of reality, as having any validity: "Naw. I don't remember that. Better to leave that. People are washing dishes now. Lupe's looking for the place again. Things are rolling right along. Why bring that up? . . . That's not me at all. That's entirely the wrong image. That must've been an accident" (*Action*, 137). For Shooter, the "me" of the present has no relationship whatsoever to the "me" of 10 minutes ago. No personality traits are gathered and stored. No events of the past need in any way influence or determine the present. He is, in Jean-Paul Sartre's words, "condemned to freedom," condemned at every instant to invent himself anew.[15]

Shepard's freshly articulated conceptual discussions of the self, of being, and of experience in *Action* shed enormous light on his early plays, giving an articulate philosophical voice to the elusive experiential images of such profoundly disturbing plays as *Chicago*, *4-H Club*, *Red Cross*, and *Icarus's Mother*. But *Action* is not simply a glance backward for Shepard; the play also serves as a prelude to the issues of identity in Shepard's jazz-inspired plays of the late 1970s and to the deceptively naturalistic theatrical style of his family dramas from that same period and later.

Chapter Six
Playing "Out"

In the fall of 1974, Sam Shepard returned to the United States, settling in the San Francisco Bay Area. Within a few months of his arrival, Shepard made contact with the Magic Theatre, an experimental company dedicated to producing the work of new American playwrights. Shepard's association with the Magic Theatre and with the close community of actors and artists in San Francisco's youthful theater scene allowed him to gather around himself an ensemble of artists like that he had first observed while working with his friend Joseph Chaikin at the Open Theatre. Shepard had attempted once before to form his own ensemble, working improvisationally with actors from Theatre Genesis during the creation of *Forensic and the Navigators* in 1967. But that collaboration was abruptly terminated when Shepard left New York to write the screenplay for Antonioni's *Zabriskie Point*.

Inacoma and a Theater for Voice and Music

In San Francisco, Shepard found both the artists and the creative climate he sought to renew his theatrical experimentation. He brought together musicians and actors and began improvising with "ways in which 'character development' might evolve directly from music and sound."[1] The immediate product of that ensemble experimentation was *Inacoma*, performed at the Magic Theatre in March 1977. Beyond *Inacoma*, the ideas and techniques developed during production led to Shepard's later, highly praised collaborations in voice and music with Joseph Chaikin on *Tongues* (1978), *Savage/Love* (1979), and *The War in Heaven* (1985).

Musical composition had always informed Shepard's style as a playwright and on several occasions in the 1960s and early 1970s he had experimented with the impact of music upon language—most notably and successfully in *The Tooth of Crime*. For Shepard, both language and music gave substance to the insubstantial: "They cut through space without having to hesitate for the 'meaning.'" Language, he once said, "retains the potential of making leaps into the unknown" ("Inner

Library" 53–54). Likewise, with music, "you could move in all these *emotional* territories."[2]

Plays such as *Mad Dog Blues*, *Back Bog Beast Bait*, *Operation Sidewinder*, and *Cowboy Mouth* employed musical numbers between and within scenes as "emotional comment" upon the characters and the stage action. But not until *The Tooth of Crime* did Shepard add music to language in a fashion intended to heighten the emotional, trance-inducing qualities of the language. In that play, Shepard combines language with music, introduced not in the form of songs alone but as a mood-evoking backdrop to the spoken speeches. When Hoss and Crow engage in their duel of verbal styles, for instances, the music is intended to function as a rhythmic, emotional amplifier:

HOSS and CROW begin to move to the music, not really dancing but feeling the power on their movements through the music. They each pick up microphones. They begin their assaults just talking the words in rhythmic patterns, sometimes going with the music, sometimes counterpointing it. As the round progresses the music builds with drums and piano coming in, maybe a rhythm guitar too. Their voices build so that sometimes they sing their words or shout. The words remain as intelligible as possible like a sort of talking opera. (*TC*, 234)

This movement toward musical enhancement of language in order to create a sort of verbal incantation seems a logical step for Shepard, who once described his use of language as experimentation "that led to rhythm discoveries in space and time . . . packing up words and stretching them out along with their size and shape and sound."[3]

The concept of the war of styles between Hoss and Crow in *The Tooth of Crime* is derived in large part from a play by one of the twentieth century's most important innovators in music theater, Bertolt Brecht. Brecht's first American genre play, *Jungle of Cities* (1923), was a confrontation between two men: a battle of style set against the gangster-ridden backdrop of Chicago. Shepard, the artistic individualist and recluse of the 1970s, was attracted to young Brecht, the emotional ruffian of the 1920s: "With Brecht, I think his attraction for me, was his 'tough guy' stance in the midst of the intellectual circle of his times. . . . his voracious appetite for the life around him and his continuous adaptability to search out a true expression and put it into practice. His concern was for a total theatre but one stripped to the bare necessity."[4]

Although antiintellectualism and a "voracious appetite for life" were apparent in the youthful Brecht of the 1920s, they were not part of his later intellectual theories on the role of music in the theater. Furthermore, while Shepard claims to have been greatly influenced by Brecht's musical dramas, *The Tooth of Crime* suggests a contradiction between Brecht's didactic intentions and Shepard's emotional ones.

Shepard has said that he intended for the music in *The Tooth of Crime* to work as an "emotional comment" upon the stage action: "I wanted the music in *Tooth of Crime* so that you could step out of the play for a minute, every time a song comes, and be brought to an emotional comment on what's been taking place in the play . . . I wanted the music to be used as a kind of sounding-board for the play" (Chubb et al., 12). Such a sounding board certainly falls within the boundaries of Brecht's intentions for music in the theater; however, Brecht utilized musical interruption within the text of his plays as a means of inducing in the audience a "critical distance" from the action on stage.[5] As Brecht saw it, music should remove the audience from the emotional pull of the stage action, offering a moment to reflect, calmly and intellectually, upon the social ramifications of the events on stage. Shepard, on the other hand, has repeatedly stated that he wants to create language and music that evoke an immediate emotional and visceral impact: "Just bam! and there it is" (Hamill, 88).

A more likely inspiration for Shepard's combination of language and music in *The Tooth of Crime* might be suggested by his relationship and collaboration with rock poet Patti Smith. Smith, as a performer, did not sing songs—she incanted poems to the accompaniment of harsh electric rock-and-roll rhythms, often in complete dissonance to the spoken rhythm of her poetry. Her album *Horses* (1975) is filled with apocalyptic, often surreal, poetry. Reminiscent of Shepard's spiraling monologues, Smith's lyrics are screamed and chanted in an apparently drug-induced, spellbinding frenzy. Her work exhibits a keen understanding of what theater theoretician Antonin Artaud called language's ability to produce "physical shock," to be distributed concretely in space, and to "shatter as well as really manifest" a rational reality (Artaud, 46). Smith's lyrics give a physical impact to heightened states of emotion and anxiety. An ecstatic encounter between lovers, for instance, is expressed in physical terms as a girl "dips into the sea of possibility," putting her hand inside the open cranium of her lover. In another song, a young girl sees "the boy break out of his skin / my heart turned over / and I crawled in."[6] These disturbing poetic images are similar to the theatrical monologues of plays such as *Red Cross*, *Icarus's Mother*, and *4-H Club* in which language seems to take possession of the speaker.

When Shepard began work with actors and musicians at the Magic Theatre in San Francisco, his experiments built upon the symbiotic blend of language and music that has been the strong suit of *The Tooth of Crime*. But with *Inacoma* Shepard abandoned the hard, pounding rhythms of rock-and-roll for the more fluid, hypnotic qualities of improvised jazz. Shepard had been exposed to jazz all of his life. His father was a jazz drummer, and during his early days in New York he shared an apartment on the Lower East Side with Charles Mingus, Jr., son of the famous jazz bassist Charlie Mingus. Shortly after moving to San Francisco, Shepard began studying musical theory and piano with a local jazz composer, Catherine Stone. In the summer of 1976, Shepard asked Stone to finish the score for his Western opera, *The Sad Lament of Pecos Bill on the Eve of Killing His Wife*. The opera, originally commissioned for the Bicentennial celebration, was performed at the Bay Area Playwrights' Festival in October 1976.

Work on *Inacoma* began soon thereafter. Stone explains how the ensemble was formed and the process began: "We started meeting, all of us, in my house. [Shepard] brought around all these actors . . . and we started 'jamming' the way musicians jam, but with actors . . . . Together we started putting together ideas of what kind of drama would surround a comatose patient on those life-machines. He wanted a big two-act musical."[7] The result was an improvisational musical fantasy about a teenage girl who falls into a coma after slipping from the speaker tower at a rock concert. The play raises questions regarding the nature of "normal" consciousness and of identity. "Who was the me that used to be?" asks the comatose girl as she slips farther and farther away from life and the "normal" state of consciousness she once knew. "What was I then when they called me by my name?"[8] Her inner tranquillity is contrasted to the moral agonizing and legal battles surrounding the decision to take her off life-support systems. "Without seeing my being, they decide on my fate,"[9] the victim laments of her doctors, parents, and lawyers.

The performance ensemble was comprised of eight actors, some of whom, like Shepard's wife, O-Lan, were also accomplished musicians. Eight musicians were also involved. Each played a variety of instruments, creating a broad range of orchestral possibilities. One of the greatest challenges of the *Inacoma* project, Stone recalls, was making the musicians and the actors sensitive to each others' conventions and techniques: "We had the horrendous problem of bridging the two worlds. I was like

the liaison. And I didn't know that much about the actor's world."[10]
Several exercises were developed in order to produce creative interaction
between the two factions. Joseph Chaikin's "sound and movement"
exercise—a process in which a sound/movement is developed by one
actor and then handed off to another who in turn can comment upon it,
change it, or leave it before handing it off to another —was adapted to
include musicians: "An actor would step out and a musician would step
out. And the musician would make the music and the actor would make
the movement and the sound. And then the actor would go over and hand
it off to another actor, and the musician would go over and hand it off to
another musician. So it's that same [Chaikin] exercise, except done with
musicians" (Stone). Another exercise central to the development of
Inacoma and to Shepard's continued use of music was the "music puppet"
exercise in which the musicians became like puppeteers, their music
being the strings that manipulated the actor: "A musician would get
behind one actor and play. And the actor couldn't do anything except if
the musician did something" (Stone). The same exercise was also re-
versed, so that the actor dictated the direction of the music. The music
could thus serve as a means of emotional comment on either the actor's
language or action: "We would take a specific character and that character would step forward like a soloist with a back-up, like a soul singer
with a back-up orchestra. And we'd say, o.k., this is the doctor . . . and
he would step forward. . . . It was like the actor would step up and the
musicians would gather something just from knowing what the character was, and knowing who the actor was. And they would start to play
something" (Stone). Many of *Inacoma*'s monologues and scenes were
developed in this fashion, the cooperative result of improvisation in
rehearsal. Shepard might initiate a situational improvisation or lead the
actors toward a particular philosophical consideration, but he brought no
material into the rehearsal process except for lyrics that Stone, as well as
members of the ensemble, set to music. *Inacoma* was the first of a string
of performance pieces for Shepard—followed by *Tongues*, *Savage/Love*,
Superstitions, and *The War in Heaven*—that combined language, sound,
and music to create a unique theatrical experience.

Stone affectionately calls *Inacoma* the "immovable object." With its
16 performers and musicians, the piece proved nearly uncontrollable.
However, the shorter pieces that followed, employing only a handful of
actors and musicians, offered a more easily manipulated structure. Shepard has called two of those pieces, *Tongues* and *Savage/Love*, "an attempt to
find an equal expression between music and the actor."[11] The same could

be said of *Superstitions*, on which Shepard collaborated with the Overtone Theatre, a musical ensemble founded by Stone, along with Shepard's wife, O-Lan, and others from the *Inacoma* cast.

Tongues, *Savage/Love*, and *Superstitions* are short pieces for voice, sound, and music—collages of monologues, poems, chants, and dialogues—comprised of snatches of everyday life and expressing a range of familiar human experience from the pain of childbirth to the fear of death. These pieces are not plays but librettos, conceived with the intent of being set to sound and music. The music is an extension of the language, working both as a subtext to the language and an environment within which the language takes place. It sometimes underlines the impact of the text, while other times it counterpoints the language or comments ironically upon it.

The "music puppet" principle of Shepard's work from *Inacoma* dominates these pieces, constantly redefining the relationship between spoken word and music. In the program notes to *Superstitions*, the members of the Overtone Theatre describe how they approached the individual segments of that work: "We worked with each piece until we found its particular musical nature. It became clear that the role of the music was as varied as the drama it surrounded. At times its presence initiates action, at other times it echoes and reflects the action. The music can be the natural sounds around the characters or the moods inside them. It can also be an equal participant in conversations, or an entry point to parts unknown."[12] Shepard initiated many experiments with the Overtone Theatre in the late 1970s, including *Drum Wars*, a "battle-of-the-drums" improvisation in which six percussionists (including Shepard) jammed conceptually, taking inspiration from words and phrases—such as "angel" or "gumbo" or "black heat"—read from placards at the center of the stage (Stone). In attempting to redefine the theatrical relationship between music and language, Shepard and Stone even undertook a project intended to reverse the usual order of musical composition for the stage: Stone first wrote an hour's worth of music, around which Shepard would later write the play. "Well, of course it didn't work," Stone recalls. The project was never realized, but the process was just one more manner in which Shepard was attempting to stretch himself as a writer.

Perhaps the most important result of Shepard's association with jazz collaborators was their philosophical reaffirmation and artistic expression of a life view that Shepard himself held and had struggled to express in his early plays. Stone explains: "I think the key word is 'freedom.' You know, that's what jazz musicians are always going on about. The freedom that you can't experience in your life, so you create an art form that you can experience it in. . . . freedom meaning flexibility—not afraid of stepping into territories and really enjoying them when you're there" (Stone). During the time Shepard was involved with the jazz scene in San Francisco, the local musicians were primarily influenced by the "outside" musicians: jazz improvisers like Ornette Coleman, John Coltrane, Denny Richmond, and Charlie Mingus who "played out" or stepped outside of the normal structured boundaries of music. These musicians, and the generation they influenced, viewed improvisation as more than a way of art: it was a way of perceiving and expressing life. The intended artistic impact of improvised jazz, then, was akin to the aim of Shepard's early plays: to take the audience into new "emotional territories," to create a change in their thinking that opened up whole new possibilities of experiencing reality for them.

As described by Stone, jazz improvisation and its impact on both musician and listener are akin to the unfixing of reality that Shepard sought to express in his early plays. Like those plays, jazz music could evoke new perceptual and emotional territories. Stone's description of what she calls "melted" music reinforces this connection:

[Unfixing] is real easy to do with music. Because it's irrational in a lot of ways to begin with because it's an emotional language that's usually put together in such a rational process. . . . It can give you the feeling that the world is a highly ordered place, it's safe and peaceful, and beautiful, right? It's so easy the minute you set that up to start having something underneath it start to be like volcanoes and 'wah-ah-ah,' meltedness and psychosis, you know. It's very easy just to layer it. We used to play a lot of what I called 'melted music.'" (Stone)

"Melted music"—music that starts off ordered and melodic but that deteriorates into distorted patterns and nightmarish wailing—is the jazz equivalent of the shattering of the realistic world in a play like *Icarus's Mother* or the descent into chaos in speeches like those in *4-H Club*.

Shepard obviously recognized and was drawn to the way in which music could evoke emotional territories with lightning quickness, much quicker than could language or dramatic action. "It's in the nature of music," he once explained, "it's when you play a note and there's a response immediately—you don't have to wait to build up to it through seven scenes" (Chubb et al., 12). His description of the process of jazz improvisation reiterates much of what Stone expresses:

Jazz could move in surprising territories, without qualifying itself. . . . You could follow a traditional melody and then break away, and then come back, or drop into polyrhythms. . . . But, more importantly, it was an emotional thing. You could move in all these *emotional* territories, and you could do it with *passion.* You could throw yourself into a passage. . . . There was a form in a formless sense. Music communicates emotion better than anything else I know, just *anything!* Just bam! and there it is. And you can't explain exactly how the process is taking place, but you know for sure that you're hooked. (Hamill, 88–89)

Shepard perceived not only the artistic ramifications of jazz improvisation as a technique that could be transferred to the art of acting and staging (as in *Angel City*) but the philosophical ramifications as well. The concept of playing "inside" the normal boundaries of music and of then "stepping outside" reflected Shepard's own vocabulary. Before meeting Stone, Shepard was already defining philosophical approaches to experience in *Action* as remaining "inside" or taking on the "outside." His association with the Overtone Theatre only served to reconfirm and give a new direction to Shepard's search for ways of theatrically manifesting unfixed reality on stage.

Angel City

While gathering his ensemble for *Inacoma*, Shepard was also working on two new scripts, *Angel City* (1976) and *Suicide in B-Flat* (1976). Written within a year of each other, both demonstrate the influence of jazz music and jazz musicians on Shepard's use of dramatic structure and language. Both plays call for onstage musicians. In some instances, these musicians are contributing characters in the action of the play. In other instances, they operate as mood evokers who comment emotionally on the spoken text.

One such musician is the saxophonist in *Angel City*. Catherine Stone recalls a saxophonist, Ed Montgomery, who lived in her house during the period that Shepard studied piano with her. Shepard was writing *Angel City* at the time, and, like the saxophonist in that work, Montgomery was an outsider, a presence and a sound in the corner of Shepard's consciousness: "[Sam] loved the saxophone player because he would come down the hall and play 'Misty' in the corner . . . Sam would be sitting there playing at the lesson and Ed would be in the kitchen with the door to the fridge open, playing to the vegetables. But I didn't realize that the fact that this guy was the kind of guy he was—outside of society, playing this beautiful music all around—was all part of Sam's mythology . . . It was right after that he started rehearsing *Angel City*" (Stone). In the surreal Hollywood landscape of *Angel City* (1976), the faceless saxophone player is the only character to remain entirely "outside" of the protective prison of the Hollywood dream machine. He is seen only as a shadowy figure who wanders past a large upstage window on stage, occasionally adding musical comment to the visionary speeches of the characters.

Angel City revolves around Rabbit Brown, a mystical writer who has been called from his Northern California home to save a faltering horror film. Dressed in a detective's tattered overcoat and covered with long leather thongs and Indian medicine bundles, Rabbit is a comic self-portrait on Shepard's part: the countercultural writer torn between art and ambition. Several years earlier, Shepard had found himself immersed in the film industry when Michelangelo Antonioni hired him to write the screenplay for *Zabriskie Point*. "I was 24 and just wasted by the experience," Shepard recalls. "It was like a nightmare" (Oppenheim, 81). In *Angel City*, Rabbit confronts a similar nightmare. Trapped by his own reputation as a "kind of magician or something,"[13] he is pressed into service by a producer whose skin is slowly turning green.

Angel City and its satirically treated themes are a constant mirror of Shepard's own aspirations and self-indulgences as an artist. The moguls who hire Rabbit seek to create a monster that will "somehow transcend the very idea of 'character' as we know it today" (*AC*, 67). Ironically, Shepard sets a similar goal for his performers in *Angel City*'s introductory "Note to the Actors": "The term 'character' should be thought of in a different way when working on this play" (*AC*, 61). Further descriptions of the terrifying special effects sought by the producers in *Angel City* are reminiscent of the disturbing qualities of Shepard's apocalyptic plays. Compare, for instance, the desired special effect (as articulated by Wheeler, the film's producer) to a description of "underground theater" from an anthology of plays including Shepard's *Red Cross*:

WHEELER:	Not simply an act of terror but something which will in fact drive people right off the deep end. Leave them blithering in the aisles. Create mass hypnosis. . . . [p]enetrating every layer of their dark subconscious and leaving them totally unrecognizable to themselves. (*AC*, 71)
OFF-OFF-BROADWAY:	It intentionally sacrifices story-line, suspense, naturalistic representation, characterization . . . for the stubbornly single-minded purpose of triggering a radically deranged and psychically liberating—or

> shall we say a "mind-blitzing" or even a "mind-blowing"—beyond-the-rational insight into the human soul.[14]

Shepard mocks not only Hollywood but himself and the "magic" that people had come to expect from his plays. "We're looking for an actual miracle," Lanx explains to Rabbit. "Nothing technological. The real thing" (*AC*, 68).

In addition to Rabbit, Shepard creates a secondary self-portrait in the character Tympani, a percussionist hired to create an original rhythm "guaranteed to produce certain trance states in masses of people" (*AC*, 72). Tympani's unusual occupation reflects Shepard's own experience in the 1960s as a drummer with the Holy Modal Rounders:

> TYMPANI: I'd never had quite that kind of feeling enter into a simple four-four pattern before. . . . Then I looked straight down at my hands and I saw somebody else playing the pattern. It wasn't me. It was a different body. Then I got scared. I panicked when I saw that, and right away I lost it. (*AC*, 79)

> SHEPARD: After periods of this kind of practice, I begin to get the haunting sense that something in me writes but it's not necessarily me. At least not the "me" that takes credit for it. This identical experience happened to me once when I was playing drums with the Holy Modal Rounders, and it scared the shit out of me. Peter Stampfel, the fiddle player[,] explained it as being visited by the Holy Ghost, which sounded reasonable enough at the time. ("Inner Library," 54)

Rabbit and Tympani worked themselves into a frenzy, chanting and beating on the drums. Only Miss Scoons, a hapless secretary possessed by their incantation, is able to bring them back down to earth: "You haven't got a thing. . . . You only got excited by the sound of your own voice," (*AC*, 87). This harsh statement might apply to any of the hundreds of . . . post-Grotowski[15] . . . incantations, including Shepard's, performed in the name of avant garde theater in the 1960s and 1970s.

Shepard's portrait of the artist also has its serious, philosophical side. "The urge to create works of art is essentially one of ambition," intones Miss Scoons during one of her many trances. "The ambition behind the urge to create is no different than any other ambition. To kill. To win. To get on top" (*AC*, 88). Rabbit wrestles with his motivations as an artist throughout *Angel City*. "I've smelled something down here," he confides in the audience, "I'm ravenous for power but I have to conceal it" (*AC*, 69). The lure of the dream machine, of a celluloid tape "telling a story to millions," has mesmerized Rabbit. Any force that so influences masses of people—"Effecting [*sic*] their dreams and actions. . . . Replacing religion, politics, art, conversation. Replacing their minds"—must be investigated by the serious artist. That this force is a billion-dollar industry also has its lure. "How can I stay immune?" Rabbit asks himself. "How can I keep my distance from a machine like that?" (*AC*, 69). The industry feeds off artists like Rabbit who are initially suspicious but who eventually "want something." Tympani explains how his superiors keep him strung out on the dream: "They'll feed off your hunger. They'll keep you jumping at carrots. And you'll keep jumping. And you'll keep thinking you're not jumping all the time you're jumping. . . . You'd be surprised how fast it happens" (*AC*, 73). Like Hoss in *The Tooth of Crime*, Tympani and Rabbit become voluntary prisoners of the system they thought they could take for a quick ride. Rabbit assumes that both Miss Scoons and Tympani are being held prisoner against their will. He slowly discovers that they have chosen to stay, as will he, to be protected from the threatening world "outside."

The set of *Angel City* is dominated by two objects: a large black chair centerstage and an upstage window, represented by a blue neon rectangle suspended in air. From the huge seat of power, characters in the play watch "all hell" pass before the window. Rabbit's attention is drawn to the window repeatedly during the play by characters begging him to "see what it's like out there." Lanx takes pride in keeping the environment in his office "controlled"—"Either we control it or it controls us," he tells Rabbit (*AC*, 65). Tympani likewise remains inside where he is "well protected."

One of the most enlightening descriptions of the characters' fears in *Angel City* comes at one of the silliest moments in the play (of which there are many). Miss Scoons runs on the stage, framed by the blue neon rectangle, and reads from a script she has "cooked up" during her lunch break: "No more pain, she cried, as they lowered half the bleeding city into a deep dark hole and covered it over with smoking rubber tires. She slowly became aware of the truth behind the power of money" (*AC*, 74). The wish for "no more pain" is a call for protection from the brutalities of life. That protection, in *Angel City*, is provided by "the power of money." Miss Scoons sets forth the equation that guides the lives of the characters: "Money equals power, equals protection, equals eternal life." Once the characters accept this equation, they become addicted to the narcotic lure of wealth and security. The outside world represents death to these characters. "What's the most frightening thing in the whole wide world?" Rabbit asks Tympani. The answer: that we will all die "and not know how or why or where!" (*AC*, 87). In the producer Wheeler's view, failure to keep the corporate machinery humming will lead not only to financial disaster but to "total annihilation."

Initially, Rabbit does not comprehend the others' fear. Having just been "out there," traveling the length of California by buckboard, he sees "nothing but a city" beyond the window. But, as Wheeler informs Rabbit, that city is turning them all into "snakes or lizards or something." *Angel City* might be seen in this light as a sort of American *Rhinoceros* (1960). Ionesco's play spoke of the mass conformity of a Nazi-like society, in which everyone is transformed into rhinoceroses. Shepard's "Angel City" is plagued by the lure of wealth, power, and material comforts, which turns its citizens into reptilian monsters so that they may better protect their position, their money, their exclusive life-styles.

The unseen force at work on the psyches of these characters is the fear of death. Rabbit thinks he is immune, but Wheeler knows better: "WHAT WE FEAR IS THE SAME! THAT MAKES US EQUAL!" (*AC*, 102). A shared fear—of death, of pain, of nonbeing (perhaps just insignificance)—eventually drags Rabbit down to Wheeler's level. "We're dying right here. Right now. In front of each other," Wheeler reminds him (*AC*, 102). Shortly thereafter, Rabbit begins turning into a lizard, just as Wheeler has.

Theatrically, *Angel City* is Shepard's most outrageous and fragmented play since *La Turista*. Saxophone music squirms and writhes its way through long, incantatory monologues, rhythm-induced trances, and orgiastic dancing. *Angel City*'s theatrical techniques are both a return to and a send-up of Shepard's apocalyptic, psychedelic images from the 1960s. Sudden disruptions of the stage action, taking the form of lightning-fast transformations of character and situation, fill the play.

In his published introduction to the play, Shepard calls for an unconventional style of acting, one which treats character as collage:

The term "character" could be thought of in a different way when working on this play. Instead of a "whole character" with logical motives behind his behavior which the actor submerges himself into, he should consider instead a fractured whole with bits and pieces of character flying off the central theme. In other words, more in terms of collage construction or jazz improvisation. This is not the same thing as one character playing many different roles. . . . If there needs to be a "motivation" for some of the abrupt changes which occur in the play they can be taken as full-blown manifestations of a passing thought or fantasy. (*AC*, 61–62)

Actors do not become different characters but instead manifest different facets of their inner selves, as though snapping in and out of self-revelatory trances. Such trances are central to *Angel City* as a means of expressing the unconscious dreams and fears of the characters.

Miss Scoons passes in and out of trances throughout the first act of the play and ultimately is possessed by demonic voices like those that speak through Cody in *Geography of a Horse Dreamer*. Shepard has ironically placed the most significant reflections of the play in the mouth of a bubble-headed secretary, the character least likely to express such insights. Miss Scoons's comments on the power of the silver screen, on the equation of money with power and eternal life, on the urge to create as one of ambition, afford the most significant moments of the play. Perhaps by placing these observations in the mouth of an innocent, Shepard is suggesting that this type of naive, eager individual most easily falls victim to the illusions generated by the film industry. Yet, as Rabbit Brown proves (and as Hoss proved in *The Tooth of Crime*), success is a trap that awaits every artist, not just the naive. In his next play, *Suicide in B-Flat*, Shepard gives life to another variation on the artist as prisoner of his own talent and success.

Suicide in B-Flat

Suicide in B-Flat was first produced at the Yale Repertory Theatre only a few months after *Angel City* appeared at the Magic Theatre in San Francisco. The play opens with the appearance of a mysterious pianist, much like the saxophonist in *Angel City*; in a tattered suit, this shadowy figure slinks across the stage hiding his face behind his sleeve. He rushes to an upright piano at the rear of the stage and begins to play. He remains at the piano, his back to the audience, throughout the play. Like *Angel City*'s saxophonist (or perhaps even more like the melodramatic pianist at a silent movie) he uses the piano to comment musically upon the text of the play, underlining the moods and nuances of individual speeches and passages.

Like *Angel City, Suicide in B-Flat* explores the world of the contemporary artist, in this case an improvisational jazz pianist, Niles, who (it appears) has committed suicide. The police have found a body in Niles's apartment with the face completely blown off; the fingerprints match those of Niles, but the nature of the death and the whereabouts of the jazz musician are still in doubt. Two comically drawn B-movie detectives, Pablo and Louis, are investigating the death. They are joined in Niles's apartment by Petrone and Laureen, two jazz musicians and Niles's longtime collaborators.

When the detectives start interrogating the two musicians, the dialogue turns philosophical, especially when improvisational jazz is the topic. The detectives represent the rational world of ironclad fact; they are here, after all, to collect the facts in a murder investigation. The musicians, on the other hand, are improvisers, in life as in music. They see the world, as they see their music, as amorphous, fluid. When pressed to define the nature of their collaboration with Niles, they offer only vague metaphysical theories of improvisation. Pablo, not satisfied with these answers, labels the free-form music and the accompanying lifestyle of the musicians as subversive, "distorting the very foundations of our cherished values!"[16] The improvisation of music, he believes, is the first fatal step toward the improvisation of reality.

Louis also expresses these opinions in the course of an argument with Laureen, who says that jazz takes her into new dimensions. When she says she is bored with "messing around in the same old dimension all the time," Louis responds as if she were proposing a psychic/political coup that could totally disrupt life. Louis has sensed the gradual dissolution of his "safe" worldview from the moment he entered Niles's apartment, an apartment where a man has committed suicide. He can neither morally accept nor rationally dismiss the suicide. The act and the apartment in which it took place leave him disoriented and frightened: "I gotta' get out of here, Pablo! Something's not right! We've gotten ourselves into deep water here! Can't you feel it? Everything's crazy! I've got to get my bearings back. It feels like we're involved in something we'd be better off not knowing about" (*SBF*, 138). Louis is driven to the edge of despair. The threat to his rational world, caused by the contemplation of suicide and "this free-form stuff," reached Louis's "inner depths." He battles with himself, rolling across the floor, fighting off a butcher knife he holds in his own hand as though struggling with an unseen assailant. In the end, Pablo, too, cries out that they are all the victims of "AN UNSEEN ENEMY" (*SBF*, 149).

At the height of Louis' despair, that intangible enemy takes physical shape as Niles appears on stage with his girlfriend, Paulette. Occupying a separate plane of reality, Niles shares the stage with the detectives and musicians, yet he is invisible to them and likewise unable to see them.

Niles's suicide has been an attempt to liberate his art and his artistic self by destroying his public persona as a well-known artist. As was Hoss in *The Tooth of Crime*, Niles is "stuck in [his] image" (*TC*, 224). As though to exorcise the various styles and images that have had an influence on his career, Niles enacts a series of ritual deaths during the play. He first dresses as a cowboy and then as a gangsterish dandy. His girlfriend, Paulette, ceremoniously slays each of these images, first shooting the cowboy with an arrow and then the gangster with a machine gun. Yet with each symbolic killing Niles seems to grow more uneasy.

Like Jeep in *Action*, Niles feels imprisoned within his accumulated self. He feels that his "real self," his existential self, has been inhabited and reshaped by other people's expectations and by his own adopted personas. Of the symbolic identities that he and Paulette systematically assassinate, Niles claims, "I want to get rid of all these ones and start over. . . . They've taken me over and there's no room left for me" (*SBF*, 141). But despite his firm intentions, Niles still fears this ritual destruction. He recalls the personal loneliness and emptiness that he experienced before he "invited" such identities into himself: "That's the reason I invited them in to begin with. So I wouldn't feel that loneliness" (*SBF*, 142).

Niles wants to be assured that he will not destroy himself. Without his adopted personas, how will he be sure he is still Niles? What constitutes "Niles" beyond his public postures? The faceless corpse, found dead in Niles's apartment, suggests that Niles has already destroyed part of himself. "WHOSE FACE DID WE BLOW OFF?" he screams at Paulette. (*SBF*, 148). Without seeing its "face," its outward physical mask, Niles cannot determine to whom the body belongs. Shepard suggests that when the individual sheds that outer identity, that "face" or "mask," he is left unrecognizable, even to himself. "How could you recognize me when I don't even recognize myself?" Niles asks Petrone (*SBF*, 152). Niles, like the man who is eliminated by his body in Shooter's story from *Action*, is indistinguishable without the guise of his created self.

At the end of the play, Niles returns to the scene of his crime and allows himself to be taken prisoner by the two detectives. In a symbolic action, he is handcuffed to them; the individual becomes one with his personal conceptual prison. "We're exactly the same," he tells them, as though he has merged with those who would permanently fix his identity (*SBF*, 155). His "self" cannot be distinguished from the elements of the public mask. Facing this revelation and the futility of his attempt to recreate himself, Niles submits to his jailers.[17]

Pointing to the dramatic equivocality of *Suicide in B-Flat*, Niles speaks directly for the playwright in the final moment of the play. Addressing the two detectives, the audience, and perhaps even Shepard's rational-minded critics, Niles refuses to explain his disappearance and the existence of the corpse in his apartment: "Am I dead or alive? Is that it? Is this me here, now? Are these questions or answers? Are you waiting for the truth to roll out and lap your faces like a Bloodhound's tongue? Are you diving to the bottom of it? Getting to the core of the mystery?" (*SBF*, 155). Although he returns to "life," that fixed plane of reality inhabited by the detectives, the seekers of objective "truth," Niles does so without rational explanation or resolution. Has he been dead or alive? Is he dreaming them, or do they dream him? Shepard refuses to disarm the surreal power of his stage image by reducing the contradictory elements of the play to a single, rational interpretation. The detectives have a prisoner, but they have solved no mystery, uncovered no truth. In a play intentionally structured as a murder investigation, no murderer is revealed, no resolution reached.

Seduced

Although first produced in 1978, well after *Curse of the Starving Class*, Shepard's *Seduced* appears to arise from the same creative impulse as *Angel City* and *Suicide in B-Flat*. A fanciful, slightly surreal play about the final days of a Howard Hughes–like millionaire (Hughes had died in 1976), *Seduced* is Shepard's final look at the role of such legendary public figures in the shaping of America's cultural consciousness. The play's protagonist, Henry Hackamore, is an eccentric and reclusive millionaire who has physically extracted himself from the world in order to gain supreme control of his life and his personal reality. Like the characters of *Angel City*, Henry seeks eternal life through power and protection. And like Niles in *Suicide in B-Flat*, he seeks to escape the public eye, leaving behind only his self-created public image. Unlike these others, however, Henry seems to have succeeded, at least temporarily, in attaining his goals. By means of his enormous wealth and power, he has virtually removed himself from "the face of the earth" and from any contact with "the world at large."

"Nothing from the outside touches me," Henry proudly proclaims of his controlled environment (sounding more than a little like Lanx in *Angel City*). Henry's living quarters, somewhere in the Caribbean, are completely insulated from the world: "Nothing from out there comes in here! No life! Not sun, not moon, not sound, not nothing!"[18] Having lived without the benefit of sunlight for several years, Henry has encased himself in an antiseptic tomb, a kind of living death. He has ceased to interact with life, blocking out the world so that his romanticized memories will not be polluted by reality. "I prefer seeing things to having them crash through my window in the light of day," he tells his servant Raul. (*Seduced*, 79).

Covering himself with tissues as though to catch germs before they reach his skin, Henry's compulsion for protection from outside contaminants extends to the microscopic level. He keeps no furniture because it creates more surfaces on which bacteria might grow. And he is so acutely tuned to his environment that, without looking, he can "feel" when one of his palm trees is out of place. He senses not only the space the tree is consuming but also "the space it's not consuming." He expects his servant Raul to share his intuitive powers and to anticipate his every wish: "What *I* want? What I want is for you to know instinctively what I want. Without any coaching. Without hints. For you to be living inside the very rhythm of my needs" (*Seduced*, 76). Henry's hypersensitivity to the unseen and microscopic forces inhabiting his environment is equal to Jim's in *Red Cross* or Jeep's in *Action*. As the man who built his fortune on "thin air"—aeronautics and jet propulsion—Henry is particularly well qualified to preach the power of the invisible. His compulsive paranoia might be looked upon as an occupational hazard.

Henry invites two movie sirens from his past to visit him before he dies. Having removed himself from the world, he asks them to tell him what "life" has been like: "Life in particular. What it smells like. What it tastes like. What it sounds like" (*Seduced*, 100). The two beautiful women appear before Henry as though they have stepped directly out of his past without aging. Henry tells Raul to watch how they carry themselves "like visions. Like moving pictures." These visions are more refined than real life, idealized images forever preserved on film. When Henry instructs the women to tell him a story, he requires that they tell it "like you were in a movie." He is accustomed to a distilled reality, once removed from the flesh and blood of real life. The real Howard Hughes is said to have watched the same films over and over because he knew they would not change. They were set images. Likewise, Henry closely regulates the events of his life, covering "all variables."

The ultimate control over life is control over death, and part of Henry's plan has been to assure himself of immortality by transforming himself into a legend. No trace of the physical Henry remains. Raul assures him that "you've disappeared off the face of the earth" (*Seduced*, 112). Like Niles, Henry has left a corpse, a pilot wearing his clothes who crashed over Nebraska. Presumably killed in his prime, Henry lives on as a mythical image in the public's mind: "I'm the demon they invented! Everything they ever aspired to. The nightmare of the nation! It's me, Raul! Only me!" (*Seduced*, 116). Henry has carefully cultivated the public image he leaves behind. He has become a living metaphor of the great American dream of supreme wealth and power. But like Niles, Henry knows he has lost a vital part of himself to the self-created image he thought he so thoroughly controlled. He has been seduced by the power of his own legend: "It happened in a second. In a flash. I was taken by the dream and all the time I thought I was taking it. It was a sudden seduction. Abrupt. Almost like rape. You could call it rape. I gave myself up. Sold it all down the river" (*Seduced*, 114).

Seduced ends with a chilling surreal image. Having forced Henry to make him sole heir to his estate, Raul pulls a gun on his master and starts firing at point-blank range. The bullets, however, have no effect. The real Henry has been dead for years. He has removed himself physically and spiritually from the earth, achieving immortality by transforming himself into a legend that surpasses his mere mortal body. "I'm dead to the world but I never been born" he chants over and over (*Seduced*, 116), suggesting the distant loss of the man who could have been but who surrendered himself to the legend. Failing to kill that legend, Raul slumps before Henry in a gesture of supplication.

Alone in his world, in his self-imposed exile, Henry is not unlike Shakespeare's Prospero in *The Tempest*. Like Prospero, Henry seeks to be a master of all things, to create his own kingdom and thus control his own destiny. At his side is the untrustworthy Raul, his Caliban. Just as Shakespeare, through Prospero, bids farewell to the stage, so Shepard's Hackamore draws the curtains on what had, until that time, been perceived as Shepard's artistic identity as a playwright. For Henry is (to the present) the last of Shepard's pop culture heroes and *Seduced* is the last of his fanciful theatrical spectacles. By the time *Seduced* was produced in 1978, Shepard had written two domestic dramas, *Curse of the Starving Class* and *Buried Child*, that would forever change the direction of his career and the implications of his reputation as a writer of American plays.

Chapter Seven

The Father, the Son, and
The Holy Ghostly

In 1978, with the American premieres of both *Curse of the Starving Class* and *Buried Child*, Sam Shepard's career took a turn neither his followers nor his critics could have anticipated. From one who had been the master of the surreal, the psychedelic, the "hipster fringe,"[1] came two powerful family dramas of an autobiographical nature more akin to Tennessee Williams or William Inge than to anything Shepard had written before. *Curse of the Starving Class* is about an impoverished Southern California ranching family on the verge of losing their home, their land, and their way of life. *Buried Child* is a homecoming mystery about the violent and incestuous family secrets of three generations of Illinois farmers. While these plays were a surprise to Shepard's audiences, they were not without precedent in his writing. Shepard's very first play in 1964, *The Rock Garden*, was about his feuding family, and in 1969 he wrote *The Holy Ghostly*, a surreal father-son drama that appears to have been based on a visit Shepard made to his estranged father. That visit may well have been the genesis of the renewed obsession with family and heritage that led Shepard to write *Curse of the Starving Class* and *Buried Child* several years later.[2]

Sometime during 1968, probably in March of that year when he traveled to Los Angeles to record an album with the Holy Modal Rounders and to watch the filming of *Zabriskie Point*,[3] Shepard traveled cross-country. Like Vince, the long-lost son in *Buried Child*, he stopped in Illinois to visit his grandparents. He then continued to the Southwest, where he found his father living alone in the desert. As do the son and father in *The Holy Ghostly*, Shepard and his father must have fought bitterly. They had not seen each other since Shepard left his parents' home in 1963; after this brief encounter, they did not see each other again for several years.

The Holy Ghostly must have seemed like little more than an anomaly from Shepard when it first appeared in 1969. While the one-act play reflects Shepard's work from that period of his career—nightmarish and apocalyptic in style, filled with long, incantatory speeches—it is, in essence, an autobiographically based father-son confrontation. In the play, Ice (whose pedigree, like Shepard's, is seven generations strong) has abandoned a successful artistic career in New York City to come to the aid of Pop, his father. Pop has been camping alone in the desert and is haunted by the figure of the Chindi, an Indian demon who Pop believes is trying to kill him. Ice and Pop are also visited by a witch, presumably the Chindi's "old lady," who deposits Pop's doppelgänger, his dead body, by their campfire.

What Pop has failed to acknowledge is that he is dead. He is a ghost, "one who has died without finishing what he had to do on the earth."[4] His life has ended with his relationship to his son unreconciled, and so he is stuck between life and death. The Chindi, the witch, the corpse, and even Ice are all manifestations of Pop's inability to accept his own end and come to terms with his failure to be a proper father to his son. Ice, too, feels that he has somehow failed in this relationship. Obsessed with Pop, he has traveled cross-country, as Shepard must have, to make one last attempt at patching things up. But, as they apparently have throughout their lives, Ice and Pop argue constantly. At the play's climax, Ice suddenly shoots Pop in the stomach and leaves him sprawled in the campfire to die.

If *The Holy Ghostly* was indeed based on a visit by Shepard to his father, he must have written it as a kind of personal exorcism; Ice shoots Pop, and thus Shepard attempts to "kill off" the memory of his father, to expel his father from his consciousness. But Pop refuses to die. At the play's conclusion, he dances in the flames of the campfire, continuing to haunt Ice's consciousness as Shepard's father haunted his.

By the time Shepard saw his father again in 1980, the playwright had moved to England, returned, and settled in the San Francisco Bay area. In 1977, with *Curse of the Starving Class*, he began a string of five plays about the American family. While the tone, settings, themes, and characters of these plays vary, one dramatic element that remains constant in each is the autobiographical presence of a young man haunted by unresolved ties to family, father, and personal heritage.

Curse of the Starving Class

In *Curse of the Starving Class*, it is not just the father's ghost who refuses to die but also a family curse, an inherited predisposition toward violence, a "nitroglycerine of the blood" that flows through the son's veins as it does through the father's. Like the unseen forces at work on Shepard's earlier characters, this blood curse, transmitted from generation to generation by "tiny cells and genes," is a powerful yet invisible force, imposing itself upon the characters in the play without their consent. And, without their consent, it turns them against each other, so that the curse of Shepard's "starving class" family is to be forever locked in battle: clinging to each other for life, yet fighting to the death.

Curse of the Starving Class starts in the wake of an act of domestic violence. The play opens to the family's teenage son, Wesley, cleaning up the pieces of a broken door. The previous night, his father, Weston, had arrived home drunk to find that the door to the house had been locked against him by his wife, Ella. In an intoxicated rage, Weston battered down the door with his body, then disappeared. The next morning, as Ella enters the kitchen setting of the play to make herself some breakfast (there is nothing in the house to eat but bacon and bread), Wesley describes the events of the previous night as he experienced them from his bed. Wesley's sensory-specific monologue, similar to those of Shepard's early plays, creates a heightened sense of the physical and emotional invasion of his being by his father's violence. He is an open receiver, sensing the "space around me like a big, black world," and aware that "any second something could invade me. Some foreigner. Something undescribable."[5] What invades Wesley's being is the sound of his father smashing down the door to the house and the terror of knowing he is vulnerable to the same violence: "Man cursing. Man going insane. Feet and hands tearing. Head smashing. Man yelling. Shoulder smashing. Whole body crashing. Woman screaming. Mom screaming. Mom screaming for police" (*CSC*, 138). Weston's violent attack upon his own home and his terrorizing of his wife and family are both literal and symbolic destruction of the protective circle of the family. He not only violates their safety, but by virtue of his absence as father and protector, he leaves them open to attack and invasion from others. Wesley is particularly sensitive to this sense of defenselessness, for he clearly wants to open himself to his father, but in so doing, he risks devastating emotional violation.

Both thematically and theatrically, *Curse of the Starving Class* contains images of violation and invasion by hostile, uncombatable forces. The play is about the all-too-sudden invasion of a small Southern California ranching community by the suburban sprawl of housing developments and superhighways; about the violation of one's physical being by poisonous "curses" such as genetic conditioning, microscopic germs, bloodlines, violence, even menstruation; about the impersonal invasion of uncontrollable socioeconomic forces into the family unit; and about the terrifying violation of a family home at night by a drunken father who smashes down the front door, leaving house and family vulnerable to even further violation.

The stage setting itself is an image of the violation of the home and family: kitchen furniture is set against a stark, open stage. There are no doors, no walls, only red-checked curtains suspended in midair to suggest the farmhouse windows. The first image one sees on this exposed kitchen set is Wesley filling a wheelbarrow (a piece of outdoor equipment) with the shattered remains of the door to the house, the only barrier between family and outside world. Any sense of interiority or of the domestic comfort of the home is immediately undermined. When the father, Weston, eventually returns midway through the play, he finds a live lamb in his kitchen. He ponders aloud this lack of differentiation between the interior and the exterior: "Is this the inside or the outside? This is inside, right? This is the inside of the house. Even with the door out it's still the inside. (to lamb) Right? (to himself) Right" (*CSC*, 156). The home—including the comforting reality the word *home* conventionally suggests—has been left exposed by the dissolution of the family and the estrangement of the mother and the father. It cannot be repaired. Even when Wesley builds a new door in an act symbolic of his desire to keep the family intact, strangers walk straight onto the stage and into the family kitchen.

Those strangers appear as the result of Weston's and Ella's individual attempts to sell the house and the farm without the other's knowledge. Ella has been dealing with Taylor, a slick attorney who has made her sexual seduction part of their business transaction. Weston has cut a deal with a sleazy bar owner, Ellis, who intends to turn the home into a steak house. Weston, it turns out, needs the money to pay off some heavy debts he has run up with local thugs.

The peculiar characterization of these intrusive strangers, with their threatening appearance and cold, criminal attitudes, is completely foreign to the domestic setting of the play and realistic characterizations of the family members. In a review of the original London production, Charles Marowitz noted that "these outside characters . . . waft on in a style peculiar to themselves with no reference to the ongoing, naturalistically pitched main situation" (Marowitz). Wesley draws attention to this peculiarity when he describes the forces at work upon his family as a zombie invasion: "It's a zombie invasion. Taylor is the head zombie. He's the scout for the other zombies. He's only a sign that more zombies are on their way. They'll be filing through the door pretty soon" (*CSC*, 163). Taylor is the first "zombie" to stroll unannounced into the kitchen, but others follow, including two moronic hired thugs, Emerson and Slater. These unannounced entrances become increasingly bizarre and threatening, climaxing with the offstage explosion of Weston's car (with his daughter, Emma, in it) as Emerson and Slater enter, giggling hysterically "as though they'd pulled off a Halloween stunt," holding out the carcass of a slaughtered lamb.

Watching these otherworldly characters burst onto the stage of this domestic drama is like watching the intersection of one plane of reality with another. Their sudden appearance is as alien and disruptive as that of Cody's cowboy brothers at the end of *Geography of a Horse Dreamer* or the business-suited men at the end of *Cowboys #2*. But, in *Curse of the Starving Class*, these figures resound with both theatrical and thematic significance. On the one hand, these characters are like the intrusive figures of Shepard's earliest plays: theatrical manifestations of the self's exposure to a world so strange as to unfix permanently one's preconceptions of reality. But they are also grounded in Shepard's personal experience as a teenager in Duarte, California. The lawyers and thugs represent the developers and real-estate hustlers who exploited Los Angeles's postwar population boom by literally wiping out the tiny farming communities that lay east of the city in the Central Valley. As superfreeways and mass housing developments began to spread into the rich farmland, small communities like the one in which Shepard grew up were literally wiped out of existence as fast as buildings could be erected and roads constructed. Postmodern America, with its shopping malls and fast-food chains, rapidly made the rural life-style of Shepard's "starving class" family obsolete.

Shepard has repeatedly claimed that such socially significant interpretations of his plays are not within his field of concern as a dramatist: "I'm not interested in the American social scene at all," Shepard has said of his family plays. "It totally bores me" (Lippman, 3). Turning to the family for inspiration, Shepard hoped to "start with something personal and see how it follows out and opens to something bigger" (Lippman, 4). The "something bigger" Shepard pursued was not the social relevance he had courted with American pop culture plays like *Operation Sidewinder* but rather the archetypal "mythic emotions" that classic tales of the family had evoked in ancient Greek tragedy. According to Shepard, his family plays are intended to strike a more universal chord; by self-consciously using the term *curse,* for instance, and employing images of hereditary violence to suggest a link between his own "starving class" family and such infamous family lines as those dramatized in Aeschylus's *Oresteia,* Shepard attempted to raise his domestic melodrama to the level of modern myth and to tap the collective contents of our repressed mythic consciousness.

Shepard employs an intricate network of images in *Curse of the Starving Class* to establish a mythic subtext in the shape of unseen forces infecting the characters and determining their fates. As in earlier plays, those forces can take on physical manifestations. For instance, long before the broader, hereditary nature of the title's curse is hinted at, a more immediate "curse" arises: Emma is stricken with her first menstrual period, the "curse" of womanhood. Her mother, Ella, warns against sanitary napkins purchased in gas stations: "You don't know whose quarters go into those machines. Those quarters carry germs . . . spewing germs all over those napkins" (*CSC,* 139).

Ella's maternal warning is the first of many images related to microscopic forces at work in the lives of the characters. Later, when Wesley brings a maggot-infested lamb into the kitchen, concern is again expressed over the presence of "invisible germs mysteriously floating around in the air" (*CSC,* 154). It is Ella who ties the power of such microscopic presences to the ancient curse of fate and heredity that condemns the family to repeated acts of violence and self-destruction:

Do you know what it is? It's a curse. I can feel it. It's invisible but it's there. It's always there. It comes onto us like nighttime. Every day I can feel it. Every day I can see it coming. And it always comes. Repeats itself. It comes even when you do everything to stop it from coming. Even when you try to change it. And it goes back. Deep. It goes back and back to tiny cells and genes. To atoms. To tiny little swimming things making up their minds without us. Plotting in the womb. Before that even. In the air. We're surrounded with it. It's bigger than government even. It goes forward too. We spread it. We pass it on. We inherit it and pass it down, and then pass it down again. It goes on and on like that without us. (*CSC,* 173–74)

Shepard once said that Greek tragedy evokes "emotional states, these forces . . . [that] go so far back that they go right to the birth of man. And we're still living in the shadow of these things" (Lippman, 4). In *Curse,* Shepard injects mythic dimensions into the lives of his characters through the presence of a biological fatalism, determined by forces "making up their minds without us," continuing into the future "on and on like that without us." The characters find themselves helpless in the grasp of an inexplicable presence in their lives: "It comes even when you do everything to stop it from coming."

The new dramatic agenda Shepard sets for himself with *Curse of the Starving Class* is not one he easily assumes. In spite of the sophistication of imagery, the domestic setting and story, and the dominant surface realism of *Curse*, the play shows definite signs of a strain between the heightened theatrical reality of many of Shepard's earlier plays and his new intentions as a family dramatist. Putting aside Shepard's use of such disparately drawn characters as Emerson and Slater to reinforce the theme of invasion, one is still left with numerous disturbing and incongruous images and events that appear to have no connection to Shepard's thematic intentions but are instead the vestiges of an earlier stage aesthetic.

Within Shepard's family plays, the mixture of surface realism and a heightened sense of a theatrical presence lurking beyond that realism led one critic to comment "one feels the need for a word such as 'novarealism' to describe the style into which Shepard's plays have settled" (Glore, 57). His stage actions and images are not just real, they are "suprareal"[6]—in the sense that, when set against the created fictional "reality" of the play, they become overwhelmingly vivid and material. *Curse of the Starving Class* opens, for instance, with a string of typically Shepardesque nonsequiturs that transform the stage reality into a series of perpetual presents. Wesley and his mother, Ella, are discussing Weston's drunken appearance of the night before when Wesley suddenly launches into an extended monologue in which he recounts the previous night's events. Just as suddenly, he leaves the stage and Ella starts speaking to the empty space. She appears to be rehearsing the lecture she will give to some (unidentified) girl who is having her first menstrual period. Perhaps a minute into this lecture, Ella's daughter, Emma, enters. Ella "talks to her as though she's just continuing the conversation" (*CSC*, 139). Emma responds, in turn, as though she has been present for the entire speech.

While some productions of the play might attempt to smooth the jagged edges of these individual moments and create a realistic narrative line, this sequence of events is far too bizarre to overlook, especially at the beginning of the play. Some directors have blocked the motherdaughter scene as though Ella is aware of Emma's presence just offstage and well within earshot.[7] But Shepard's stage directions indicate no such assumption, stressing that Ella "speaks alone" at the beginning of the speech and that Emma does not enter, nor is she heard offstage, until later (*CSC*, 138–39). The causal and temporal reality of the scene are thus unfixed, and the sequence of events resembles a description of schizophrenic reality: "an experience of isolated, disconnected, discontinuous material signifiers which fail to link into a coherent sequence" (Jameson, 119).

But to what end? Neither Wesley's transfixing monologue nor Emma's dreamlike materialization in the middle of her mother's discourse serves to reinforce any apparent dramatic or thematic intention on Shepard's part. Such irrational, discontinuous images are without context in this play, seeming to exist for their own sake as unqualified material images. The same is true of Shepard's startling use of the unqualified physical presence of the actor playing Wesley.

Early in the play, this actor must, without warning or explanation, unzip his pants and urinate on Emma's 4-H club charts. Later, he is required to walk naked onto the stage, again without warning, and scoop a live lamb into his arms, carrying it off. Linked to the unexpectedness and inexplicability of his actions, the purely physical reality of the actor—either exposing his genitals to urinate or entering naked—is so strong that the created illusion of his character and the fictional stage reality are shattered. Such physical nudity creates a heightened stage reality: there is no such thing as a naked "character" on stage. When the actor sheds his clothing, he sheds the illusion of character, of acting, and brings a new level of physical immediacy or "suprapresence" to the stage. This effect is intensified by the presence of the live lamb. The unqualified existence of the animal—that is, its immediate physical presence without the created pretense of character or performance—is far more "real" than the fictional reality of the play. The image of the naked actor scooping the live lamb into his arms and carrying it offstage transcends the realm of scripted reality in favor of the suprareal.

Had these events occurred in just about any Shepard play previous to this one, they would have been equally shocking perhaps, but they would also have been an integral, vital part of Shepard's phenomenological stage consciousness. However, in *Curse of the Starving Class*, Shepard is both telling a conventional story and introducing sustained characters and a narrative discourse into his writing. If he is "dramatizing a condition," as Robert Corrigan might suggest, that condition is the thematically anchored state of invasion in which the characters find themselves. If these instances of heightened reality have any relation to that condition, it is only to intensify the physical and psychic discomfort suggested by the presence of a pervasive curse and of microscopic physical forces. They add, in John Glore's words, "a tone of foreboding anxiety" by virtue of their "erratic disruption of a surface realism" (Glore, 64). More likely, though, is that Shepard, trying to find his way through a full-length domestic drama for the first time in his career, turned without thinking to the techniques of a stage aesthetic that had been part of his highly intuitive modus operandi for more than 10 years.[8]

The stories that open and close *Curse of the Starving Class* indicate the direction Shepard's drama is to take from this point on in his career. The play begins, as mentioned earlier, with Wesley's vivid account of the violent events from the previous night. The story is extremely sensory-specific, allowing the stillness and silence of the night to stretch the perceptual boundaries of the boy in his bed, and allowing the sense of sound to become acute, dominating all other experience. The telling of the story is a solo riff, in which Wesley steps out of the action of the play to create a moment, much like those in Shepard's early plays, in which the incantatory power of the language takes the audience beyond the confines of the stage.

By contrast, the final story of the play is far more literary, intended as far less of a visceral experience and more of a metaphorical comment on the events of the play. Weston begins the story at the top of the third act, and Ella finishes it as she stares at the gutted lamb that Emerson and Slater have dropped in the middle of her floor. Weston tells of a day he was castrating lambs and of an eagle that began swooping down out of the sky to grab the testes as Weston threw them over his shoulder onto the roof of a small shed. Each time the eagle would snatch the testes up in his talons, Weston would jump involuntarily to his feet, yelling, "with this icy feeling up my backbone" (*CSC*, 183). When Ella tells what she claims is the same story at the play's conclusion, she describes a substantially different course of events in which the eagle accidentally scoops up a cat and carries it off into the sky: "And they fight. They fight like crazy in the middle of the sky. That cat's tearing his chest out, and the eagle's trying to drop him, but the cat won't let go because he knows if he falls he'll die. . . . And they come crashing down to the earth. Both of them come crashing down. Like one whole thing" (*CSC*, 200). This story, so clearly a metaphor for the self-destructive way in which the family members cling most desperately to those with whom they fight most savagely (namely themselves), ends the play on a powerful but dramatically conventional note. Wesley's incantatory monologue is the last of its kind in Shepard's family plays, and Ella's heavily laden metaphor is the first of many that Shepard will employ in the plays that follow. Yet, with each successive family play, Shepard's use of such traditional literary and dramatic conventions increases as his talents as a realistic dramatist grow. With each new play he also makes a greater effort to forcibly subjugate his highly theatrical intuition—the trademark of the "old Shepard"—to his new dramatic strategies and thematic concerns as a family dramatist.

Buried Child

Close on the heels of *Curse of the Starving Class* came *Buried Child*, which premiered at the Magic Theatre in June 1978. Again, Shepard borrows from the classical Greek family myths, incorporating such archetypal narratives as the Orestean homecoming, Oedipal incest, the battles of fathers and sons, as well as patricide and infanticide. *Buried Child* also exhibits a particular indebtedness to Henrik Ibsen's modern family classic, *Ghosts* (1881), both in its narrative pursuit of a dark family secret and in its thematic preoccupation with the revelation of the son's true identity and spiritual inheritance.

But at the same time that *Buried Child* courts the conventions of classical drama, it demonstrates a subversive scorn for the rational closure of such narratives. *Buried Child* is propelled by two mysteries having to do with the family's inability to recognize a returning son, Vince, and with the identity of an unacknowledged infant corpse that has been buried for over 30 years behind the family's farmhouse. Neither of these mysteries is ever, in the final analysis, satisfactorily unraveled. Like Shepard's contemporary detective play, *Suicide in B-Flat*, the rational mystery structure of *Buried Child* proves to be a Möbius strip of contradictory memories and realities that never comes to narrative resolution.

Curse of the Starving Class's final metaphoric image of the members of the family as cat and eagle caught in a mutually destructive embrace is reimagined in *Buried Child*. Here, the family is a black hole that holds its offspring in a deadly grip, eventually sucking them back into its vortex. Vince, who has not seen his family in six years, has returned to his grandparents' farmhouse in Illinois. Like Oswald in Ibsen's *Ghosts*, he has been living the "debauched" life of the artist in the big city, and he has undertaken a journey toward what he thought was home to seek out his father and to face his personal ghosts. His girlfriend, Shelly, tells us that he has stopped in "every stupid little donut shop he ever kissed a girl in"[9] searching for his heritage. Shelly, who expected Vince's family to be something out of a Norman Rockwell illustration with "turkey dinners and apple pie and all that kinda stuff," is confronted by a radically different vision that, in one critic's words, is "as if Grant Wood's American Gothic family were perceived while on a bad acid trip."[10]

When Vince arrives at his grandparents' house, neither his father, Tilden, nor his grandfather, Dodge, claims to remember him. The only child missing from the family as far as they are concerned is the one buried in the backyard. Tilden and Dodge are just two of the emotional and physical cripples who inhabit the once-flourishing household. Dodge cannot, or will not, move from the sofa where he sits wrapped in a blanket, taking guarded sips from the whiskey bottle he has hidden under the cushions. Tilden, who has recently returned after years of living alone in the desert, is more like a gigantic child, his brain numbed by too much sun and alcohol.

Vince's arrival marks the near-completion of a cycle that began more than 30 years earlier. He is the last of the men in his family to return to his grandparents' house, to be drawn into the vortex of communal family secrets that has given birth to this crippled brood and that seems to be a final resting place for the family's men. Among those men are Vince's deranged uncle, Bradley (who cut his leg off in a chain-saw accident), his dead uncle, Ansel (who mysteriously perished on his honeymoon), and the buried child of the play's title.

The house's only female inhabitant is Dodge's wife, Halie. The play begins with the sound of Halie's disembodied voice coming from her bedroom upstairs, where she watches the rain come down "in sheets" outside her window while Dodge sits downstairs staring at a blank television screen. Both Halie and Dodge inhabit worlds of their own creation. Permanently rooted to his sofa, Dodge isolates himself from the outside world, trying to hide from and forget his family and his past. Halie, meanwhile, surrounds herself with pictures of the past and of her family in its prime. Early in the play, she leaves the house to meet with a local pastor, Father Dewis, in order to re-create the past and repopulate her world with heroes to replace the monsters to which she has given birth.

Rather than create the kind of immediately disorienting stage image and action he used in *Curse of the Starving Class*, throwing the audience into turmoil before it had the opportunity to settle into the rhythm of the play, Shepard applies a stage aesthetic in *Buried Child* akin to that he used in one of his earliest plays, *Icarus's Mother*. In that play, the action began in a relatively realistic manner and only gradually came unfixed.

The lesson had been, as director Michael Smith noted, that the play "needs reality in order to transcend reality" (Smith, *Notes*, 28). *Buried Child* opens upon what appears to be a conventional realistic situation within a traditional domestic setting: Dodge watching television in the front room of his Illinois farmhouse. An old wooden staircase with frayed carpet leads "off stage left up into the wings with no landing." Dodge sits on a dark green sofa "with the stuffing coming out in spots," facing the television with the "blue light flickering on his face." Behind the sofa is a large, screened-in porch with a screen door "leading from the porch to the outside. Beyond that are the shapes of dark elm trees" (*BC*, 63).

Since writing *Buried Child*, Shepard has acknowledged that he can unfix stage reality more effectively by starting a dramatic action with a surface realism that places the audience (falsely) at ease: "I like to set it up at the beginning so that everybody's happy, so that nobody's trying to figure anything out. Everything's okay to begin with. To begin with something that is immediately unrecognizable [, too] immediately mysterious is confusing, because no one knows where to go. But if everybody starts out thinking they know where they're going, *then* you can go in a different direction. *Then* you can go off into territory unknown" (Lippman, 45). In *Buried Child*, this principle is achieved both through the seemingly ordinary stage setting and through the presence of Dodge, a likable old curmudgeon, whose wry humor and mocking disdain for Halie's attempts at dialogue quickly disarm the audience.

Even before the action in *Buried Child* starts to turn surreal, one begins to sense that there is more to the play than this cantankerous old man. The strange quality of Halie's voice, coming from the unseen wings of the stage, serves as an aural reminder of the theatrical space beyond the realistic setting and of the limitations or peculiarities of the set itself. Like the play, the set is realistic only to a point. In both the original San Francisco production at the Magic Theatre and in the subsequent New York City production, the screened-in porch and the stairway leading into the wings created a particularly disturbing effect. Walter Kerr, in his review of the New York production, noted the peculiar visual impact: "In *Buried Child* it is the abrupt staircase that seems to vanish into nothingness, and the further curious nothingness of a useless corridor at the rear of the stage. . . . Anyone entering or leaving must pass through a void. If the precise meaning of the added space is less than clear, a suggestive dimensionality is created—not in the characters . . . but in the planes that extend their world. Provocative."[11] Photographs of the Magic Theatre production reinforce Kerr's observations. The screen separating the porch from the main area of the stage is more like a broad scrim that covers the entire upstage wall of the stage; the action behind it therefore takes place in the kind of separately lit theatrical space that is more conventionally used to suggest dreams or apparitions. The "dark elm trees" Shepard mentions in his stage directions are absent, and the blank upstage wall, brightly lit, suggests a vast expanse of emptiness just outside the house. The stairs, leading offstage, extend beyond the stage-left wall of the set and are highlighted against a black backdrop. In one photo, what appears to be an unfinished two-by-four or other wooden support beam can be clearly seen offstage.[12]

When Halie enters in the first act, descending the stairs a step at a time, she appears to be materializing from some off-stage limbo, as though the stairs, continuing beyond the edge of the stage setting, led to some other dimension. The screened-in porch, likewise, becomes a strange corridor linking the ghostly happenings of the household, which has escaped the passage of time during the last 30 years, with a frightening and unpredictable outside world. At one point, Dodge screams after his son Tilden: "Don't go outside. There's nothing out there. . . . Everything's in here. Everything you need" (*BC*, 80). Later in the play, Vince threatens Shelly from the porch: "No man or woman has ever crossed the line and lived to tell the tale! . . . Don't come out here! I'm warning you! You'll disintegrate!" (*BC*,127, 128). In truth, it is Dodge who risks disintegration by leaving the house where he has holed himself up for 30 years, hiding from the child buried in the yard and the consequences of his actions. He is the only character never to leave the stage.

Shepard's grounding of the surreal in surface realism carries over into his use of suprareal props in *Buried Child*. In *Curse of the Starving Class*, the suprapresence of real food, as well as a live lamb and a naked actor, disrupted the stage reality by physically transcending it. In *Buried Child*, it is the fresh vegetables Tilden brings onstage that fulfill this function. In the first act, for instance, Tilden carries an armload of fresh corn onto the stage, husking it to assure the audience that it is a fresh vegetable and not some prop maker's masterpiece. However, like the lamb in *Curse of the Starving Class* or the barbecue pit in *Icarus's Mother*, that real corn takes on a surreal quality by virtue of the context in which it is used. Part of a mysterious bumper crop that has sprouted overnight behind the house after 30-some years of barrenness, the corn husks are employed in a ceremonious rite of regeneration in which they are strewn, without apparent psychological motive, over the sleeping Dodge: "[Tilden] moves center stage and gathers an armload of corn husks then crosses back to the sofa. He stands holding the husks over DODGE and looking down at him[,] he gently spreads the corn husks over the whole length of DODGE's body. He stands back and looks at DODGE. . . . He gathers more husks and repeats the procedure until the floor is clean of corn husks and DODGE is completely covered in them except for his head" (*BC*, 81). Much like the "found objects" of the surrealists, the corn suddenly assumes unfamiliar dimensions by virtue of its irrational and highly suggestive new function. Shepard's transition from the familiar to the deeply disturbing embraces Antonin Artaud's intent to create a sense of metaphysical danger on the stage by the "abrupt, untimely transition from an intellectual image to a true image" (Artaud, 43–44). As John Glore has rightfully noted, "Shepard's vegetables come as close as anything in Western drama to satisfying Artaud's call for the 'objective unforeseen'" (Glore, 55).

Tilden's silent ceremony is followed closely by the entrance of Bradley, a creature who fits Artaud's demand for "the sudden appearance of a fabricated Being . . . capable of reintroducing on the stage a little breath of that great metaphysical fear which is at the root of all ancient theater" (Artaud, 44). Bradley, Dodge's son and Tilden's brother, is no fabricated monster, yet he creates an overpowering aura of foreboding: "His left leg is wooden, having been amputated above the knee. He moves with an exaggerated, almost mechanical limp. The squeaking sounds of leather and metal accompany his walk coming from the harness and hinges of the false leg. His arms and shoulders are extremely powerful and muscular due to a lifetime dependency on the upper torso doing all the work for the legs. . . . He moves laboriously" (*BC*, 81–82). Sigmund Freud has noted that the ability of such beings to induce terror and psychic discomfort arises from an "uncertainty whether a particular figure in the story is a human being or an automaton."[13] While Bradley is undoubtedly human, his mechanical movement and general menacing appearance raise his entrance to the level of a Freudian nightmare. He embodies a new plane of threatening reality foreign to that already onstage. Through the introduction of the corn husk ceremony and this primordial being, Shepard subtly yet rapidly transports the play out of the realm of realism and into that of a horrifying fantasy.

Bradley's slightly inhuman appearance is enhanced by the specific act of menace he subsequently performs; that is, the shaving of Dodge's head:

He pulls out a pair of black electric hair clippers from his pocket. Unwinds the cord and crosses to the lamp. He jabs his wooden leg behind the knee, causing it to bend at the joint and awkwardly kneels to plug the cord into a floor outlet. He pulls himself to his feet again by using the sofa as leverage. He moves to DODGE's head and again jabs his false leg. Goes down on one knee. He violently knocks away some of the corn husks then jerks off DODGE's baseball cap and throws it down center stage. DODGE stays asleep. BRADLEY switches on the clippers. Lights start dimming. BRADLEY cuts DODGE's hair while he sleeps. (*BC*, 82)

Although Halie says early in the play that Bradley will be coming to cut Dodge's hair, she does not begin to prepare us for the appearance of this frightening being, nor for the ritual act of emasculation he performs upon his father.

During the second act, Tilden again enters with an armful of vegetables from the presumably barren back field. This time, he brings carrots, which he gives to Shelly to clean and cut. As do the corn husks in the first act, the carrots assume an unvoiced significance as Shelly cradles them in her arms like an infant and refuses to let Vince take them from her. Bradley's second entrance, signaled by the chilling mechanical squeak of his harness offstage, brings the act to a close. His very presence sends Tilden running from the house, leaves Dodge crumpled on the floor, and freezes Shelly in her tracks. Bradley performs a vaguely sexual rite of domination upon her:

BRADLEY: Open your mouth.

SHELLY: What?

BRADLEY: (motioning for her to open her mouth) Open up.
(She opens her mouth slightly.)

BRADLEY: Wider.
(She opens her mouth wider.)

BRADLEY: Keep it like that.
(She does. Stares at BRADLEY. With his free hand he puts his fingers into her mouth. She tries to pull away.)

BRADLEY: Just stay put!
(She freezes. He keeps his fingers in her mouth. Stares at her. Pause. He pulls his hand out. She closes her mouth, keeps her eyes on him. BRADLEY smiles.) (*BC*, 106–7)

This highly charged image, like the strewing of the corn husks or the savage haircut, is both physically explicit and at the same time without narrative or psychological precedent. It is both an obvious act of rape and an image, intrinsic to itself, that does not have to be compared to rape or to any other form of sexual domination in order to affect the audience. When the third act begins, almost no mention is made of this encounter. Shepard creates an extremely specific image, yet he refuses to reduce it to psychologically motivated terms by discussing it once it has happened. The image is thus both charged with meaning and "entirely invented, corresponding to nothing, yet disquieting by nature" (Artaud, 44).

The dual nature of such unresolved images in *Buried Child* is representative of Shepard's attempt, as a dramatist, to incorporate his talent for creating disquieting stage pictures, especially those using the suprapresence of material objects and actors, into his new dramatic agenda. The images that end the three acts of *Buried Child*—the haircut, the fingers in the mouth, and the infant corpse—do not so much disrupt the action of the play as they intensify the sense of foreboding that has been realistically introduced through the action. When Tilden enters in the final moments of the play with the infant corpse cradled in his arms, the image is both a final physical manifestation of the decay of this family and, tied as it is to the unresolved mysteries of the play and the inexplicable appearance of the crops in the field, the embodiment of the impossibility of giving meaning to the play's contradictions. It intensifies the significance we draw from the events that have come before it yet still denies us a definitive interpretation of those events.

The stage is set for Tilden's final entrance by the gradual and contradictory unraveling of a family secret about Halie's illegitimate baby, a baby that we are led to believe Dodge drowned and buried behind the house years earlier. At one point, Tilden says, "I had a son once but we buried him," suggesting that his mother's child is also his. Dodge immediately dismisses any such possibility: "That happened before you were born! Long before!" (*BC*, 92). Earlier, Dodge had claimed the child as his own, stating that his "flesh and blood's buried in the back yard" (*BC*,77). In the third act, he changes his story once again: "Then Halie got pregnant again. . . . We had enough boys already. In fact, we hadn't been sleepin' in the same bed for about six years. . . . Halie had this kid. This baby boy. She had it. . . . It wanted to grow up in this family. It wanted to be just like us. It wanted to be part of us. It wanted to pretend that I was its father. She wanted me to believe in it. Even when everyone around us knew. Everyone. All our boys knew. Tilden knew. . . . Tilden was the one who knew. Better than any of us"

(*BC*, 123–24). Dodge not only denies that the buried child is his but also suggests that Tilden is the father, a possibility he earlier dismissed.

The matter is further complicated by the fact that Vince is Tilden's son, or claims to be Tilden's son. Yet none of the family, with the notable exception of Halie, recognizes Vince or remembers that Tilden ever had a son. This confusion suggests an unconfirmed link between Vince (whose mother is never identified) and the illegitimate child born to Halie and Tilden. Thus, one possible interpretation of the play (and the mystery of Vince's identity as well as the baby's) is that Vince is the "buried child" that might have been, returned as an adult. This reading of the play is encouraged by the strong suggestion that it is Tilden's digging behind the house—that is, his decision to accept the role of father and nurturer that Dodge has denied—that is responsible for Vince's sudden appearance. Tilden has, in a sense, called forth the presence of the son that might have been. In the final moment of the play, both sons—the young child grown to adulthood and the rotting corpse, representing both planes of possibility—simultaneously inhabit the stage.

One other interpretation might be given to the complex mystery of the buried child. Halie speaks fondly, throughout the play, of her dead son, Ansel, a war hero and All-American basketball star. At the beginning of the play, Halie's tales of Ansel seem almost a fantasy she has formulated and that she trots out from time to time as a substitute for the disappointment of her real sons. The effect is similar to that of Edward Albee's *Who's Afraid of Virginia Woolf?* (1962), in which George and Martha have created a fantasy child in order to compensate for their sterility. As *Buried Child* progresses, one wonders whether Ansel is the child buried in the back yard whom Halie has transformed into a hero to compensate for his death.[14] When Halie speaks of Ansel's prowess on the basketball court, Bradley silences her by announcing that Ansel "never played basketball." Yet, Halie is supported by the seemingly objective Father Dewis, who recalls having seen Ansel play on several occasions. Later, however, even Dewis's interjection is brought into question when Halie lavishes upon Vince the attributes of "perfect child" and "hope of the family" that she earlier ascribed to Ansel. Where Ansel was a "hero" who "would have taken care of us," Vince is now a "guardian angel" whom everyone loves and who is going to "watch over all of us." While Halie's stories, like those of the other characters, may well be the fantasies of the deranged, Shepard never offers a clue as to who is mad in this family and who is not.

Tired of these endless contradictions, Vince's girlfriend, Shelly, eventually demands the "truth of the matter." From her first appearance, Shelly has served as a perceptual guide for the audience. The only outsider, she is an unbiased observer in the play trying to make sense of the various versions of the past. Dodge berates Shelly's obsession with objective fact in much the same way that Niles taunted the detectives in *Suicide in B-Flat*. He even accuses her of acting "like a detective or something": "She wants to get to the bottom of it. (to SHELLY) That's it, isn't it? You'd like to get right down to bedrock? You want me to tell ya'? You want me to tell ya' what happened? I'll tell ya'. I might as well" (*BC*, 122). Although Dodge's story about Halie's baby (quoted earlier) appears to be as specific a truth as anyone has spoken in the play, it does not resolve the many contradictions of both past and present. No version of the past nor interpretation of the present is entirely objective or exclusive of the others. Shepard has created an environment in which both the characters' memories and the present reality of the play are brought into question. He gives dramatic form to a principle of reality expressed by Harold Pinter (whose play, *The Homecoming* [1965], *Buried Child* vaguely resembles), treating the present as if it were as malleable as an imperfect memory: "If we can speak of the difficulty of knowing what in fact took place yesterday, one can I think treat the present in the same way. What's happening now? We won't know until tomorrow or in six months' time, and we won't know then, we'll have forgotten, or our imagination will have attributed quite false characteristics to today. A moment is sucked away and distorted, often even at the time of its birth" (Pinter, 11). Contradictions transcend the possible madness of the characters in *Buried Child* and become part of the fabric of reality itself.

Vince's journey into his past and into the vortex of his personal heritage comes full circle at the play's conclusion. Although Vince tries, midway through the play, to run from his heritage, he is drawn back into it by a vision of his own inescapable destiny: "I studied my face. Studied everything about it. As though I was looking at another man. . . . And every breath marked him. Marked him forever without him knowing. And then his face changed. His face became his father's face. Same bones. Same eyes. Same nose. Same breath. And his father's face changed to his Grandfather's face. And it went on like that. Changing. Clear on back to faces I'd never seen before but still recognized" (*BC*, 130). Like Oswald Alving in Ibsen's *Ghosts*, Vince finds his father, his family, and his personal heritage within himself. Against his will and without his knowing it, they have inhabited his body. He is the spiritual and biological inheritor of what Ibsen called "ghosts": the decaying doctrines and diseased genetic traits, unavoidably handed down from parent to child, that predetermine one's life. They flow through Vince's veins like the curse of Shepard's "starving class."

Buried Child concludes with Vince assuming ownership of his grandparents' house. In a last will and testament that Dodge recites aloud before he dies unnoticed by the others, he leaves the house to Vince, whom he now claims as his grandson. He asks that the rest of his possessions be "pushed into a gigantic heap and set ablaze in the very center of my fields" (*BC*, 129). Vince covers Dodge's stiffening corpse with his blanket. He then lies down on the sofa, taking Dodge's usual spot, his posture mirroring that of his grandfather's dead body. The play ends where it began. But Halie's voice, heard only by Dodge at the play's beginning, now serves as backdrop to a far more devastating sight. As she describes the bright sun that has finally broken through the rain clouds (much like the final image of Ibsen's *Ghosts*) Tilden enters, unseen by Vince. With the infant corpse in his arms, he begins to climb the stairs toward his mother. As in *Ghosts*, the play ends with mother and child finally reunited. But this image of rebirth is set astride the grave, for Halie's child, whether seen as Vince or the infant corpse, has long ago been sacrificed to the crippling disease of heredity that dictates the family's fate.

True West

The third of Shepard's family plays, *True West* (1980), offers none of *Buried Child*'s unveiling of the past nor *Curse of the Starving Class*'s disruptive fragmentation of reality. Instead, the play represents a conscious effort on Shepard's part to maintain a strict adherence to psychological and scenographic realism. In an interview given before the London premiere of the play, Shepard explained in musical terms his efforts to stay within the boundaries of conventional dramatic realism: "Musicians have this terminology—playing in and out. Playing out roughly means to improvise, whereas playing in means developing inside a structure. For me, now, it's much more interesting, though more difficult, playing in."[15] Since his move to San Francisco, Shepard had played "out" with improvisationally inspired musical works such as *Inacoma* and *Angel City*. Even his first two family plays, *Buried Child* and *Curse of the Starving Class*, reflected Shepard's spontaneous flair for the irrational. But *True West* is grounded in and propelled by the psychological opposition of two conflicting brothers. In terms of character, playing "in" meant that Shepard was "determined in this play, no matter what, to ride the characters out" (McFerran, 25)—standard operating procedure for almost any playwright but Shepard. This intention does not mean that *True West* abandons the irrational; the theme and physical staging, while well within the realm of psychological and physical realism, still exhibit elements of the unfixing of reality and of character that had become Shepard's trademarks.

The play opens with Austin, a successful young scriptwriter, attempting to finish work on an artistic "project" he hopes to sell to Saul Kimmer, a Hollywood producer. He is staying at his mother's Southern California home while she is vacationing in Alaska. When Austin's older brother, Lee, unexpectedly appears, his threatening, untamed presence and persistently annoying attempts at conversation prevent Austin from progressing with his work. Lee is an outlaw who prowls the desert, sleeping in abandoned cars and making a living by stealing and gambling. Austin, by contrast, writes for and is a product of the Hollywood system and of the suburban society of shopping malls and superhighways. From the opening moments of the play, it is clear that these Cain and Abel siblings embody the struggle between the clashing life-styles of the "old" West and the "new" West. One lives off the land; the other has helped to pave over it. While each is openly disdainful of the other's life-style, they are secretly envious of each other. When Saul drops Austin's project in favor of an old-style western script proposed by Lee, the two brothers suddenly, almost eagerly, trade personas. Austin gets drunk, abandoning his own work and yearning for the desert, while Lee sheds his criminal self in an attempt to write a screenplay.

When Austin informs Lee that Saul "thinks we're the same person," he is not only suggesting a motivation for Saul's unexpected shift in allegiance— he is also hinting at the central dramatic conceit behind Shepard's creation of these two warring brothers. According to Shepard, Lee and Austin "are each other. . . . I've just divided one person in two" (McFerran, 25). Their opposing characters represent a split that Shepard feels within himself and within the human psyche in general, an "unresolvable clash" between our "social selves" and those darker "galaxies inside of us" that we try not to explore (Lippman, 6). In *Curse of the Starving Class*, those darker, uncivilized traits were manifest in the uncontrollable savagery passed by blood from parent to child. In *Buried Child*, it was the infant corpse that embodied the inherited brutality of the family's males. In *True West*, it is a primal capacity for violence and mayhem that Lee seems to bring into the house and that is unleashed in Austin as he feels what it is like to be his brother.

The reversal of characters in *True West* is both a reflection of Shepard's personal demons and a continuation of his examination of the individual as "a composite of different mysteries" ("Inner Library," 55). From his early days writing transformational plays in the style of the Open Theatre, through the objectification of self in *Action*, to his exploration of character as improvisational jazz collage in *Angel City*, Shepard has looked upon character as malleable. The self, according to Shepard, is unstable; it is constantly recreated. "You act yourself out," Shooter reminds us in *Action*.

The first act of *True West* juxtaposes the world of the civilized self to a more primal plane of experience. "I just don't want to get all worked up about it," Austin tells Lee at one point.[16] The phrase serves to define his civilized, self-disciplined life-style; in the face of Lee's gradual domination of events, Austin attempts to maintain self-control, to play "inside" the rules. He has painstakingly developed a relationship with Saul, and he carefully nurtures it, expecting fair reward for his hard work. Lee, on the other hand, cannot summon enough patience to play inside the game. He is, as Saul calls him, a "raw talent." Whereas Austin lives by his refined skills, Lee survives on his instincts. He has the creative ability to concoct a winning western, but he lacks the self-imposed discipline to put it on paper. Lee short-circuits the system, lives outside the law, stealing, cheating, gambling, and using force to achieve immediate, if not lasting, gratification. If Lee is the "raw talent," then Austin is the discipline and technique needed to harness that talent. Together, they represent the opposing sides of Shepard's psyche as artist.

When Lee applies his hardball tactics to Austin's world, using his threatening powers of persuasion to make Saul look at his script, Austin claims, "You don't understand the way things work down here" (*TW*, 14). As it turns out, Lee does know how things work; he understands how to tap into Saul's less civilized emotions—fear and greed—in order to cut through the businesslike system to which Austin is enslaved. By the end of the first act, the separate worlds of the brothers, so carefully isolated at the play's beginning, have begun to merge. The final image of the first act, Lee's description of two cowboys disappearing into the desert at night, mirrors the brothers' situation: "So they take off after each other straight into an endless black prairie. The sun is just comin' down and they can feel the night on their backs. What they don't know is that each one of 'em is afraid see. Each one separately thinks that he's the only one that's afraid. And they keep ridin' like that straight into the night. Not knowing. And the one who's chasin' doesn't know where the other one is taking him. And the one who's being chased doesn't know where he's going" (*TW*, 27). Each brother explores unknown territory within himself. Lee's world, as well as Austin's, is subtly unfixed during the adventure. Each pushes the other out of his conventional mode of dealing with life, opening up new ways of viewing reality.

The second act maps the total collapse of the civilized self. Austin discovers that Saul has dropped his project in favor of Lee's outlandish western. Austin's sense of self dissolves and his ordered world is shattered as he witnesses the impossible. Reality, as he knows it, is turned upside down. The tight-lipped, businesslike Saul gambles with Austin's livelihood and loses. Lee wins an improbable game of golf and sells a terrible script that defies everything for which Austin stands as a writer. The tenets upon which Austin has based his personal integrity and behavior prove an illusion. Feeling as though his once-stable life view is no longer valid, he transforms himself (or tries to) into his brother Lee, drinking heavily and combing the neighborhood for household appliances to steal. Lee, meanwhile, apes Austin's behavior of the first act: typing by candlelight and complaining when Austin tries to break his concentration. Each recreates himself based on his image of the other. Although these transformations are, in the realistic framework of the play, too sudden, Austin reminds us that realism is an illusion, as is the concept of stable character: "Those aren't characters. . . . Those are illusions of characters" (*TW*, 40).

Perhaps the most memorable stage image in *True West* is the opening of scene 8, the "typewriter-toasters" scene, in which Shepard offers a tour de force of suprareal staging. At the end of the previous scene, Lee was left pounding out a script on the typewriter as Austin stumbled off into the night, determined to prove himself to his brother by stealing a toaster. Scene 8 opens several hours later:

Very early morning, between night and day. No crickets, coyotes yapping feverishly in distance before light comes up, a small fire blazes up in the dark from alcove area, sound of LEE smashing typewriter with a golf club, lights coming up, LEE seen smashing typewriter methodically then dropping pages of his script into a burning bowl set on the floor of alcove, flames leap up, AUSTIN has a whole bunch of stolen toasters lined up on the sink counter along with LEE's stolen TV, the toasters are of a wide variety of models, mostly chrome, AUSTIN goes up and down the line of toasters, breathing on them and polishing them with a dish towel, both men are drunk, empty whiskey bottles and beer cans litter the floor of kitchen. . . . LEE keeps periodically taking deliberate ax-chops at the typewriter, using a nine-iron[.] (*TW*, 42–43)

In this scene, the psychologically farfetched transformation of the two brothers is provided with both a material grounding and a sharp surreal edge by the introduction of suprareal staging techniques. Shepard's disruption of ordered reality is physically anchored in the use of several operative toasters popping up burnt toast throughout the scene and a previously functional typewriter rendered into a lump of twisted metal by the persistent swing of Lee's nine iron. The toast is carefully buttered, only to be scattered across the floor, the contents of the kitchen drawers and cabinets are strewn across the stage, and the phone is literally ripped from the wall. This wonderful Walpurgisnacht of suprarealism is so accurate in its reproduction of material reality that one loses track of where the rational action ends and the surreal takes over. As William Kleb noted in his review of the original Magic Theatre production, "objective and subjective realities are not juxtaposed [as they were in many of Shepard's earlier plays], they are superimposed."[17]

Once Shepard draws the audience into the undomesticated midnight landscape of the second act, like the unseen coyotes in the play who lure "innocent pets away from their homes," he sheds the light of day on his creation. In the midday heat of the final scene, "all the debris from the previous scene is now starkly visible in intense yellow light" (*TW*, 50); Mom's clean, tidy kitchen has been transformed into a "desert junk-yard." To accentuate the distance he has taken his audience, Shepard suddenly redirects the flow of the action by introducing a new character whose unintegrated presence, like the thugs at the end of *Curse of the Starving Class*, is completely foreign to the stage environment. The surreal intruder is none other than Mom herself, who has returned from the Alaskan frontier. While her presence might not have seemed unreal at the play's beginning, by the end of the play the stage has been transformed into a wasteland in which Mom, an anemic and emotionless little woman, dressed in white with matching red shoes, shoulder bag, and luggage, is completely out of place. She has cut short her vacation to the Alaskan wilds in order to return to the civility of her home. Upon entering, however, she is confronted by a savage battle between her sons that leaves her feeling "worse than being homeless." Her reaction, however, is completely bland, completely disproportionate to the wreck-age in her kitchen and the violent struggle of her two sons. "You boys shouldn't fight in the house," she drones, as Lee and Austin pose on the verge of killing each other.

In the light of day and with his mother's entrance, Lee quickly dismisses the previous night's dreamlike activities, abandoning the script and his aspirations as a scriptwriter. Austin, however, is not as willing to drop his newly adopted persona. When Lee decides to back out of an earlier promise to take Austin to the desert, Austin turns savage. Throwing Lee to the floor and wrapping the phone cord around his neck, he chokes Lee until the older brother falls limp in his arms.

In the final moments of the play, Shepard creates an archetypal image that both encompasses and transcends all that has preceded it. With Lee lying motionless on the floor, Austin is free to take the car and escape into the desert. In the first act, he told Lee, "We're not insane. We're not driven to acts of violence" (*TW*, 24). But in this final scene, as if to prove the complete adoption of his new primal persona, Austin expresses the remorselessness of his newly uncovered violence. With the phone cord still wrapped around his brother's neck, he tells his mother: "I can kill him! I can easily kill him. Right now. Right here" (*TW*, 58). At the moment of his escape, however, Austin hesitates. Moral consciousness seems to creep back into his psyche as he stares at the inert body of his brother. In that instant of hesitation, Lee is on his feet, blocking Austin's escape. The lights suddenly change as the two brothers "square off to each other . . . the figures of the brothers now appear to be caught in a vast desert-like landscape, they are very still but watchful for the next move, lights go slowly to black as the after-image of the brothers pulses in the dark, coyote fades" (*TW*, 59). This final image is not a resolution, as Shepard himself has pointed out, but a timeless confrontation. The pulsing of the after-image suspends the moment in time and space, transporting it beyond the relatively realistic realm of the play. It is a "postplay" (in the sense of "posthypnotic") suggestion in which the brothers are transformed into archetypal figures, facing off, fighting hopelessly on against the backdrop of eternity. In Austin's moment of hesitation arises the germ of moral consciousness that forever separates him from Lee and places him at irresolvable odds with the amoral "Lee" in himself. As Ross Wetzsteon said of his moving exposure to the final image of Shepard's *La Turista,* it was a moment that "dramatized the themes of the play far more precisely than could any words, an image that communicated the emotional texture of the characters' lives far more vividly than could any speech" (Wetzsteon 1984, 1–2).

Fool for Love

By the time *Fool for Love* was produced in 1983, theatergoers had begun to forget the "old" Sam Shepard with his experimental plays, his hallucinatory flights of language, and his metatheatrical stage images. In his place had appeared a "new" Sam Shepard, a ruggedly handsome movie star and icon of American popular culture whose film presence had been compared to that of Gary Cooper and whose dark, humorous family dramas were now held up alongside those of Eugene O'Neill, Tennessee Williams, and Arthur Miller.

When Shepard directed the premiere production of *Fool for Love* at the Magic Theatre in San Francisco, he had already finished filming *The Right Stuff* in which he played the role of the daring test pilot Chuck Yeager, the first man to break the sound barrier. It was Shepard's fifth film appearance in as many years and the part that would complete his rise to film stardom. His face began to appear on the covers of magazines across America, and his image as the "thinking woman's beefcake" (Shewey, 11), both on-screen and off-, was never stronger. *The Right Stuff* was released late in 1983, while the transplanted production of *Fool for Love* was still enjoying a successful run in New York City. Among those in the film's cast were many of the actors with whom Shepard had worked at the Magic Theatre. Sharing the combined success of *The Right Stuff* and *Fool for Love* with Shepard was actor Ed Harris, who played astronaut John Glenn in the film and who originated the role of Eddie in *Fool for Love.*

Fool for Love both fulfilled and denied the expectations of theatergoers. It was Shepard's ultimate work of psychological realism to date, with subtly drawn, complex characterizations, as well as a continuation of his exploration of the American family, of the secrets that bind it together, and of the poisons that pass from parent to child. But at the same time, *Fool for Love* represents an apparent return to the self-consciously theatrical and dreamlike stage imagery of Shepard's earlier work with its juxtaposed stage realities and expressionistic use of space and sound. Central to the dreamlike and disturbing quality of *Fool for Love* is the presence of "the old man," a father figure who seems to exist simultaneous to, but in a dimension removed from, the action of the play. He is both a surreal specter and a reinforcement of Shepard's continuing obsession with his own personal heritage and his father.

Lee and Austin's absent father was mentioned sporadically in *True*

West, serving as one of the many sources of conflict between the brothers. In that play, Lee has stayed in contact with his derelict father who, like Lee himself, spends most of his time living alone in the desert. Austin, who has little in common with his father, has seen him only on rare occasions and out of a seeming sense of guilt and remorse. Austin's strange tale of how his father lost his false teeth while drinking in bars "up and down the highway" in Mexico is the only real piece of storytelling in *True West*, and as such it carries much of the weight of the old man's unspoken presence in Lee and Austin's lives.

But in *Fool for Love*, the absent father appears not only in the stories of his offspring but as a ghostlike character on stage as well. Like some eccentric visiting dignitary who has been offered the best seat in the house, or a ghostly witness to a ceremonial family rite, the old man's unintegrated onstage presence takes the play out of the realm of realism, placing the reunion of Eddie and May, two incestuous half siblings, within a metatheatrical framework.

In a tiny, bleak motel room on the edge of the Mojave Desert, Eddie and May rehash the worn-out differences of their 15-year romance. Eddie is a veteran rodeo cowboy. May, his sometime lover, is currently working as a short-order cook in a diner; she has taken whatever work she can get while running from Eddie.[18] The conflict between May and Eddie is quickly established: Eddie has only just returned to May, tracking her down after a long and passionate affair with a mysterious countess whose black Mercedes Benz appears repeatedly outside the motel in the course of the play. May does not wish once again to become the victim of Eddie's macho, romantic delusions, nor of his hopeless infidelity and restless need for flight. Eddie's cowboy dreams reflect the western ideals of his profession: he envisions a quiet, hard-working future with May, settled on that notoriously proverbial "patch of land" up in Wyoming. All May sees are the long hours she has spent cooped up in Eddie's trailer, waiting for him to appear, while the hot, dry wind howls through the walls. Of Wyoming, she gibes, "What's up there? Marlboro Men?" Her own hope is to free herself of Eddie; she tells him that she has a new boyfriend, Martin (who appears later in the play). But May is not as free of Eddie as she would like to be. She is inexplicably tied to him, as he is to her, in a consuming love/hate relationship, the incestuous nature of which is only gradually revealed.

At first glance, the subject matter of *Fool for Love* is deceptively mundane, almost stereotypically romantic. But, the play quickly develops an aura of theatrical significance far beyond that of the surface plot by virtue of the old man's presence. Sitting in his rocking chair, with his bottle of sourmash close at hand, he watches the action from a small alcove in the downstage left corner of the playing area. He is present at this meeting between Eddie and May but not really part of it. Or, he is part of it but not really present.

The old man represents a plane of reality that, while it shares the stage with the two lovers, is in complete juxtaposition to them. One frustrated critic wrote: "The Old Man and the pair of lovers exist on two different planes of reality: one exists only as a figment of the other's imagination. The underlying question of the play is: *Whose* imagination?"[19] Although Shepard's published text of the play suggests a response to this concern (as will be discussed later), the play in performance offers no easy answers. The result is a state of juxtaposed realities in which the spectator becomes uncertain of the seemingly metaphysical relationship between the motel room and the alcove. By refusing to rationally reduce the contradictory stage realities, by denying the audience any theatrical or narrative verification that the old man is dreaming the two lovers or that they are dreaming him, Shepard negates the possibility of an objective reality in the play or even of a *raisonneur* whose viewpoint the spectator might take as "truth."

At the top of the play, it is unclear whether May and Eddie are even aware of the old man's presence. For nearly 20 minutes he sits silently without soliciting any response from either of the other two characters. He finally speaks to Eddie while May is offstage. In a physically poignant manifestation of their relationship, May allows Eddie to gull her into a long and passionate embrace only to knee him sharply in the groin, thus fulfilling her earlier promise that "right in the moment when you're sure you've got me buffaloed. That's when you'll die."[20] As Eddie lies writhing on the floor, gasping for breath, the old man laughs at his embarrassing and clearly uncomfortable predicament. "I thought you were supposed to be a fantasist," he says. "Isn't that basically the deal with you? You dream things up. Isn't that true?" (*FFL*, 26). The old man seems to indicate that Eddie is somehow performing for him, creating a romantic masculine fantasy for his approval. But Eddie's painful condition suggests that if this is a fantasy, he has momentarily lost control of it. The old man, as if to set an example, points to the empty wall of the motel room:

THE OLD MAN: I wanna' show you somethin'. Somethin' real, okay? Somethin' actual.

EDDIE:	Sure.
THE OLD MAN:	Take a look at that picture on the wall over there. (He points at wall stage right. There is no picture but EDDIE stares at the wall.) Ya' see that? Take a good look at that. Ya' see it?
EDDIE:	(staring at wall) Yeah.
THE OLD MAN:	Ya' know who that is?
EDDIE:	I'm not sure.
THE OLD MAN:	Barbara Mandrell. That's who that is. Barbara Mandrell. You heard a' her?
EDDIE:	Sure.
THE OLD MAN:	Well, would you believe me if I told ya' I was married to her?
EDDIE:	(pause) No.
THE OLD MAN:	Well, see, now that's the difference right there. That's realism. I am actually married to Barbara Mandrell in my mind. Can you understand that?
EDDIE:	Sure.
THE OLD MAN:	Good. I'm glad we have an understanding. (*FFL*, 26–27)

This humorous lesson verbally reinforces the strange, irresolvable relationship between fact and illusion that has been suggested from the play's beginning by the old man's inexplicable presence on stage. It also introduces the importance of belief and acknowledgment in discerning reality from simple self-delusion. In the twisted logic of *Fool for Love*, to acknowledge illusion as such and to control it is to make that illusion a reality. Eddie later tells May's boyfriend, Martin, that "lying's when you believe it's true. If you already know it's a lie, then it's not lying" (*FFL*, 58). This strange paradox cuts not only to the theatrical heart of Shepard's stage metaphor but to the philosophical heart of human existence as perceived by the playwright. "Reality" as we know it is a constructed lie that has been repressed to the level of an unconscious assumption about life. To face life openly, one must be able to recognize and acknowledge the illusion of reality, yet show the strength to control and to live in the face of such knowledge. The old man's "marriage" demonstrates the principles of such strength. By acknowledging that Barbara Mandrell is his wife only in his head, the old man's reality is stronger than Eddie's; conscious of his lie, he controls it and can still live it in spite of it. That is, he lives as though life and reality were meaningful, although he recognizes the folly of such an assumption. Still, there is a great difference, which Shepard recognizes, between acknowledging the harmless lie of an imaginary marriage and acknowledging the more substantial lies upon which one's entire life is built. Can illusion be controlled? Can one face the destruction of the lies upon which he or she has based a life and continue living? Shepard's old man answers these questions at the play's conclusion.

Shepard builds to a powerful climax in *Fool for Love* through the careful dramatic use of one of his most characteristic and popular techniques as a playwright: storytelling. In previous plays, many of Shepard's spoken narratives, like Wesley's monologue in the early moments of *Curse of the Starving Class*, took the form of a pause in the play, what Shepard saw as jazzlike riffs that stepped out of the flow of the action without adding to the dramatic development. However, the stories told by Eddie and May, leading to *Fool for Love*'s climax, are neatly integrated into the play's retrogressive action. They do not interrupt the flow, but rather build tension, collecting information from the past like a tragic Sophoclean puzzle and revealing to the old man the fatal fruit of his bigamous and incestuous family tree.

As in *Buried Child, Fool for Love* is created around the contradictory memories and gradual shocking disclosure of a closely kept family secret. But more so than in *Buried Child*, control of the past and of language becomes a commodity of power, and he or she who controls the past controls the present. Eddie and May each offer their own version of the past. While May is supposedly changing in the bathroom, Eddie recounts to the captive Martin how for years the old man split his time between two families, arriving and departing without warning or explanation. An absolute fool for the love of two women, he was possessed with an overpowering and irreconcilable need for them both. "It was the same love," the old man interjects, "just got split in two, that's all" (*FFL*, 63). Eddie and May were the offspring of his divided love, living with their separate mothers, never suspecting each other's existence. Eddie conjures up a romantic memory in which his father takes him for a long walk one evening, traveling across freshly plowed fields, stopping at a liquor store to buy a bottle, and finally approaching a house on the far side of town:

Then, finally, we reached this little white house with a red awning, on the far side of town. I'll never forget the red awning because it flapped in the night breeze and the porch light made it glow. . . . And then this woman comes to the door. This real pretty woman with red hair. And she throws herself into his arms. And he starts crying. He just breaks down right there in front of me. . . . And then through the doorway, behind them both, I see this girl. . . . She just appears. She's just standing there, staring at me and I'm staring back at her and we can't take our eyes off each other. It was like we knew each other from somewhere but we couldn't place where. But the second we saw each other, that very second, we knew we'd never stop being in love. (*FFL*, 66–67)

As Eddie describes this scene, May opens the bathroom door, the light behind her catching her red hair, giving substance to Eddie's description. She is momentarily entranced, caught up in the mutually tender memory, but her trance is fleeting. May slams the bathroom door, breaking the spell of Eddie's narrative. She screams to Martin not to believe a word he has heard. An innocent bystander, Martin is forced to sit in unwilling judgment over May and Eddie's tales of the past as they compete for his credulity and sympathy. The sole earthly witness to their battle, he possesses the power to verify the past, to decide which of them is living a lie and which the truth—if any truth exists at all.

May's subsequent story does not contradict Eddie's so much as it broadens the perspective, continuing past the romantic conclusion Eddie has reached for the old man's sake. She includes the woman's side of the story: her mother's painful and obsessive love for a husband who repeatedly deserted her. In May's version, she and Eddie are not brought together by the old man. They are lovers before they learn of their paternal ties. It is May's mother who tracks down the old man, "hunting for him from town to town" (*FFL*, 70). May acknowledges the passion she shared with Eddie but juxtaposes it to her mother's consuming agony. While Eddie and May fall more deeply in love, May's mother endures torment each moment she is forced to live without her husband. In her daughter's passionate attachment to Eddie, May's mother begins to recognize her own dangerous obsession. She begs May and Eddie to stop seeing each other. Unsuccessful, she is determined to confront Eddie's mother with the truth. The other woman's reaction is simple and violent: "Eddie's mother—Eddie's mother blew her brains out" (*FFL*, 73). On this note, May ends her story.

Throughout May's story the old man tries to prod Eddie into supporting an alternate view. "Boy, is she ever off the wall with this one," he taunts Eddie. "You gotta' do somethin' about this" (*FFL*, 72). But Eddie allows May to complete her tale and her words to bear the burden of truth. When May falls silent, the old man stands for the first time in the play. He leaves his corner, breaks the imaginary plane separating him from the lovers—thus shattering the theatrical barrier between their juxtaposed realities—and steps out onto the stage to confront Eddie. But Eddie confirms May's story, adding that it was the old man's rifle his mother used.

May's story somehow purges Eddie of his need to defend "the male side" of the past. As the old man attempts to discredit May's revelation and to defend himself before his estranged children, the lights of the countess's car flash past the upstage window as they have earlier in the play. This time, however, an explosion is heard offstage. The countess has set fire to Eddie's truck. The bright colors of the burning gasoline splash across the walls of the motel room like a UFO landing.

The explosion, coming as it does at the moment the old man is forced to confront the violence he has engendered, represents more than a burning truck. It is the material realization of the explosion of truth upon the old man's romantic memories: the destruction of his controlled illusion of the past and of his manipulation, through the lives of Eddie and May, of his hereditary male fantasy. As he crumples into an upstage corner of the room, flickering lights engulf him; the previously undisclosed death of his wife suddenly shakes the ground on which he stands. Eddie and May come together in a final moment of tenderness. In what has amounted to a ritual of exorcism, they have purged themselves of their inherited obsessions and of the undying grip of the old man's memory. Whether present in the flesh or only in spirit at this ritual, the old man is forced to recognize that violent death and suffering, not these two lovers, are the offspring of his selfish love. Eddie and May leave him huddled in the flames of his exploded knowledge and go their separate ways. The play concludes with the old man repeating his earlier convictions regarding the imaginary picture on the wall. But now, his rambling takes on a new meaning. Barbara Mandrell is no longer a fantasy that the old man controls and in which he chooses to indulge. She represents a life lie, an escape from a tragic truth too painful for him to endure. He does not control the lie, as he claimed earlier—the lie controls him. Lacking the strength to face his past, he is a slave to his self-imposed blindness.

This powerful finale is indicative of the combination of dramatic text with highly physical staging that Shepard, as playwright and director, employed throughout the original Magic Theatre production of *Fool for Love.* Both the stage space itself and the physical movement of the actors within the space commented on the play's theme of passionate entrapment. The motel room setting, painted in garish tones of yellow and green, was bare-walled and raked up and in toward the rear in a forced, expressionistic perspective. The actors crept around the edges of the set, flattening themselves against walls, throwing themselves into corners, and crawling along the floorboards. Sometimes they were animals trapped in a cage, while at other times they seemed more like inmates in a padded cell. To reinforce the violence of the movement and the sense of entrapment, Shepard placed microphones behind the walls of the set so that each slamming of a door, each pounding of a wall, each blow from an elbow, knee, and fist—of which there were many—was amplified and broadcast through speakers beneath the audience. Entrances and exits, escapes and returns, were all given amplified emotional significance. Shepard's experience as a percussionist was apparent in speeches punctuated by the slamming of bodies against flat surfaces.

This physical immediacy creates not only powerful emotional effects but humorous ones as well—especially when Eddie chooses to adopt the macho attitude of the rodeo hothead. Like so many of Shepard's western men—especially Lee in *True West*—Eddie possesses the undaunted desire and uncanny ability to make everyone else in the room uncomfortable in his presence. His mock-threatening domination of the space includes the use of a gun, a saddle, metal spurs, and coiled lassos, which he slaps with boyish glee against the walls of the room. Eddie's use of the bed, chairs, and table as practice targets for his cowboy rope tricks caused one critic to liken the play to "an indoor rodeo."[21] At one point, Eddie tries to impress May by strapping on his rodeo spurs, or "hooks" as he calls them. With sharp kicks that take him off his feet, he demonstrates for May how he will kick Martin "into a fig" if the other man dares to make an appearance. Even more so than Austin in *True West*, who at least holds his own against his brother Lee's irritating harassment, Martin becomes the perfect victim of Eddie's (and Shepard's) caustic cowboy wit.

In spite of the work in both theater and film that Shepard has done since *Fool for Love*, it is difficult not to see this play as the culmination of his career as a dramatist to date. Director Jacques Levy once said of Shepard's early work that "Sam is more interested in *doing* something to audiences than in saying something to them" (Levy, 98). With *Fool for Love*, Shepard fulfills the intention of "doing something" to his audience; that is, he reaches the audience on a visceral level with the play's ambiguous dreamlike setting and with its fierce expressionistic staging. But the achievement of *Fool for Love* is that it works not only on this theatrical level but also on a dramatic and thematic level as well. *Fool for Love* both does something to the audience and tells them something at the same time. It successfully blends form and content, creating a theatrical spectacle of juxtaposed realities that embodies the play's thematic preoccupation with illusion and the subjectivity of reality.

The irony of Shepard's achievement in *Fool for Love* is that it seems to have been accomplished almost against his will. Shepard has said in numerous interviews that he wrote as many as 16 drafts of *Fool for Love* before he felt he had a play that remained true to the realistically drawn lovers and their naturalistically pitched situation.[22] What Shepard does not mention in those interviews is that it was not until the final draft of the play that he introduced the spectral presence of the old man into the script.[23] Until that draft, the play had been a conventional romantic confrontation between the long-separated lovers, Eddie and May. That Shepard would write well over a dozen drafts of a realistic play, and then finally complete a satisfactory draft only after the inspired addition of the old man, suggests the power of Shepard's intuitive theatricality over his conscious attempts to write within the self-imposed restraints of psychological realism. The solution to Shepard's writing problem was not a psychological or dramatic one but a theatrical one, involving the presence of a character who suspends the play between fantasy and reality.

The struggle between the "old" Shepard's theatrical intuition and the "new" Shepard's conscious restraint can be further felt in the published text of *Fool for Love*. In that text, Shepard states that the old man "exists only in the minds of MAY and EDDIE" (*FFL*, 15). This rationalization of the old man's presence would have been totally unnecessary for the "old" Sam Shepard, who felt perfectly comfortable with intersecting planes of reality in *Suicide in B-Flat*. As noted earlier, when *Fool for Love* is performed live, there is no suggestion in the play itself that the old man is being imagined or dreamed by either Eddie or May. In fact, one has the distinct impression on several occasions, especially at the end of the play when May and Eddie have both left the stage, that the old man may well be dreaming them. And yet Shepard felt obliged, when publishing the play, to rationalize the old man's existence.

While many reviewers, including myself,[24] wished to see *Fool for Love* as the final triumphant resurrection of the "old" Shepard in a new glorious incarnation as an innovative family dramatist, the inclusion of this single stage direction in the text of the play should have served as a sobering indicator of the conservative direction Shepard's career was continuing to take in spite of *Fool for Love*. He has since rejected anything about his family plays that "smacks of the 'old' Shepard," citing examples of suprareal and surreal staging from *Curse of the Starving Class, Buried Child*, and *Fool for Love* as sources of embarrassment (Allen, 150).

Shepard's most recent family play is the sadly conventional, tamely self-imitative *A Lie of the Mind.*

A Lie of the Mind

Sam Shepard once lamented that drama critics wanted him to "stop playing around and give us a really MAJOR NEW AMERICAN PLAY."[25] For most of his career, Shepard has sought to avoid the canonical mainstream of American drama, pursuing his own interests in his own fashion, publicly rebuffing the lure of Broadway and the New York theater establishment, and denying the title of "Great American Dramatist." Shepard has never had any of his plays produced on Broadway and has told the press that it is "ridiculous to look on New York as *the* arena, or the New York audience as the ultimate audience."[26] Only twice has he agreed to have his work premiered in commercial New York venues: *Operation Sidewinder* at the Lincoln Center in 1970, and *A Lie of the Mind* at the Promenade Theatre in 1985. Yet, in both these instances, especially the latter, Shepard appears to have acquiesced to the wishes of his critics, to the myth of New York, and to his popular image by writing plays that court mainstream audiences as well as encompass the complexity of that vague entity, "the American experience."

The parallel between *Operation Sidewinder* and *A Lie of the Mind* is not significant because of any stylistic or thematic similarities between the two plays. In most respects, they are as different as they could be. The first is a satirical tale of counterculture revolutionaries and a snakelike computer run amok in the desert wilderness of the American Southwest. The second is a love story of domestic violence and unreconciled families. What is significant is the position each occupies in Shepard's career. Both came at the end of highly productive and stylistically distinct periods in Shepard's writing. Both have been followed by periods of relative artistic silence. Both are uncharacteristic of Shepard in their use of short cinematic scenes and multiple settings. And, most significantly, these two plays—Shepard's two most ambitious forays into mainstream American drama—were both written during periods of time when Shepard was working on films that served to reinforce his public image as chronicler of the American people: Michelangelo Antonioni's *Zabriskie Point* in 1970 and Robert Altman's *Fool for Love* in 1985. This fact certainly sheds light on the uncharacteristically cinematic structure of both plays. But, more importantly, it helps to explain the rather forced attempt on Shepard's part, in both these instances, to write what he has always claimed he did not wish to write: major new American plays.

Shepard's distaste for Hollywood and the film industry, like his distaste for the New York theater establishment, has been well documented in plays as well as interviews.[27] Yet throughout his career he has been conspicuously influenced by Hollywood images of America and unwillingly lured by the power of such images to communicate in sweeping social generalities to a vast audience. As Rabbit says in *Angel City*, "The vision of a celluloid tape with a series of moving images telling a story to millions. Millions anywhere. . . . And I ask myself, how can I stay immune?" (*AC*, 69). The young Sam Shepard who worked on *Zabriskie Point* was "wasted by the experience. It was like a nightmare" (Oppenheim, 81). But by 1985, Shepard's increasing exposure as a movie star had apparently changed his mind about film and about the archetypal images of the family and the American dream perpetuated by that industry.

Shepard has said of Hollywood that "everything there is contrived to make you believe your own publicity. . . . It's easy to be seduced by that" (Goodman, 77). *A Lie of the Mind*, in many respects, appears to be the product of such a seduction. Nearly everything about the play—from the story line, with its archetypal American families and conventional themes of love and domestic violence, to the choice of a chic New York venue for the premiere, the casting of film and Broadway veterans, and the careful scheduling of the opening to coincide with the nationwide release of the film version of *Fool for Love*—suggests that Shepard was actively influenced by both Broadway and Hollywood and that he was pursuing, for his play and himself, a place within both popular culture and the classical canon of mainstream American drama. It is as though, persuaded by his own press clippings and his on-screen persona that he is indeed an icon of the great American male, Shepard set out to write a play worthy of his image.

But these blanket statements may serve to oversimplify the case for what is actually a complex and powerful play. Paul Berman underestimates Shepard and overstates the case when he says of Shepard that "he's not a major playwright and the effort to become more than what he is has led to fiascoes like *A Lie of the Mind*."[28] Shepard is without doubt one of America's major playwrights, and while *A Lie of the Mind* disappoints in some ways, it is far from being a fiasco. Nevertheless, the play does show the strain of Shepard's attempt to manipulate consciously his personal vocabulary of archetypal family images into a significant statement about America for widespread public consumption. As Gordon Rogoff expressed it, "[Shepard] can't decide if he wants to tell a tale about people or a parable about the nation."[29]

A Lie of the Mind is a symmetrically structured tale of two families, one in California, the other in Montana, linked by the marriage of Jake and Beth. The play opens with Jake at a roadside pay phone. Appearing slightly drunk and crazed, Jake pounds the receiver against the phone booth's metal hood. "I never even saw it comin'," he says to his brother Frankie on the other end of the line. "I never did."[30] At first it sounds as though Jake has been in an automobile accident—that he has killed a woman in a car crash. But what Jake did not foresee was his own outburst of violence: he has severely beaten his wife, Beth, left her for dead, and taken to the road. At one point he says, "She's right here with me now!" A moment later, he claims, "She's dead!" Frankie is confused by this apparent contradiction, but it is Beth's presence in Jake's heart, rather than her physical presence, that he is trying to express.

Frankie's confusion introduces one of the central literary motifs of the play: lingering love translated into terms of death and life, murder and resurrection. "My whole life is lost from losing her," Jake laments. "I'll die like this" (*LM*, 14). Likewise, Beth, who has survived Jake's beating, but with serious brain damage, tells her brother, Mike, "Hee killed us both. . . . I'M DEAD!" A moment later she insists that Jake still lives inside of her: "You gan [can't] stop him in me. . . . HEEZ MY HAAAAAAAAAAAAAAAAAART!!!" (*LM*, 19, 20). The play is crowded with images of lovers who have been "killed" by neglect and of love that still "lives" inside of them. Jake's mother, Lorraine, states firmly that all traces of her husband are "dead and gone," only to contradict herself in nearly the same breath: "He put stuff into me that'll never go away" (*LM*, 91). Absent lovers haunt their partners and offspring just as the old man haunted May and Eddie in *Fool for Love*.

Shepard treats Jake as well as Beth as a victim of sorts who must be nursed back to health after a cataclysmic experience. Shortly after Jake phones Frankie, he collapses into a delirious semicoma. His mother, Lorraine, a dominant matriarchal figure, retrieves Jake from his brother and takes him home to his old bedroom. She tries to reaffirm her role as maternal protectress, ignoring all that has happened, even denying Beth's existence, and feeding her son his favorite childhood soup. "I'm gonna take him on a permanent basis," she announces to Frankie and to Jake's sister, Sally (*LM*, 26). Later, with Jake tucked securely in his old bed, his model airplanes dangling on wires above his head and his pants carefully locked away to ensure his compliance with her wishes, Lorraine tells her son, "You can stay here as long as ya want to. . . . You don't ever have to go outa this room again if you don't want to" (*LM*, 39). For a while, it seems as though Jake will comply; he tells Sally, "I'm not goin' outdoors anymore. I'm not leavin' this room" (*LM*, 61). But when he learns that Frankie has gone in search of Beth, his ability to convince himself of her death slowly wanes. He knows he must face the world and eventually face his wife and his own brutality.

While convalescing, Jake confronts another ugly reminder of his own past brutality: his involvement in his father's death. Despite his failure to kill Beth and erase her from his life, Jake succeeded years earlier in indirectly killing his father. He has since suppressed the memory. The specific facts of the incident are revealed late in the play, but Jake's unnatural obsession with his father is manifested throughout the action. He dons the dead man's leather flight jacket, pins medals to his chest, and opens the small box containing his father's cremated remains. In a visually arresting moment, Jake sits cross-legged on the floor and, holding the box in his hands, blows a cloud of his father's ash into the air. When Jake later escapes his mother's house, he is without pants, but he carries the American flag from his father's coffin wrapped around his shoulders.

Unfortunately, Shepard never allows Jake to articulate the nature of his sudden obsession with nor his feelings for his father. Although that obsession is clearly manifested in symbolic images like those mentioned here and is closely linked (though how or why, Shepard does not say) to Jake's decision to search out Beth, it is never discussed. Near the end of the play, Jake arrives on Beth's doorstep, still wrapped in the flag. It is clear that he has completed a personal spiritual odyssey, yet the nature of Jake's odyssey and his motives remain veiled. His personal journey has taken place offstage, between acts, and is never revealed.

One benefit of this inadequate treatment of Jake is that Shepard spends as little time as possible focusing on the self-pity of a wife beater and instead concentrates on the victim of that abuse. Beth's side of the story begins in a hospital room. Having been severely beaten about the head, she suffers from partial amnesia and from aphasia, a brain dysfunction that robs the individual of the power to use or understand words. She must relearn both the use of language and the motor functions of speech and general muscle coordination. Beth first regains consciousness in an abrupt nightmare, screaming aloud, lurching upright in her bed, and pouring forth a stream of garbled sounds that her mouth will not articulate. Her speech is primitive; she cannot operate her vocal mechanism, and, more importantly, she has lost command of the complexities of spoken language. "Who fell me here?" she asks her brother Mike, remembering only vaguely at first the "name" who beat her.

Shepard created a brain-damaged girl once before in his rock musical, *Inacoma*. That play employed the young victim's comatose state to raise questions about the nature of identity and of "normal" states of consciousness and perception. "Who was the me that used to be?" the girl asks herself, having been stripped of her former identity and fixed perceptions. Shepard also had tragic personal exposure to the effects of brain damage and aphasia. In 1979, his wife O-Lan's mother, Scarlett Johnson Dark, suffered an apparent stroke resulting in aphasia. In 1984, Shepard's close friend and artistic collaborator, Joseph Chaikin, had a stroke during open-heart surgery resulting in aphasia that seriously impaired his speech.[31] These real-life incidents left Shepard with first-hand knowledge of the type of perceptual dysfunction he had often attempted to explore in his plays. As he said in reference to *Inacoma*, many of his plays centered on "a character in a critical state of consciousness" (Weiner, 14).

The most fascinating developments of character and theme in *A Lie of the Mind* arise from the acute state of awareness brought about by Beth's injury and recovery. Shepard utilizes Beth's mental state as a perceptual rebirth that allows her to view the world and her life without the enforced preconceptions of experience. "If something broken . . . ," she tells her brother Mike, "parts still float. For a while" (*LM*, 47). Beth's mind has been unfixed by her injuries; the victim of partial amnesia, her existential slate of personal experience has been nearly wiped clean. Gathering experience and utilizing language only in fragments, she reorients her perceptions and recreates reality around her only as she is able to create a language to articulate it. In one of her many moments of stunning perception, Beth reinforces the love and death images of the play when she explains that her father has given up love: "Love is dead for him. My mother is dead for him. Things live for him to be killed" (*LM*, 57). Although the language is stilted, Beth's description of her father—a hunter who passes his time in a game blind behind the house, coming inside only to have his wife rub mink oil into his frostbitten feet—demonstrates a quality of perception that transcends that of ordinary observation. The strange new syntax of her speech reflects the new connections with which she perceives her surroundings: "Your whole life can turn around. Upside down. In a flash. Sudden. . . ." she announces. "This whole world can disappear" (*LM*, 81). Having seen the fixed world disappear, she now consciously explores and manipulates her potential to create a new world, to order the fragments into a new perception.

Remembering little of her past, Beth also has the opportunity to recreate herself, an opportunity that many of Shepard's past characters sought desperately. Sensing instinctively that her feminine role in the past has been a passive and consequently unfortunate one, she takes advantage of her present situation to construct a more satisfying self. When Beth's mother, Meg, offers her a choice of shoes—either men's boots or soft, fuzzy women's slippers—Beth chooses to remain barefoot, as though she does not wish to be categorized or locked into a particular sexual role. Returning home, she selects one of her father Baylor's rough, woolen fishing shirts for herself. In a moment of uncanny, childlike insight, she illuminates the sexual symbolism and role playing of such clothing, explaining that the "shirt scares man" so man wears the shirt in order to internalize its threat and "become" the shirt. Beth dons her father's shirt and becomes, in her own playful words, a "shirt-man."

When Baylor accidentally shoots the prowling Frankie, mistaking him for a deer in the snow, Beth decides that Frankie can be part of her recreated universe. "You could be the woman . . . ," she tells him. "Between us we can make a life. . . . You could pretend to be in love with me. With my shirt" (*LM*, 75). Having recognized Frankie's voice and associating it with Jake, she tells him to pretend to be Jake, "Just like him. But soft. With me. Gentle. Like a woman-man" (*LM*, 76). Beth wants to recreate her old life but without the rigidly enforced male/female categories and distinctions that led to her beating and present misfortune.

Such pretending "fills" Beth, in her words, because her "ordinary" life, the victimized life that she led with Jake and that she sees her mother lead, is "no good. Empty." In fact, it is Beth's penchant for pretending that originally brings about Jake's outburst of violence. Jake tells Frankie early in the play that Beth's acting career has become "the real world" for her, and that she transforms herself into whatever character she is playing to the point of believing that she is that character. When Jake becomes convinced that Beth is living out a fantasy life with her scene partner ("some actor jerk," as Jake calls him), his imagination overtakes him and he tries to kill her. It is this imagined infidelity, generated by jealousy, from which the play takes its title. As Jake eventually realizes, Beth's sexual transgression was nothing more than "a lie of the mind."

Beth's exploration of the boundaries between "being" and "acting" is nothing new to Shepard's work. "You act yourself out," says Shooter in *Action*; and he is just one of many characters in Shepard's plays to draw attention to the fabricated performance quality of our created "social selves." What is new in *A Lie of the Mind* is the application of such a discussion to issues of gender. Never before has Shepard associated this rather existential theme with sexual roles, nor has he ever placed such considerations in the mouth of one of his female characters.

The other women in *A Lie of the Mind* make equally noteworthy contributions to the examination of gender roles and male/female relations. Having watched Beth's new self-creation, her mother, Meg, comments to Baylor that their daughter has changed: "All I recognize anymore is her body. And even that's beginning to change" (*LM*, 99). Meg believes Beth has "male" in her, and she proceeds to describe the "two opposite animals" that are male and female: "The female—the female one needs—the other. . . . The male" (*LM*, 105). But the male doesn't really know what he needs, and so he goes off alone, leaving the female. In precisely this manner, Baylor has left Meg. He spends his days hunting, believing that his whole life "went sour" because of women. "I could be up in the wild country huntin' antelope," he tells Meg. "But no, I gotta play nursemaid to a bunch a' feeble-minded women down here in civilization who can't take care a' themselves" (*LM*, 106).

Jake's father also sought to escape the "civilization" of women. We learn over the course of the play that he long ago left his wife and family, needing something he was unable to identify. He wandered off and eventually ended up living alone in the desert. Like the old man in *Fool for Love* and the father in *Curse of the Starving Class*, Lorraine's husband disappeared for long stretches of time, finally deserting his family completely and settling in a trailer in Mexico. "Is there any good reason in this Christless world why men leave women?" Lorraine asks her daughter Sally (*LM*, 86). In the third act of the play, Jake repeats his father's behavior when he "runs away" from his mother to find Beth.

Sally is conspirator both to Jake's escape and to a much greater sibling mystery involving their father's death. Like May in *Fool for Love*, Sally shares a solemn pact with her brother, carrying a secret burden inside herself, "like some disease he left behind." In a story much like the one that climaxes *Fool for Love*, Sally reveals to her mother the truth about her father's death. She recounts how she and Jake visited the old man in Mexico. Jake took his father out for a drink. "At first it was like this brotherhood," Sally recalls. But as the two men get drunk, their conversation acquires a competitive edge, "the way an animal looks for the weakness in another animal" (*LM*, 92, 93). The men determine to prove their mettle in a footrace and drinking contest, drinking their way from one bar to the next, racing to the American border. The old man eventually trips and sprawls headlong in the street where he is too drunk to escape an oncoming truck. Jake sits in the next bar up the road, unmoved even when he hears the ambulance arrive. "It was just the same as if he'd had a gun," Sally tells her mother (*LM*, 94). Jake convinces Sally to call the police, who in turn inform Lorraine of her husband's death. Jake never tells his mother of his involvement.

At first Lorraine refuses to believe Sally. Then, irrationally, she blames her daughter for not stopping the race. Eventually, however, the two women are purged by the confession; like May and Eddie at the end of *Fool for Love*, they collapse into each other's arms. "What're we doin' in this room now?" Sally eventually asks, suddenly aware that she and her mother have been living in Jake's bedroom—and hence in the male-dominated past—since his disappearance. "What're we supposed to be hiding from?" (*LM*, 96). The scene ends with Lorraine wishing for "one of those winds" that blow everything away, leaving the sky without a cloud, "pure, pure blue."

In their final scene together, Sally and Lorraine create such a wind. Gathering old belongings from the house—vestiges of men and boys, model planes, sports equipment, photos, remembrances of the past—they set the room and the house itself ablaze. Like Beth, they seek to erase their past, to free themselves of the men and the memories that have accumulated in their hearts and stifled their beings. Shepard has said, "[You feel] . . . jailed by all of your cultural influences and your psychological influences from your family, and all that" (Chubb et al., 16). In a phoenixlike blaze, these women suggest that only through the incineration of the personal past and of their servitude to the men they have loved can they achieve rebirth and freedom.

Beth and her mother, Meg, achieve a different kind of rebirth. Rather than incinerate the past, they rekindle old flames in order to resurrect life. In the final moments of the play, Jake leaves Beth in Frankie's care, while Meg, having been touched with affection by her husband for the first time in 20 years, gazes meditatively out over the audience. Snow has been falling outside her house during the entire play. As Meg watches it, she glimpses a distant image: "Looks like a fire in the snow. How could that be?" (*LM*, 131). On stage, the fire in Lorraine's house still flickers across a symbolic gulf that separates the two households onstage. The softened flames, which only moments earlier suggested the final immolation of a dead past, now suggest the rekindling of a long-forgotten tenderness in a cold and barren household. Shepard's final image is one of twofold hope and rebirth. The two households have come to opposite but equally rewarding renewal.

While this final poetic image is a rich and touching one, *A Lie of the Mind* is generally lacking in the dense mythic imagery and powerful stage tableaux of Shepard's best work. Shepard creates several striking stage images in this play, yet none of them have the chilling theatricality of, for instance, the old man who sits unexplained in his alcove during *Fool for Love* or of Tilden who enters again and again in *Buried Child* bearing armloads of fresh vegetables and finally a muddied infant corpse. Like Tilden, Beth's brother, Mike, repeatedly enters from the snowstorm outside their house. At one point, he even carries onstage the freshly slaughtered flank of a deer he has shot. His claim that the woods are suddenly full of bucks is reminiscent of Tilden's claim that the fields behind his home are buried in vegetables, sprouted overnight. But such images seem watered down in *A Lie of the Mind*, never inclining toward the archetypal or surreal. The characters in the play, as well, frequently appear to be the weak reworking of earlier successes. As Robert Brustein notes, "The brothers in *A Lie of the Mind* remind us of the ones in *True West*; the husband and wife recall the brother and sister in *Fool for Love*; the California family comes from *Curse of the Starving Class*, the Montana family from *Buried Child*."[32] The play, at times, almost seems to be a commercialized imitation of Shepard's work, especially in moments of clichéd symbolism like the one involving an American flag that comes near the end of the play.

When Beth and Jake finally meet face to face in the last scene of the play, the moment is both undercut and sentimentalized by the sight of Baylor and Meg, working in unison for the first time in the play (and perhaps for many years), ceremoniously folding the American flag that Jake earlier wrapped around his shoulders. When they finish, Baylor affectionately sweeps his wife up into his arms, kissing her on the cheek, and holding up the flag as he shouts, "We did it! We did it, Meg!" This absurd image of an American couple suddenly and inexplicably revitalized by an act of symbolic patriotism might be an appropriate ending to the glamorized Hollywood visions of America that Shepard's career has sought to deconstruct. But coming at the conclusion of Shepard's most ambitious play to date, it is an embarrassing bit of heavy-handed and inappropriate symbolism, inconsistent with his more complex concerns as an American dramatist.

Shepard's lack of theatrical originality extends to the physical staging of *A Lie of the Mind* as well. Beth's unfixed perception would seem to offer a perfect opportunity for Shepard's lightninglike flashes of expanded consciousness. In plays such as *Action, Angel City,* or *Suicide in B-Flat,* Shepard presented a world completely unfixed from its rational framework. Yet *A Lie of the Mind* offers no outward manifestation of Beth's condition to suggest that the world is indeed as malleable as she perceives it to be. The only theatrical support offered Beth's vision is in the evolution of the stage setting from scene to scene. Locations are established in the first act with only isolated pieces of furniture in vague areas of light. The extremities of the set are filled in only gradually during the course of the play, with the "perimeters of the area[s] more fully lit" (*LM,* 28) as if to suggest that, as Beth and Jake reconstruct their lives, their perceptual universe begins to expand and order itself as well. By the second act of the play, walls, doors, and other touches of realistic detail have appeared. Nevertheless, the limitations of Beth's recovery are clearly indicated by the "black void" beyond the set's windows and doors. While this scenic concept may be said to "reflect" Beth's gradual reconstruction of self and reality, it does not theatricalize her condition but only takes timid license with scenic realism. Shepard's treatment of space here pales in comparison to the bold theatrical strokes of *True West* or the visceral use of the stage as emotional signifier in *Fool for Love.*

While critical response to *A Lie of the Mind* has been mixed, of one point there is little doubt. As Jack Kroll put it, "'A Lie of the Mind' is likely to gain Shepard his widest audience yet as a playwright; there's no doubt that this play will be produced all over the country."[33] Sadly, this acclamation may come less from Shepard's achievement than from his conscious attempts to render his work accessible to a larger audience. At the heart of *A Lie of the Mind,* artistic concessions have been made that place the soul of the piece in limbo. No unseen force ripples beneath the surface of this play, nor does the action ever threaten to explode off the stage.

Shepard appeared, with *A Lie of the Mind,* to have created the "major new American play" critics and the American public expected of him. Yet, with Shepard's mythic density and wild theatricality sacrificed for the sake of accessibility, America had lost its most uncompromising theatrical genius. Not until 1991, after an artistic silence of more than five years, did Shepard demonstrate that he still carried the renegade spirit for which he was first celebrated in the Off-Off-Broadway of the 1960s.

Chapter Eight
States of Shock:
A Nonconclusion

Early in 1991, Sam Shepard was in New York City working with Joseph Chaikin on *The War in Heaven (Angel's Monologue)*. Shepard and Chaikin had collaborated on the piece off and on during the early 1980s. Having performed it at various times and in various drafts around the country, Chaikin was now preparing to perform the work for the first time in New York City.[1] *The War in Heaven* is a poetic monologue about an angel who dies on the day he is born and who, drifting aimlessly in the afterlife, has lost all sense of personal order and destiny. The quality of existence the angel recounts is best described in a letter Shepard wrote to Chaikin in October of 1983. In that letter, Shepard told Chaikin that he had been pondering the idea of being "lost," of "one's identity being shattered under severe personal circumstances—in a state of crisis where everything that I've previously identified with in myself suddenly falls away."[2] Shepard suggested that one might call this Pirandellian condition a "shock state." He proposed to focus not on the trauma or the shock itself but on the "resulting emptiness or aloneness." Little did Shepard know when he wrote those words that his friend and collaborator was less than a year away from the stroke that would leave him in just such a state of crisis, suffering from aphasia. Nor did Shepard know that seven years later, working again with Chaikin on *The War in Heaven*, he would combine the extremely personal concept of a "shock state" with a current world crisis in order to create a timely political play, *States of Shock*.

When Shepard and Chaikin joined forces in 1991 to rework *The War in Heaven* for its New York premiere, the political climate in the United States had added a new dimension to their collaboration. With American troops massed in the Persian Gulf, about to invade Iraq, the angel's voice took on a new political tone for both Chaikin and Shepard.[3] The sense of personal loss and of emptiness was no longer a purely spiritual state, nor one that spoke solely of Chaikin's disorienting experiences with aphasia, but one that spoke as well for all of postmodern, post-Vietnam America, suddenly at war again. The result was not only a newly inspired reading of *The War in Heaven* on Chaikin's part but a new play on Shepard's part, *States of Shock*, which opened at the American Place Theatre only weeks after Chaikin's performances ended.

Produced for only a brief run,[4] *States of Shock* was unlike anything Shepard had written for nearly two decades. The play is, on one level, an overtly political response to the American government's military invasion of Iraq in February of 1991 and to the compliant and complacent reaction of the American public to that invasion. But *States of Shock* is not simply a political tract; it is a fluid, dreamlike event of hypnotic, archetypal images, as full of visual poetry as it is of current politics.

Stylistically, *States of Shock* immediately reminds one of Shepard's short, hallucinatory plays from the mid-1960s. Like those plays, it is more concerned with expressing a highly personal state of consciousness than with telling a story. Yet, like such later Shepard dramas as *Buried Child* and *Fool for Love*, *States of Shock* is propelled by the unraveling of a family secret.

Here, as in so many of Shepard's plays, family eventually comes down to fathers and sons. *States of Shock* is, on its most obvious level, a confrontation between a father figure and a disinherited son. But unlike the autobiographical images of Shepard and his father that populate the family plays of the late 1970s and 1980s, these two figures take on both sociopolitical dimensions and mythic proportions, embodying universal qualities of manhood, young and old. The father, known only as the Colonel, is dressed in bits and pieces of historical uniforms, military decorations, and combat gear from various American wars. He is an archetypal military man: a firm believer in the noble myths of war that men like himself have served to perpetuate. Stubbs, the Colonel's self-proclaimed son, is the disabled veteran of an unnamed war. He is a Christ-like martyr who has been technologically resurrected after surviving a direct hit from incoming artillery. Their confrontation, enacted before symbolic representatives of the American public, suggests a battle between those fathers who make war and those sons who must do battle, between the patriarchal, pre-Vietnam myths of a righteous American military and the shattered, post-Vietnam realities of young men killed and traumatized in a costly and paranoid war of expansionism. The gas masks that appear late in the play also make it clear that these two men represent George Bush's America, attempting to flex its global muscle in the Persian Gulf, and the unquestioning soldiers who participated in that lopsided war of rampant destruction. In Shepard's apparent world-view, fathers (and the governments they support and represent) will always be struggling to perpetuate their own patriarchal myths, and sons will always be called, unwittingly or unwillingly, to serve their fathers' unwholesome ends.

In *States of Shock*, the Colonel publicly claims that Stubbs is a war hero, a valiant soldier who attempted to save the life of the Colonel's son by putting his own body between that son and an incoming enemy missile. As the Colonel tells it, the missile went straight through Stubbs and killed his unfortunate son anyway. Stubbs, "the lucky one," has lived to tell the tale.

But Stubbs's recollection of events is somewhat different from the Colonel's. Partially paralyzed and confined to a wheelchair, Stubbs cautiously suggests that he is, in fact, the Colonel's son and that he was running from battle when he was struck by a missile fired by his own forces. Like the angel in *The War in Heaven*, Stubbs once felt he "had a mission," that he was "part of something." But all that disappeared in battle. Betrayed by the patriarchal myths that guided him into battle, shot upon and abandoned by his countrymen, Stubbs is ultimately denied his own identity by a father who will no longer acknowledge his kinship. The experience has left Stubbs, in his own words, "eighty per cent mutilated," dead and rotting from the inside out. He has also been left spiritually, emotionally, and literally impotent. As he screams at the top of his lungs on a number of occasions during the play, "My thing hangs like dead meat!"[5]

Stubbs's physical and emotional mutilation is graphically manifest in a wound that he regularly reveals to the audience and to the other characters on stage. If, as Shepard has said of his earliest plays, he started with a single image and created his play around that image, then *States of Shock* was undoubtedly created around the image of Stubbs, slumped in his wheelchair, tugging his sweatshirt up around his neck to reveal a round, red scar, the size of a softball, through the middle of his chest. This startling image, usually accompanied in the play by a shrill blast on the whistle Stubbs wears around his neck, speaks simply and eloquently of the physical devastation and emotional havoc wreaked upon those who go to war, those who die, and those who return "mutilated" to the families that sent them off to fight. Stubbs is the image of inglorious war and its brutal aftermath, known to Shepard's generation—the Vietnam generation—but carefully avoided by the media coverage of the Persian Gulf War. As if to remedy that myopic media coverage and to remind Americans of the physical and emotional reality behind the masculine myths of war, Stubbs frequently wheels himself to the front edge of the stage, pulls up his shirt, blasts on his whistle, and thrusts his wound in our faces.

Stubbs's wound is a classic Shepard manifestation of life and self unfixed: it represents Stubbs's life, suddenly gutted of everything from which he gathered meaning and a sense of self. The trauma and betrayal of his war experience have torn through him like a missile, stripping him not just of his name but of the very core of his being. As Shepard wrote in his 1983 letter to Chaikin, he explores a character in whom "everything which [he's] previously identified with [him]self suddenly falls away." Like the angel in *The War in Heaven*, adrift in the afterlife, Stubbs finds himself adrift in an America that no longer exists for him.

In spite of its timely statement on America's military presence in the Persian Gulf, *States of Shock* is closer in tone to the spiritual world of *The War in Heaven* than to a "political" play in any conventional sense. It is a personal poetic response to a specific moment in American history. The images, like those of Shepard's best work, are both simple and at the same time startling in their ability to carry profound meaning.

The scenic elements are minimal: the set is supposedly a "family restaurant" (as we are reminded repeatedly during the play), but it is more like the dreamscape of such a restaurant, consisting of a few isolated properties placed on a bare stage in front of a large white cyclorama. During moments of intense emotion or extended descriptions of battle, that cyclorama is illuminated from behind with bursts of light, color, and the stylized images of war. Beyond the cyclorama, two percussionists underscore such moments with intense rhythmic drumming and the stylized sounds of a battle in progress.

One of the most singular visual images of the play is the presence on stage throughout the action of an elderly, seemingly affluent couple dressed from head to foot in white. They sit at a table, also white, waiting for a long overdue order of clam chowder. Detached and unaffected, they are anemic white America, watching unmoved as father and son debate the terrible cost of war. More a symbolic scenic element than actual customers in a restaurant, they are occasionally annoyed at the minor inconvenience that the war and its aftermath have caused them. They seem to take more interest in their missing clam chowder or in the shopping they could be doing than in the issues at hand.[6] Only when the Colonel savagely beats Stubbs do they reveal shades of the desperate impotence and bitterness buried beneath their postures of indifference: as the beating progresses, the white man masturbates under a napkin while the white woman encourages the Colonel to act like a proper parent and strike again.

States of Shock was poorly received by New York critics who saw it as a regression on Shepard's part after so long a silence.[7] But in spite of the play's heavy-handed political symbolism and its uneven tone and tempo, the striking imagery and theatrical energy of *States of Shock* suggest not so much a regression as a rejuvenation of the impassioned (and sometimes reckless) theatrical genius who, in the 1960s, projected his inner emotional landscapes onto the stages of Off-Off-Broadway.

With *States of Shock*, Sam Shepard has demonstrated once again that attempts to draw hard and fast conclusions about his work or the eventual course of his career eventually prove meaningless. He has once more reinvented himself and, for the moment, the family dramatist has vanished and a new incarnation of the one-time rebel of Off-Off-Broadway has taken his place. The only conclusion I would dare draw about Shepard, who I hope has many more plays still within himself, is that he has given a new term to the vocabulary of dramatic criticism: "Shepardesque." But as *States of Shock* illustrates anew, the qualities of that term are difficult to pin down. Certainly the fragmented reality of *La Turista* is Shepardesque, but so too is the family in *Buried Child*. The language in *The Tooth of Crime* is Shepardesque, and so are the suprareal toasters in *True West*. But what ties these elements of Shepard's work together? What, for that matter, is the connection between the cowboys, the space freak, and the cheerleader in *The Unseen Hand*? Surely they are all Shepardesque.

There is no one characteristic of Shepard's writing that defines his work exclusive of all the others. One may state rather vaguely, as many have, that Shepard's work is unified by his vision of America; however, the America of *Mad Dog Blues* has little to do with that of *A Lie of the Mind*. Shepard is not a one-issue writer. His career has been a series of artistic reincarnations in which various issues, interests, and artistic trademarks have come to the forefront or stepped temporarily to the rear.

In defining the qualities of Shepard's work, one must consider the constantly changing interrelationship of a number of thematic and theatrical elements and intentions: the disappearing West; the loss of and search for a harmony with the land; the juxtaposition of the old and the new, the authentic and the fabricated, the spiritual and the technological, the father and the son; the cultural fixing and entombing of artists and public heroes; a language rich in American vernacular and idiolects; a cast of characters equally rich in American popular culture genres; the uncertain nature of identity and at the same time the seeming inescapability of cultural, genetic, and familial inheritance; and, finally, an unstable stage reality—sometimes hypnotically malleable, other times terrifyingly fragile.

As I have said throughout this study, the one element of Shepard's work that I feel appears with any consistency, both thematically and theatrically, is the sense of the world and the self as unfixed—the sense of loss that Shepard described in his letter to Chaikin. And while even this element of Shepard's intent as a theater artist neither belongs exclusively to Shepard nor exclusively defines him, it is, for me, the single most dominant feature of his writing. It is present in the plight of cowboys who have lost touch with the land, in hallucinatory monologues that push the limits of reality into heightened states of consciousness, and in the suprapresence of fresh food, functional properties, and live actors and animals whose materiality transcends and thus disrupts the fictional reality of the stage. It is even present in the traumatic experience of a war veteran who has been physically and emotionally emptied by the instruments of his country's aggression. These are all variations on the unfixing of the assumptions and beliefs upon which we construct our fragile lives. Unique to Shepard is the ability to manifest that unfixing through plot, language, imagery, and especially live theatrical staging.

Reality unfixed is also, Shepard's plays suggest, the condition of postmodern America, and thus it is intimately tied to the various "American" themes present in his work. Shepard's fantastic spectral palette of spoken American vernaculars, of the rival idiolects his characters speak, is an extension of the fragmentation of our land into a growing number of self-generating subcultures. In *The Rock Garden*, such cultural fragmentation has invaded the family itself: mother, father, and son experience reality so differently that they no longer speak a common language. Instead, they have each generated a personal vernacular to give expression to the world they see.

This same juxtaposition of incongruous realities is evident in the intertextual patchwork of various cultural genres in plays such as *The Unseen Hand*, where western outlaws, a futuristic space freak, and a high school cheerleader all share the stage. While these characters inhabit radically different landscapes, they are all part of America's media-fed collective consciousness. That consciousness, jammed with so many of these inbred codified images, has lost contact with their origins and significance. Thus, the world of *The Unseen Hand* is not the identifiable product of any single guiding culture or mythology but is identifiable only by its total lack of such guidance. Reality is not a unified experience but rather a patchwork of discontinuous moments and images.

When Shepard turns to the family, this type of fragmentation is still present in a discontinuity of stage action (such as the string of perpetual presents at the beginning of *Curse of the Starving Class*). Thematically, however, Shepard uses the family plays to bring to the forefront the inverse side of his preoccupation with the postmodern condition: the search for origins. For at the same time that Shepard chronicles a media-simulated and fragmentary reality, he still demonstrates a faith in and a desire to reconnect with an authenticated state of being in which reality and the self are given meaning. Vince's homecoming in *Buried Child* is a search for authentic origins, as is the Indian ritual in *Operation Sidewinder* or Stubbs's attempt to gain the recognition and acceptance of his father in *States of Shock*. In addition, while Shepard's cowboys have lost touch with the land and have been turned into meaningless matinee images by their mass simulation in popular culture, Shepard seems to believe that they once enjoyed an authentic spiritual and emotional harmony with the West. Shepard's return to the family, along with his adoption of increasingly conventional dramatic methods in the early 1980s, is thus a struggle to deny and to transcend the disturbing reality of the postmodern condition as experienced in his earlier plays.

Shepard's silence following *A Lie of the Mind* in 1985 led many in the theatrical community and in critical circles to speculate on his future in the American theater. Concern was expressed that, with his stature as a film star, Shepard would turn his creative energies entirely to film. Such a possibility is neither implausible nor without precedent. Hollywood has robbed the American theater of many of its great writers, directors, and actors in the past. But Shepard's approach to film has always been a cautious one: he has been unwilling to compromise his own artistry for the sake of those in power or those who see film primarily as a means of making money. "I tend to accept parts only with friends and work with people I know and like . . . with creative people," Shepard explained in 1983 (Goodman, 76). But Shepard now lives with Jessica Lange, one of the most highly respected film actresses. As Lange has introduced Shepard to her circle of peers, the number of Shepard's "friends" in the film industry has grown, as have his film appearances. Furthermore, as his film-directing debut in *Far North* (1988) demonstrated, Shepard's on-screen clout, combined with Lange's, has allowed him to begin wrestling artistic control away from those clutching the purse strings.

The surprising appearance of a play like *States of Shock* after so long a silence on Shepard's part makes one take a long look backward at his public persona and at his plays to date. Both comprise a string of disappearing acts. Shepard is a self-made myth, a man who created an artistic identity at the age of 19 and who has successfully reinvented himself, leaping into new areas of artistic expression, as the need or impulse has arisen. At the same time, he had been unable to erase his personal heritage. As his family plays demonstrate, he has gradually accepted the spiritual, cultural, and familial inheritance of being Samuel Shepard Rogers VII. So Shepard has both succeeded and failed in disappearing, in erasing himself.

"Nobody can disappear," Austin says in *True West*. "You'll never erase me," chimes in Stubbs in *States of Shock*. Let us hope that Shepard will fail in erasing that part of himself that is compelled to write innovatively for the stage and that he will succeed in re-emerging again and again in new artistic guises.

Notes and References

Chapter One

1. *Motel Chronicles* (San Francisco: City Lights Books, 1982), 49.

2. "Azusa Is a Real Place," *Plays and Players*, May 1973, I.

3. Fredric Jameson, "Postmodernism and Consumer Society," in *The Anti-Aesthetic: Essays on Postmodern Culture*, ed. Hal Foster (Port Townsend, Wash.: Bay Press, 1983), 124–25; hereafter cited in text.

4. Bernard Weiner, "Sam Shepard Goes into a Trance for His New Play," *San Francisco Chronicle*, 20 March 1977, 14; hereafter cited in text.

5. Samuel G. Freedman, "Sam Shepard's Mythic Vision of the Family," *New York Times*, 1 December 1985, H1.

6. Amy Lippman, "A Conversation with Sam Shepard," *Harvard Advocate*, March 1983, 3; hereafter cited in text.

Chapter Two

1. Of these early typescripts, the only one publicly accessible is *Up to Thursday*, available both in Shepard's personal archives at Boston University's Mugar Library and in agent Toby Cole's archives at Shields Library, the University of California, Davis. I first saw the *Up to Thursday* script as part of a packet of Shepard scripts lent to me in 1984 by Patrick Fennell, who had written his Ph.D. dissertation on Shepard in 1977 at the University of California, Santa Barbara. That packet, which also contained the typescripts of *Dog*, *The Rocking Chair*, and *Blue Bitch*, was stamped "Toby Cole: actors and authors agent" on the front page. According to Fennell, Shepard gave him personal permission to acquire the unpublished typescripts from Cole in 1977.

Also in 1984, I acquired the original stage-manager's production script of *Cowboys*, along with memorabilia from the Theatre Genesis, from Ralph Cook. The final page of that typescript is missing. Other than the photocopy of *Cowboys* that I left with Cook, the production script in my possession is, to the best of my knowledge, the only extant copy of the play.

2. Michael Bloom, "Visions of the End: The Early Plays," in *American Dreams*, ed. Bonnie Marranca (New York: Performing Arts Journal Publications, 1981), 73; hereafter cited in text.

3. According to Ralph Cook, the first scene did not exist at the time of the Theatre Genesis production. This claim is corroborated by both the original program and the published version of the play, neither of which lists the girl in the cast.

Ralph Cook, interview with author, Berkeley, California, 12 December 1984; hereafter cited in text as Cook interview.

4. *The Rock Garden*, in *Angel City, Curse of the Starving Class, and Other Plays* (New York: Urizen Books, 1976), 224; hereafter cited in text as *RG*.

5. Chaikin's remarks are cited in Robert Goldberg, "Sam Shepard: American Original," *Playboy*, March 1984, 192; hereafter cited in text.

6. The dialogue in *Cowboys #2* is roughly the same. However, in the original *Cowboys*, Chet responds to Stu's question with "Maybe" before asking him what he said. So, Chet—perhaps in his sleep—has heard the question, and he knows Stu is talking about the rain.

7. Jerry Tallmer, "Tell Me about the Morons, George," *New York Post*, 12 October 1964, 67.

8. Michael Smith, "Theatre: *Cowboys* and *The Rock Garden*," *Village Voice*, 22 October 1964, 13.

9. "Under the Flag," *Newsweek*, 2 February 1965, 93.

10. Kenneth Chubb et al., "Sam Shepard: Metaphors, Mad Dog Blues, and Old Time Cowboys," *Theatre Quarterly* 4 (August–October 1974), 8; hereafter cited in text.

11. Both Ellen Oumano and Don Shewey make this suggestion in their biographies of Shepard. Ellen Oumano, *Sam Shepard: The Life and Work of an American Dreamer* (New York: St. Martin's Press, 1986), 37; hereafter cited in text; Don Shewey, *Sam Shepard* (New York: Dell, 1985), 53; hereafter cited in text.

12. *Up to Thursday* actually previewed on 23 November 1964 at the Village Gate South before being moved to the Cherry Lane.

13. Robert Lewis Shayon, "Theater of the Ear," *Saturday Review*, 9 April 1966, 52.

14. Luigi Pirandello, *Henry IV*, in *Naked Masks*, trans. and ed. Eric Bentley (New York: E. P. Dutton, 1952), 192.

15. Robert W. Corrigan, *The Theatre in Search of a Fix* (New York: Dell, 1973), 94; hereafter cited in text.

Chapter Three

1. See Bloom for an in-depth discussion of the apocalyptic elements of these early plays.

2. Sam Shepard, *4-H Club*, in *The Unseen Hand and Other Plays* (New York: Bobbs-Merrill, 1972), 205–6; hereafter cited in text as *4H*.

3. Kenneth Chubb, "Fruitful Difficulties of Directing Shepard," *Theatre Quarterly* 4 (August–October 1974), 18; hereafter cited in text as Chubb.

4. Ross Wetzsteon, "Introduction," in *Fool for Love and Other Plays* (New York: Bantam Books, 1984), 7; hereafter cited as Wetzsteon 1984.

5. *Icarus's Mother*, in *Chicago and Other Plays* (New York: Urizen Books, 1967), 48; hereafter cited in text as *IM*.

6. Harold Pinter, "Introduction: Writing for the Theatre," in *Complete Works: One* (New York: Grove Press, 1976), 11; hereafter cited in text.

7. Michael Smith, "Notes on *Icarus's Mother*," in *Chicago and Other Plays* (New York: Urizen Books, 1967), 27; hereafter cited in text as Smith, *Notes*.

8. Gerald Weales, *The Jumping-Off Place: American Drama in the 1960s* (Toronto: Macmillan, 1969), 237.

9. Peter Feldman, "Notes on the Open Theatre Production [of *Keep Tightly Closed*]," in *Viet Rock and Other Plays* by Megan Terry (New York: Simon & Schuster, 1967), 200–1; hereafter cited in text.

10. Robert Pasolli, *A Book on the Open Theatre* (New York: Bobbs-Merrill, 1970), 21.

11. "Language, Visualization, and the Inner Library," *Drama Review (TDR)* 21 (December 1977), 55; hereafter cited in text as "Inner Library."

12. Published letter, in "Symposium—Playwriting in America," *Yale/Theater* 4 (Winter 1973), 26.

13. Ren Frutkin, "Paired Existence Meets the Monster," in *American Dreams*, ed. Bonnie Marranca (New York: Performing Arts Journal Publications, 1981), 108; hereafter cited in text.

14. John Glore, "The Canonization of Mojo Rootforce: Sam Shepard Live at the Pantheon," *Theater* 12 (Summer 1981), 55; hereafter cited in text.

15. Antonin Artaud, *The Theater and Its Double*, trans. Mary Caroline Richards (New York: Grove Press, 1958), 44; hereafter cited in text.

16. This is similar to Artaud, who writes: "Carried along by the paroxysm of a violent physical action which no sensitivity can resist, the spectator finds his over-all nervous system becoming sharpened and refined, he becomes more apt to receive the wave-length of rarer emotions and the sublime ideas of the Great Myths which through the particular performance will attempt to reach him with their physical conflagration-like force." Cited in Eric Sellin, *The Dramatic Concepts of Antonin Artaud* (Chicago: University of Chicago Press, 1968), 33.

17. Ralph Cook, "Notes on *Chicago*," in *Chicago and Other Plays* (New York: Urizen Books, 1967), 2; hereafter cited in text.

18. *Chicago*, in *Chicago and Other Plays* (New York: Urizen Books, 1967), 5; hereafter cited in text as *Chicago*.

19. Robert Pasolli, "Theatre" [review of *Chicago*], *Nation*, 4 April 1966, 405.

20. Jacques Levy, "Notes on *Red Cross*," in *Chicago and Other Plays* (New York: Urizen Books, 1967), 96; hereafter cited in text.

21. *Red Cross*, in *Chicago and Other Plays* (New York: Urizen Books, 1967), 102; hereafter cited in text as *RC*.

22. Robert Coe, "The Saga of Sam Shepard," *New York Times Magazine*, 23 November 1980, 120.

23. Elizabeth Hardwick, "Introduction," in *La Turista* (New York: Bobbs-Merrill, 1968), xiii; hereafter cited in text.

24. C. W. E. Bigsby, Kenneth Chubb, and Malcolm Page, comp. "Theatre Checklist No. 3: Sam Shepard," *Theatrefacts*, August–October 1974, 6.

25. *La Turista* (New York: Bobbs-Merrill, 1968), 19; hereafter cited in text as *LT*.

26. Lewis Funke, "Singing the Rialto Blues," *New York Times*, 5 March 1967, sec. 2, p. 5.

27. *Five Plays* (New York: Bobbs-Merrill, 1967). At the time this collection was prepared for publication, *Melodrama Play* was, as yet, unproduced. The collection places it with other plays from 1965 to 1966.

28. Shepard's personal archives in the Mugar Library Collection at Boston University contain unfinished and unproduced scripts from every period of Shepard's career.

29. *Cowboys #2*, in *Angel City, Curse of the Starving Class, and Other Plays* (New York: Urizen Books, 1976), 229; hereafter cited as *C#2*.

30. The only known copies of the original typescript are missing the final page. But according to Ralph Cook, who directed *Cowboys*, the ending was never fixed, and it changed from night to night (Cook interview).

Chapter Four

1. Robert Brustein, "Sam Shepard's America," *New Republic*, 21 April 1973, 23.

2. Sam Shepard, "Back in the 1970's," in *Hawk Moon* (New York: Performing Arts Journal Publications, 1981), 12.

3. Mel Gussow, "Sam Shepard: Writer on the Way Up," *New York Times*, 12 November 1969, 42; hereafter cited in text as Gussow 1969.

4. Jack Kroll, "Desert Apocalypse," *Newsweek*, 23 March 1970, 69.

5. Sam Zotolow, "Black Students Block Yale Play," *New York Times*, 27 December 1968, 38.

6. The original version of *Operation Sidewinder*, with the questionable scenes intact, appears in *Esquire*, May 1969, 152 et passim.

7. Brendan Gill, "Getting On with the Story," *New Yorker*, 21 March 1970, 116.

8. *Operation Sidewinder* (New York: Bobbs-Merrill, 1970), 62–63; hereafter cited in text as *OS*.

9. *The Unseen Hand*, in *The Unseen Hand and Other Plays* (New York: Urizen Books, 1972), 5; hereafter cited in text as *UH*.

10. *Mad Dog Blues*, in *Angel City, Curse of the Starving Class, and Other Plays* (New York: Urizen Books, 1980), 156; hereafter cited in text as *MDB*.

11. I have never located the source of this legend, but it has appeared frequently, including in Michael ver Meulen, "Sam Shepard: Yes, Yes, Yes," *Esquire*, February 1980, 81.

12. *Cowboy Mouth*, in *Angel City, Curse of the Starving Class, and Other Plays* (New York: Urizen Books, 1976), 200; hereafter cited as *CM*.

13. Ruby Cohn has commented that the play's "drive and intensity" suggest a single author, thus crushing the amusing and romantic myth of coauthorship. Ruby Cohn, *New American Dramatists: 1960–1980* (New York: Grove Press, 1982), 180; hereafter cited in the text.

14. The phrase is adapted from W. B. Yeats's 1921 poem, "The Second Coming": "And what rough beast, its hour come round at last, / Slouches toward Bethlehem to be born?"

15. Shepard noted in 1980 that he had started reading classical drama roughly 10 years earlier. Scott Christopher Wren, "Camp Shepard: Exploring the Geography of Character," *West Coast Plays* 7 (Fall 1980), 86.

16. Irving Wardle, "Return of Theatrical Fireball," *Times* (London), 6 June 1974, 9.

17. *The Tooth of Crime*, in *Seven Plays* (New York: Bantam Books, 1981), 220; hereafter cited in text as *TC*.

18. Leonard Wilcox, "Modernism vs. Postmodernism: Shepard's *The Tooth of Crime* and the Discourse of Popular Culture," *Modern Drama* 30 (December 1987), 560–73.

Chapter Five

1. The play opened 18 January 1973, directed by Murray Mednick. It was also filmed for BBC Television in England in the spring of 1973. To my knowledge, the only publicly accessible copy of the script is in Shepard's archives in the Mugar Library at Boston University.

2. Martin Washburn, "Cosmic Knockouts and a Mean Mama," *Village Voice*, 25 January 1973, 69; hereafter cited in text.

3. The plot is loosely based on the 1930s film comedy, *Three Men and a Horse*, in which a greeting card writer with a knack for picking winners is kidnapped because of his special talent.

4. Ross Wetzsteon thoroughly exposes the link between Cody as dreamer and Shepard as artist, rightfully pointing out the inferiority of the play's allegory to true stage metaphor. Ross Wetzsteon, "Looking a Gift Horse Dreamer in the Mouth," *Village Voice*, 5 January 1976, 71.

5. Harold Clurman, "Theatre" [review of *Geography of a Horse Dreamer*], *Nation*, 10 January 1976, 27.

6. *Geography of a Horse Dreamer*, in *The Tooth of Crime and Geography of a Horse Dreamer* (New York: Grove Press, 1974), 93; hereafter cited in text as *GHD*.

7. First performed 17 September 1974 at the Theatre Upstairs, London. Shepard had also written and produced *Little Ocean*, a musical review, in March 1974.

8. Rodney Simard has made this observation about Shepard's work in general in his book, *Postmodern Drama: Contemporary Playwrights in America and Britain* (Lanham, Md.: University Press of America, 1984).

9. See, for example, Irene Oppenheim and Victor Fascio, "The Most Promising Playwright in America Today Is Sam Shepard," *Village Voice*, 27 October 1975, 81–82; hereafter cited in text, and David Savran, "Sam Shepard's Conceptual Prison: *Action* and the Unseen Hand," *Theatre Journal* 38 (March 1984), 57–73; hereafter cited in text.

10. Edith Oliver, "Off-Broadway" [review of *Action*], *New Yorker*, 5 May 1975, 81.

11. *Action*, in *Angel City, Curse of the Starving Class, and Other Plays* (New York: Urizen Books, 1976), 128; hereafter cited in text as *Action*.

12. This final speech appears only in the London publication of *Action*. *Action* (London: Faber & Faber, 1975), 38.

13. See Savran for a detailed analysis of self-objectification in *Action*.

14. Such stasis is discussed in detail in Gerry McCarthy's "'Acting it Out': Sam Shepard's *Action*," *Modern Drama* 24 (March 1981), 1–12.

15. Jean-Paul Sartre, "Existentialism Is a Humanism," in *Existentialism from Dostoevsky to Sartre*, ed. Walter Kauffmann, trans. Philip Mairet (New York: World Publishing, 1965), 295.

Chapter Six

1. "Proposed Project," an undated, typewritten document in Magic Theatre publicity archives.

2. Peter Hamill, "The New American Hero," *New York*, 5 December 1983, 88; hereafter cited in text.

3. "Playbill for Premiere Production [of *Red Cross*]," in *The New Underground Theatre*, ed. Robert J. Schroeder (New York: Bantam Books, 1968), 80.

4. Cited in Doris Auerbach, *Sam Shepard, Arthur Kopit, and the Off Broadway Theater* (Boston: Twayne Publishers, 1982), 30.

5. Bertolt Brecht, *Brecht on Theatre*, ed. and trans. John Willet (New York: Hill & Wang, 1964), 88.

6. Patti Smith, "Kimberly" and "Land," from *Horses*, Arista Records, 1975.

7. Calvin Ahlgren, "Shepard with Music," *San Francisco Chronicle*, 16 December 1984, 57.

8. "Deep Water," from the personal papers of Catherine Stone.

9. "Watching Myself," from the personal papers of Catherine Stone.

10. Catherine Stone, interview with author, San Francisco, California, 14 March 1985; hereafter cited in text as Stone.

11. "Program Note" for productions of *Savage/Love* and *Tongues*, Eureka Theatre, San Francisco, 1979.

12. The Overtone Theatre, "Program Note" for productions of *Supersti-*

tions and *The Sad Lament of Pecos Bill on the Eve of Killing His Wife*, Magic Theatre, San Francisco, 1984.

13. *Angel City* in *Fool for Love and Other Plays* (New York: Bantam Books, 1984), 67; hereafter cited in text as *AC*.

14. Robert Schroeder, ed., *The New Underground Theatre* (New York: Bantam Books, 1968), x–xi.

15. Jerzy Grotowski, founder of the Polish Laboratory Theatre and author of *Towards a Poor Theatre* (New York: Simon and Schuster, 1968).

16. *Suicide in B-Flat*, in *Buried Child and Seduced and Suicide in B-Flat* (Vancouver: Talon Books, 1979), 130–31; hereafter cited in text as *SBF*.

17. In his approach to the issue of artistic identity in this play, Shepard reflects the ideas of Italian dramatist Luigi Pirandello. Niles is similar to the unnamed hero of Pirandello's play *When One Is Somebody* (1933). This firmly established poet and essayist is permanently imprisoned in his own celebrity. He must look, dress, act, think, and, above all, write as his public expects him to do. He eventually turns into stone, a perfect, unwavering monument to his artistic identity, completely entombed by his public's expectations.

18. *Seduced*, in *Buried Child and Seduced and Suicide in B-Flat* (Vancouver: Talon Books, 1979), 79; hereafter cited in text as *Seduced*.

Chapter Seven

1. Charles Marowitz, "Is This Shepard or Saroyan?" *New York Times*, 15 May 1977, sec. 2, p. 3; hereafter cited in text.

2. Events that appear to be based on that encounter appear in the plays *Buried Child, Mad Dog Blues*, and especially *The Holy Ghostly*.

3. While my reconstruction of this trip is conjectural, based on bits of information from several official (and a few unoffficial) sources, the trip to Los Angeles is documented in Oumano (72) and Shewey (63). The stop at his grandparents' home is recreated in *Hawk Moon* (68) and *Motel Chronicles* (43–46).

4. *The Holy Ghostly*, in *The Unseen Hand and Other Plays* (New York: Urizen Books, 1972), 100; hereafter cited in text as *HG*.

5. *Curse of the Starving Class*, in *Seven Plays* (New York: Bantam Books, 1981), 137; hereafter cited in text as *CSC*.

6. This term is my own coinage, and I do not mean to suggest any connection whatsoever to the "hyper-realism" of postmodern criticism, the Hyperrealism of a playwright like Franz Xavier Kroetz, or to the "Super-Realist" school of American painters. I say "suprareal" in the sense that such images and moments transcend the fictional "realism" of the play. This means that, while I agree with many of the points made by Toby Silverman Zinman in her article "Sam Shepard and Super-Realism," *Modern Drama* 29 (September 1986), 423–30, I feel the parallels between Shepard and the Super-Realist painters fall short of explaining the disturbing quality of what I call the suprareal.

In my description of such moments as overwhelmingly vivid and material, I am indebted to Jameson, who uses the terminology of schizophrenia to describe what I would call the suprareal (119–20).

7. I am reminded, in particular, of the 1982 Magic Theatre production, directed by John Lion, in which this scene was presented in an entirely causal and realistic fashion.

8. This type of suprarealism is also manifest in Shepard's use of operative stage props, such as a functional stove and refrigerator, and of real food, including frying bacon and the especially acrid smell of boiling artichokes, which my late colleague, George House of the University of California, found particularly agitating in the 1979 Berkeley Stage Company production directed by Andrew Doe.

9. *Buried Child*, in *Seven Plays* (New York: Bantam Books, 1981), 119; hereafter cited in text as *BC*.

10. Bernard Weiner, "Sam Shepard's 'Buried Child'—A Major, Bitter New Play," *San Francisco Chronicle*, 6 August 1978, 19.

11. Walter Kerr, "Sam Shepard—What's the Message?" *New York Times*, 10 December 1978, D3.

12. I originally noticed these features of the set when looking at production photographs by Ron Blanchette from the Magic Theatre production. One of Blanchette's photos, which clearly illustrates these features, can be seen in *American Theatre* 1 (April 1984), 11.

13. Sigmund Freud, "The 'Uncanny,'" in *On Creativity and the Unconscious*, ed. Benjamin Nelson (New York: Harper & Row, 1958), 132.

14. This interpretation is corroborated by an early (and quite different) draft of the play, contained in the Yale Repertory Theatre archives, in which Bradley is responsible for the murder of the infant Ansel.

15. Ann McFerran, "Poet of Post-War Americana," *Time Out* (London), 4–10 December 1981, 25; hereafter cited in text.

16. *True West*, in *Seven Plays* (New York: Bantam Books, 1981), 24; hereafter cited in the text as *TW*.

17. William Kleb, "Worse Than Being Homeless: *True West* and the Divided Self," in *American Dreams*, ed. Bonnie Marranca (New York: Performing Arts Journal Publications, 1981), 121.

18. May's character represents, to a limited extent, a step forward for Shepard; she is the first three-dimensional woman to assume a major role in one of his plays. Shepard sought, with May, to "sustain a female character and have her remain absolutely true to herself." See Michiko Kakutani, "Myths, Dreams, Realities—Sam Shepard's America" [interview with Shepard], *New York Times*, 29 January 1984, sec. 2, p. 27.

19. Mimi Kramer, "In Search of the Good Shepard," *New Criterion* 2, no. 2 (October 1983), 56.

20. *Fool for Love* (San Francisco: City Lights Books, 1983), 20; hereafter cited in text as *FFL*.

21. Frank Rich, "'Fool for Love,' Sam Shepard's Western," *New York Times*, 27 May 1983, C3.

22. Shepard discusses the composition of *Fool for Love* in Lippman and in Jennifer Allen, "The Man on the High Horse: On the Trail of Sam Shepard," *Esquire*, November 1988, 141–44, et passim; hereafter cited in text.

23. A draft of the script dated only "1982," which I read in the offices of the Magic Theatre in San Francisco, has no old man in it. The final draft of the script, used in production, was dated "12/82." Advance publicity from the Magic Theatre, which appeared in the spring of 1982, announced that Shepard's new play would have "two men and two women"—that is, Eddie, May, Martin, and the countess. In John Lion's *American Theatre* article, he also makes reference to the fact that he auditioned "about a hundred actresses" for the role of the "princess" before Shepard ever showed him a draft of the script. That draft, which Lion estimates was number 11, had no "princess" and no old man. See John Lion, "Rock 'n Roll Jesus with a Cowboy Mouth," *American Theatre* 1 (April 1984), 6.

24. See David J. DeRose, *"Fool for Love"* [theatre review], *Theatre Journal* 36 (March 1984), 100–101.

25. Sam Shepard [contributor], "American Experimental Theatre: Then and Now," *Performing Arts Journal* 2 (Fall 1977), 14.

26. Joan Goodman, "The Good Shepard," *US*, 11 April 1983, 77; hereafter cited in text.

27. Among many other examples, see Allen, Chubb et al., Goodman, and Oppenheim.

28. Paul Berman, "Theater," *Nation*, 22 February 1986, 218.

29. Gordon Rogoff, "America Screened," *Village Voice*, 17 December 1985, 118.

30. *A Lie of the Mind* [and *A War in Heaven*] (New York: New American Library, 1987), 3; hereafter cited in text as *LM*.

31. Joseph Chaikin and Sam Shepard, *Joseph Chaikin and Sam Shepard: Letters and Texts, 1972–84*, ed. Barry Daniels (New York: Plume, 1990), 153.

32. Robert Brustein, "The Shepard Enigma," *New Republic*, 27 January 1986, 26.

33. Jack Kroll, "Savage Games People Play," *Newsweek*, 16 December 1985, 85.

Chapter Eight

1. *The War in Heaven* was part of a one-man double bill performed by Chaikin at the American Place Theatre. The other play was *Struck Dumb*, a collaboration between Chaikin and Jean-Claude Van Itallie about a victim of aphasia. Performances began on 19 March 1991 and ran for two weeks.

2. The letter is dated 29 October 1983, Waterloo, Iowa. See Barry Daniels, ed., *Joseph Chaikin and Sam Shepard: Letters and Texts, 1972–84* (New York: Plume, 1990), 128.

3. Chaikin attests to this fact on behalf of himself and Shepard in Eileen Blumenthal's article on *The War in Heaven*, entitled "The Voyage Back," *American Theatre* 8 (June 1991), 53.

4. *States of Shock* began performances on 30 April 1991. It officially "opened" on the fifteenth of May, and it closed just two weeks later on the second of June. The production was directed by Bill Hart. Since, at this writing, *States of Shock* has not been published, I am relying on my memory and my notes from the performance of 15 May 1991.

5. The connection between *The War in Heaven* and *States of Shock* is reinforced in performance by the fact that Stubb's stark, blunt language and stiff delivery are not unlike the vocal patterns of an individual with aphasia.

6. The only other character in the play is a black waitress named Glory Bee. Treated in a highly symbolic fashion, her name reflects her belief in America as the land of promise, while her status—as a member of the serving class, as a woman, and as a person of color—confirms the subservient role that such marginalized groups must play in the power games of authoritarian white men like the Colonel. It is Glory Bee, image of America's powerless majority, who must wait on the Colonel and Stubbs, who must clean up when they make their boyish messes, and who must become the sexual object for whom and over whom they eventually fight.

7. Characteristically leading the way in articulating such negative sentiments was *New York Times* critic Frank Rich, who called Shepard's conviction that the stage is still an effective platform for political dissent "quaint" and wondered if Shepard had been hibernating since the Vietnam War. See Frank Rich, "Sam Shepard Returns, on War and Machismo," *New York Times*, 17 May 1991, C1.

Selected Bibliography

PRIMARY SOURCES

Plays

Action and The Unseen Hand. London: Faber & Faber, 1975. [Contains variant text of *Action*].

Angel City, Curse of the Starving Class, and Other Plays, with an Introduction by Jack Gelber. New York: Urizen Books, 1976. [Contains *Angel City, Curse of the Starving Class, Killer's Head, Action, Mad Dog Blues, Cowboy Mouth, The Rock Garden, Cowboys #2*.]

Blue Bitch. Unpublished typescript [photocopy]. Sam Shepard Collection. Mugar Library, Boston University, 1972.

Buried Child and Seduced and Suicide in B-Flat. Vancouver: Talon Books, 1979.

Cowboys. Unpublished typescript. In possession of David J. DeRose, from private papers of Ralph Cook. 1964.

Five Plays. Indianapolis: Bobbs-Merrill, 1967. Reprinted as *Chicago and Other Plays*. New York: Urizen Books, 1967. [Contains *Chicago, Icarus's Mother, Red Cross, Fourteen Hundred Thousand, Melodrama Play*.]

Fool for Love. San Francisco: City Lights Books, 1983. [Also contains libretto and music for *The Sad Lament of Pecos Bill on the Eve of Killing His Wife*, 82–112.]

Fool for Love and Other Plays, with an Introduction by Ross Wetzsteon. New York: Bantam Books, 1984. [Contains *Fool for Love, Angel City, Geography of a Horse Dreamer, Action, Cowboy Mouth, Melodrama Play, Seduced, Suicide in B-Flat*.]

Four Two-Act Plays, with an Introduction by Elizabeth Hardwick. Indianapolis: Bobbs-Merrill, 1976. [Contains *Operation Sidewinder, The Tooth of Crime, La Turista*, and *Geography of a Horse Dreamer*.]

La Turista, with an Introduction by Elizabeth Hardwick. Indianapolis: Bobbs-Merrill, 1968.

A Lie of the Mind. New York: New American Library, 1987. [Also contains *The War in Heaven: (Angel's Monologue)* with Joseph Chaikin, 137–55.]

Little Ocean. Unpublished typescript [photocopy]. Sam Shepard Collection. Mugar Library, Boston University, 1974.

Mad Dog Blues and Other Plays, with an Introduction by Michael McClure. New York: Winter House, 1972. [Contains *The Rock Garden, Mad Dog Blues, Cowboys #2, Cowboy Mouth*.]

Operation Sidewinder. Indianapolis: Bobbs-Merrill, 1970.

Operation Sidewinder. Esquire, May 1969, 152 et passim. [Variant text.]

Seven Plays, with an Introduction by Richard Gilman. New York: Bantam Books, 1981. [Contains *Buried Child, Curse of the Starving Class, The Tooth of Crime, La Turista, Tongues, Savage/Love, True West.*]

The Tooth of Crime and Geography of a Horse Dreamer. New York: Grove Press, 1974.

True West. Garden City: Nelson Doubleday, 1981.

The Unseen Hand and Other Plays. Indianapolis: Bobbs-Merrill, 1972. Reprint. New York: Urizen Books, 1981. [Contains *The Unseen Hand, Forensic and the Navigators, The Holy Ghostly, Back Bog Beast Bait, Shaved Splits, 4-H Club.*]

The Unseen Hand and Other Plays, with an Introduction by Sam Shepard. New York: Bantam Books, 1986. [Contains *The Unseen Hand, The Rock Garden, Chicago, Icarus's Mother, 4-H Club, Fourteen Hundred Thousand, Red Cross, Cowboys #2, Forensic and the Navigators, The Holy Ghostly, Operation Sidewinder, Mad Dog Blues, Back Bog Beast Bait, Killer's Head.*]

Up to Thursday. Unpublished typescript [photocopy]. Sam Shepard Collection. Mugar Library, Boston University, 1965.

The War in Heaven (Angel's Monologue). Performing Arts Journal, 4:2–3.

Screenplays

Far North. Unpublished filmscript. 1988.

Fool for Love. Unpublished filmscript adapted from Shepard's stage play. 1985.

Me and My Brother. With Robert Frank. Unpublished filmscript. 1968.

Paris, Texas. Adaptation for publication by L. M. Kit Carson. Berlin: Road Movies, 1984.

Renaldo and Clara. With Bob Dylan. Unpublished filmscript. 1978.

Zabriskie Point. Filmscript with Michelangelo Antonioni, Fred Gardner, Tonino Guerra, and Clare Peploe. New York: Simon & Schuster, 1972.

Short Prose, Poems, Nonfiction, and Dramatic Monologues

Hawk Moon. Los Angeles: Blacksparrow Press, 1973. Reprint. New York: Performing Arts Journal Publications, 1981.

"The House and the Fish." In *Three Works by the Open Theatre.* Edited by Karen Malpede. New York: Drama Book Specialists, 1974. [A monologue in the play *Nightwalk.*]

Jacaranda. Unpublished monologue [photocopies]. Sam Shepard Collection, Mugar Library, Boston University; Magic Theatre Collection, Bancroft Library, University of California, Berkeley. 1978. [A monologue to be accompanied with dance by Daniel Nagrin.]

Motel Chronicles. San Francisco: City Lights Books, 1982. Reprint. London: Faber & Faber, 1985.

Red Woman. Unpublished monologue [photocopy]. Magic Theatre Collection, Bancroft Library, University of California, Berkeley, 1978.
[Written/performed at Padua Hills Playwrights Workshop, July 1978.]

Rolling Thunder Logbook. New York: Viking Press, 1977. Reprint. New York: Limelight Editions, 1987.

Essays and Other Publications

"Azusa Is a Real Place." In *Action and The Unseen Hand*, 43–44. London: Faber & Faber, 1975. Reprinted in *Plays and Players* (May 1978): I.

"Introduction." In *The Unseen Hand and Other Plays*. New York: Bantam Books, 1986.

Joseph Chaikin and Sam Shepard: Letters and Texts, 1972–1984. With Joseph Chaikin. Edited by Barry Daniels. New York: Plume, 1990.

"Time." *Theater* 9 (Spring 1978): 9. Reprinted in *American Dreams: The Imagination of Sam Shepard*, edited by Bonnie Marranca, 210–11. New York: Performing Arts Journal Publications, 1981.

"True Dylan." *Esquire*, July 1987, 59–68.

Untitled statement. In "American Experimental Theatre: Then and Now." *Performing Arts Journal* 2 (Fall 1977): 13–14. Reprinted in *American Dreams*, ed. Marranca, 212–13.

Untitled statement. In "Symposium: Playwriting in America." *Yale/Theater* 4 (Winter 1973): 26–27.

"Visualization, Language, and the Inner Library." *Drama Review* 21 (December 1977): 49–58. Reprinted in *American Dreams*, ed. Marranca, 214–19.

Interviews and Articles Based on Interviews

Allen, Jennifer. "The Man on the High Horse." *Esquire*, November 1988, 141–44, 146, 148, 150–51.

Chubb, Kenneth, et al. "Metaphors, Mad Dog Blues, and Old Time Cowboys." *Theatre Quarterly* 4 (August–October 1974): 3–16. Reprinted in *American Dreams*, ed. Marranca, 187–209.

Coe, Robert. "Saga of Sam Shepard." *New York Times Magazine*, 23 November 1980, 56–58, 118, 120, 122, 124. Reprinted as "Sam Shepard— Playwright Laureate of the West." *San Francisco Chronicle*, 21 December 1980, Datebook section, 35–38.

Cott, Jonathan. "The Rolling Stone Interview: Sam Shepard." *Rolling Stone*, 18 December 1986 to 1 January 1987, 166–72, 198, 200.

Dark, John. "A Conversation with Sam Shepard about a Very Corny Subject." *San Francisco*, September 1983, 68–72.

Dark, John. "The 'True West' Interviews." *West Coast Plays* 9 (Summer 1981): 51–71.

Fay, Stephen. "The Silent Type." *Vogue*, February 1985, 213, 216, 218.

Goldberg, Robert. "Sam Shepard, American Original." *Playboy*, March 1984, 90, 112, 192–93.

Goodman, Joan. "The Good Shepard." *US*, 11 April 1983, 76–77.

Gussow, Mel. "Sam Shepard: Writer on the Way Up." *New York Times*, 12 November 1969, 42.

Hamill, Pete. "The New American Hero." *New York*, 5 December 1983, 75–76ff.

Kakutani, Michiko. "Myths, Dreams, Realities—Sam Shepard's America." *New York Times*, 29 January 1984, B1, B26–28.

Lippman, Amy. "A Conversation with Sam Shepard." *Harvard Advocate* (March 1983): 2–6, 44–46. Reprinted as "Rhythm and Truths: An Interview with Sam Shepard." *American Theatre* 1 (April 1984): 9–13, 40–41.

Oppenheim, Irene, and Victor Vascio. "The Most Promising Playwright in America Today Is Sam Shepard." *Village Voice*, 27 October 1975, 81–82.

Sessums, Kevin. "Geography of a Horse Dreamer." *Interview*, September 1988, 70–78.

ver Meulen, Michael. "Sam Shepard: Yes, Yes, Yes." *Esquire*, February 1980, 79–81, 85–86.

White, Michael. "Underground Landscapes." *Manchester Guardian*, 20 February 1974, 8.

Library Collections

Shepard's personal archives are housed in the Mugar Library at Boston University. The contents include scores of unpublished and unproduced plays, monologues, and fragments; manuscripts, typescripts, and variant scripts of published plays; unproduced screenplays; poetry; short prose; journals and notebooks; articles; juvenalia; correspondence; and audio tapes.

Other library collections that have proved useful in locating unpublished documents by Shepard, as well as variant and unpublished scripts, are the Magic Theatre archives in the Bancroft Library at the University of California, Berkeley; the Toby Cole collection in the Shields Library at the University of California, Davis; and the Yale Repertory Theatre archives in the Yale School of Drama Library.

SECONDARY SOURCES

Bibliographies

Dugdale, John. *File on Shepard.* London: Methuen Drama, 1989. Part of Methuen's pocket companion "File" series on modern playwrights. Includes a chronology of Shepard's life and dramatic works with brief synopses of all plays and selected critical quotations on each from reviews. Also contains quotes from Shepard on Shepard, a bibliography of dramatic and nondramatic writings, and of selected secondary sources. Limited in scope, but an extremely handy source of names, dates, titles, and famous quotations by and about Shepard.

King, Kimball. *Ten Modern American Playwrights: An Annotated Bibliography*, 197–213. New York: Garland Publishing, 1982.
Very good bibliography of early plays in their various American and British editions and publications. Some gaps and inaccuracies. Selected secondary sources are annotated individually and production reviews are organized in a play-by-play format for easy reference. Stops short of 1980.

Kleb, William. "Sam Shepard." In *American Playwrights Since 1945: A Guide to Scholarship, Criticism, and Performance*, edited by Philip C. Kolin, 387–419. New York: Greenwood Press, 1989.
A bibliography of primary and secondary sources on Shepard accompanied by various short essays assessing Shepard's critical reputation, tracking the history of his plays in production, and giving an overview of the major critical studies that have been made of his work. Exceptionally thorough and accurate. Supersedes all other previous bibliographies on Shepard, but inconveniently lumps all secondary sources and reviews together.

Books and Parts of Books

Bachman, Charles R. "Defusion of Menace in the Plays of Sam Shepard." In *Essays on Modern American Drama: Williams, Miller, Albee, and Shepard*, 163–73. Toronto: University of Toronto Press, 1987.
Discusses inability of Shepard's early plays to reach a point of dramatic cataclysm. Volume includes three other essays on Shepard.

Bank, Rosemarie. "Self as Other: Sam Shepard's *Fool for Love* and *A Lie of the Mind*." In *Feminist Rereadings of Modern American Drama*, edited by June Schlueter, 227–40. Rutherford, N.J.: Fairleigh Dickinson University Press, 1989.
Feminist examination of doubling and gender transformations in Shepard's two most recent family plays.

Bigsby, C. W. E. *A Critical Introduction to Twentieth-Century American Drama*. 3 Vols. Cambridge: Cambridge University Press, 1985.
Best when dealing with Shepard as an American writer and a mirror of his times. Ties Shepard to modern dramatic influences, theatrical contemporaries, and to American literary traditions.

Cohn, Ruby. "The Word Is My Shepard." In *New American Dramatists: 1960–1980*. New York: Grove Press, 1982.
Chapter offers a brief overview of Shepard's contributions to contemporary American drama, both thematically and stylistically, through *True West*.

Hart, Lynda. *Sam Shepard's Metaphorical Stages.* Contributions in Drama and Theatre Studies, No. 22. New York: Greenwood Press, 1987.
Cross-section of 10 Shepard plays: 5 from Shepard's early and middle period; and the 5 family dramas. Traces Shepard's dramatic practices to those of major modern European dramatists and theorists.

Hart, Lynda. "Sam Shepard's Spectacle of Impossible Heterosexuality: *Fool for Love.*" In *Feminist Rereadings of Modern American Drama*, edited by June Schlueter, 213–26. Rutherford, N.J.: Fairleigh Dickinson University Press, 1989.
Discusses Shepard's failure to create a "heterosexual encounter" between May and Eddie.

King, Kimball, ed. *Sam Shepard: A Casebook.* Vol. 2 of Casebooks on Modern Dramatists Series. New York: Garland Publishing, 1989.
Collection of thematic essays on Shepard, some using new critical and poststructuralist approaches, others uneven in scholarship. Of special note is essay by Patrick J. Fennell on "lost" Shepard plays. This essay is the only place where any of Shepard's unpublished plays are quoted directly.

McNamara, Brook, Jerry Rojo, and Richard Schechner. "*The Tooth of Crime.*" In *Theatres, Spaces, Environments: Eighteen Projects*, 130–37. New York: Drama Book Specialists, 1975.
Transcribed conversations by collaborators on Schechner's "environmental" production of *The Tooth of Crime.*

Marranca, Bonnie, ed. *American Dreams: The Imagination of Sam Shepard.* New York: Performing Arts Journal Publications, 1981.
Widely read collection of Shepard criticism, reviews, and interviews. Includes the best of the early critical writing on Shepard as well as the Chubb interview with Shepard, interviews with and essays by some of Shepard's collaborators, and three essays by Shepard on writing. Stops short of the family plays with the exception of an essay on *True West.*

Marranca, Bonnie, and Gautam Dasgupta. *American Playwrights: A Critical Survey.* New York: Drama Book Specialists, 1981.
Chapter on Shepard. Overview of Shepard's style, themes, career, and critical reception.

Mottram, Ron. *Inner Landscapes: The Theater of Sam Shepard.* Columbia: University of Missouri Press, 1984.
Noteworthy as the first full-length study of Shepard's plays. Ends with *Fool for Love.*

Oumano, Ellen. *Sam Shepard: The Life and Work of an American Dreamer.* New York: St. Martin's Press, 1986. Reprint. London: Virgin, 1987.
A celebrity biography of Shepard as playwright turned film star. Of interest to Shepard scholars are the anecdotal reminiscences of Shepard's friends, lovers, and collaborators from his early days in New York City.

Parker, Dorothy, ed. *Essays on Modern American Drama: Williams, Albee, and Shepard.* Toronto: University of Toronto Press, 1987.
Includes four essays on various aspects of Shepard's work reprinted from *Modern Drama.*

Patraka, Vivian M., and Mark Siegel. *Sam Shepard.* Boise State University Western Writers Series, no. 69. Boise: Boise State University, 1985. A short monograph discussing Shepard's thematic concerns as a western American writer.

Shewey, Don. *Sam Shepard.* New York: Dell Publishing, 1985. Deceptively marketed as a celebrity biography, but Shewey is a theater critic who grasps the complexities of Shepard's voluminous writings and the interplay between his life and his plays.

Simard, Rodney. "Sam Shepard: Emotional Renegade." In *Postmodern Drama: Contemporary Playwrights in America and Britain.* Lanham, Md.: University Press of America, 1984. Simard places Shepard in context of Beckett, Pinter, Stoppard, and others, identifying him as the first truly postmodern American playwright and interpreting his work in terms of its thematic and theatrical manifestation of a postabsurdist or postmodern reality.

Wilcox, Leonard, ed. *Sam Shepard: Contemporary Critical Interpretations.* London: Macmillan Press, 1992. A collection of original essays, suggesting postmodern, feminist, and poststructuralist "rereadings" of works from throughout Shepard's career. Includes essay by DeRose on family plays.

Articles

Blumenthal, Eileen. "The Voyage Back." *American Theatre* 8 (June 1991): 12–17, 53. Documents the long-standing friendship between Shepard and Joseph Chaikin and the process by which they collaborated on *The War in Heaven* after Chaikin suffered a stroke in 1984 that left him with aphasia.

Carroll, Dennis. "The Filmic Cut and 'Switchback' in the Plays of Sam Shepard." *Modern Drama* 28 (March 1985): 125–38. Analyzes discontinuous action in Shepard's plays in light of "switchback" techniques of film.

Chubb, Kenneth. "Fruitful Difficulties of Directing Shepard." *Theatre Quarterly* 4 (August–October 1974): 17–25. Explores Shepard's rejection of conventional dramatic structure and the challenges that rejection poses for directors of his early plays.

Cima, Gay Gibson. "Shifting Perspectives: Combining Shepard and Rauschenberg." *Theatre Journal* 38 (March 1986): 67–81. Compares Shepard's fragmentation of dramatic narrative and conventional character to the shifting perceptual framing of artist Robert Rauschenberg's collagelike "combines."

Falk, Florence. "The Role of Performance in Sam Shepard's Plays." *Theatre Journal* 33 (May 1981): 182–98. Defines Shepard's plays in terms of performance rituals, proposing the performance of the self and of national myths as a strategy for imposing meaning on life where none exists.

Glore, John. "The Canonization of Mojo Rootforce: Sam Shepard Live at the Pantheon." *Theater* 12 (Summer–Fall 1981): 53–65.

First essay to identify Artaudian aspects of Shepard's work. Charts struggle in Shepard's work, especially family plays, between the avant-garde impulse, descended from Artaud, and the desire to enter the canonical mainstream of modern realistic drama.

Londré, Felicia Hardison. "Sam Shepard Works Out: The Masculinization of America." *Studies in American Drama 1945–Present* 2 (1987): 19–27.

Examines Shepard's attempt to create a balanced masculine-feminine nexus in his recent stage and film work.

McCarthy, Gerry. "'Acting It Out': Sam Shepard's *Action*." *Modern Drama* 24 (March 1981): 1–12.

Explores moments of self-objectification and self-conscious performance in *Action*.

Putzel, Steven. "Expectation, Confutation, Revelation: Audience Complicity in the Plays of Sam Shepard." *Modern Drama* 30 (June 1987): 147–60.

Discusses the expectations made of and demands placed upon the audience by the unconventional stage realities of various Shepard plays in performance.

Rabillard, Sheila. "Destabilizing Plot, Displacing the Status of Narrative: Local Order in the Plays of Pinter and Shepard." *Theatre Journal* 43 (March 1991): 41–58.

Examines Shepard's *A Lie of the Mind* and Harold Pinter's *Old Times* in terms of how "traditional storied plot" is displaced in both by alternative principles of organization.

Rabillard, Sheila. "Sam Shepard: Theatrical Power and American Dreams." *Modern Drama* 30 (March 1987): 58–71.

Proposes that Shepard's drama be regarded as explorations of theatricality by examining how Shepard exploits or rejects certain conventional semiotic practices to create a spellbinding power over his audience rather than to convey traditional meaning.

Savran, David. "Sam Shepard's Conceptual Prison: *Action* and the Unseen Hand." *Theatre Journal* 38 (March 1984): 57–73.

Examines *Action* as a self-referential theatrical exploration of the impossibility of absolute presence or authenticity in either performance or existence.

Wilcox, Leonard. "Modernism vs. Postmodernism: Shepard's *The Tooth of Crime* and the Discourses of Popular Culture." *Modern Drama* 30 (December 1987): 560–73.

Defines characters of Hoss and Crow in *The Tooth of Crime* respectively as modernist hero and postmodern antihero, discussing Shepard's ambivalence toward both.

Wilson, Ann. "Fool of Desire: The Spectator to the Plays of Sam Shepard." *Modern Drama* 30 (March 1987): 46–57.

Examines the function of onstage spectators and the primacy of visual and stage images over text in selected plays.

Wren, Scott Christopher. "Camp Shepard: Exploring the Geography of Character." *West Coast Plays* 7 (Fall 1980): 75–106.

Personal journal written during playwriting workshop led by Shepard at Bay Area Playwrights Festival, summer of 1980.

Wren, Scott Christopher. "Duck Hunting in Marin: On the Second Shepard Workshop." *West Coast Plays* 11–12 (Winter–Spring 1982): 210–19.

Report on second playwriting workshop with Shepard, summer of 1981.

Zinman, Toby Silverman. "Sam Shepard and Super-Realism." *Modern Drama* 29 (September 1986): 423–29.

Explores similarities between Shepard's staging techniques and the work of Super-Realist painters, especially their shared emphasis on "surface."

Zinman, Toby Silverman. "Shepard Suite." *American Theatre* 1 (December 1984): 15–17.

Feature on musical and physical qualities of Shepard's writing and on collaboration between director George Ferencz and jazz composer Max Roach during festival of Shepard plays.

Zinman, Toby Silverman. "Visual Histrionics: Shepard's Theatre of the First Wall." *Theatre Journal* 40 (December 1988): 509–18.

Discusses Shepard's theatrical use of the upstage wall in such plays as *La Turista* and *Angel City* and the violation of that wall as a violation of the histrionic imperative of the stage.

Play-by-Play Production Reviews

Cowboys and *The Rock Garden*
  Smith, Michael. "Theatre: *Cowboys* and *The Rock Garden*." *Village Voice*, 22 October 1964, 13.
  Tallmer, Jerry. "Tell Me about the Morons, George." *New York Post,* 12 October 1964, 16.

Up to Thursday
  Smith, Michael. "Theatre: New Playwrights—I." *Village Voice*, 18 February 1965, 12.
  "Under the Flag." *Newsweek,* 2 February 1965, 93.

Icarus's Mother
  Albee, Edward. "Icarus's Mother." *Village Voice*, 25 November 1965, 19.

Icarus's Mother and *4-H Club*
  Shayon, Robert Lewis. "Theatre of the Ear." *Saturday Review*, 9 April 1966, 52.

Red Cross
  Barnes, Clive. "Where Is U.S. Theatre? It's Alive Off-Broadway." *New York Times*, 28 May 1968, 41.

Chicago

Kauffmann, Stanley. "6 from La Mama." *New York Times*, 13 April 1966, 36.

Pasolli, Robert. "Theatre." *Nation*, 4 April 1966, 402–6.

La Turista

Hardwick, Elizabeth. "Introduction." In *La Turista*. New York: Bobbs-Merrill, 1968.

The Unseen Hand

Brustein, Robert. "Sam Shepard's America." *New Republic*, 21 April 1973, 23.

Sharman, Jim. "It'll Get You in the End." *Plays and Players* (May 1973): xiii–xv.

Operation Sidewinder

Barnes, Clive. "Stage: Lizard vs. Snake." *New York Times*, 13 March 1970, 33.

Gill, Brendan. "Getting On with the Story." *New Yorker*, 21 March 1970, 115–16.

Kerr, Walter. "'I Am! I Am!' He Cries—But Am He?" *New York Times*, 22 March 1970, sec. 2, p. 1.

Kroll, Jack. "Desert Apocalypse." *Newsweek*, 23 March 1970, 69.

Zolotow, Sam. "Black Students Block Yale Play." *New York Times*, 27 December 1968, 38.

Mad Dog Blues

Gussow, Mel. "Stage: 'Mad Dog Blues.'" *New York Times*, 9 March 1971, 25.

Stambolian, George. "Shepard's *Mad Dog Blues*: A Trip through Popular Culture." *Journal of Popular Culture* 7 (Spring 1974): 776–86.

Cowboy Mouth

Ansorge, Peter. "Cowboy Mouth / Little Ocean." *Plays and Players* (May 1974): 45.

The Tooth of Crime

Barnes, Clive. "Theater: Shepard's 'Tooth of Crime.'" *New York Times*, 8 March 1973, 34.

Clurman, Harold. "Theatre." *Nation*, 26 March 1973, 410–12.

Cushman, Robert. "The Tooth of Crime." *Plays and Players* (September 1972): 49–50.

Feingold, Michael. "Biting Shepard." *Village Voice*, 16 November 1972, 75.

Kerr, Walter. "The Audience Helped Write the Play." *New York Times*, 18 March 1973, D3.

Kroll, Jack. "American Pie." *Newsweek*, 27 November 1972, 77–78.

Lahr, John. "The Tooth of Crime." *Village Voice*, 8 March 1973, 55.

Novick, Julius. "Frank Langella as Aging Rock Star." *New York Times*, 19 November 1972, 77.

Oliver, Edith. "Fractured Tooth." *New Yorker*, 17 March 1973, 92, 94.

Wardle, Irving. "Return of Theatrical Fireball." *Times* (London), 6 June 1974, 9.

Wardle, Irving. "The Tooth of Crime." *Times* (London), 18 July 1972, 11.

Blue Bitch

Washburn, Martin. "Cosmic Knockouts and a Mean Mama." *Village Voice*, 25 January 1973, 69.

Geography of a Horse Dreamer

Clurman, Harold. "Theatre." *Nation*, 10 January 1976, 27.

Gussow, Mel. "Stage: *Horse Dreamer*." *New York Times*, 13 December 1975, 21.

Lahr, John. "Geography of a Horse Dreamer." *Plays and Players* (April 1974): 46–47.

Wetzsteon, Ross. "Looking a Gift Horse Dreamer in the Mouth." *Village Voice*, 5 January 1976, 71.

Action and *Killer's Head*

Barnes, Clive. "Theater: 2 by Shepard." *New York Times*, 17 April 1975, 54.

Clurman, Harold. "Theatre." *Nation*, 3 May 1975, 542.

Coveney, Michael. "Action." *Plays and Players* (November 1974): 29.

Feingold, Michael. "Everything's So Shocking Inside." *Village Voice*, 21 April 1975, 87.

Lahr, John. "Action." *Village Voice*, 31 October 1974, 90.

Oliver, Edith. "Off Broadway." *New Yorker*, 5 May 1975, 81.

Wardle, Irving. "Futile Stamp in the Animal Pit." *Times* (London), 18 September 1974, 14.

Weiner, Bernard. "Sam Shepard's Powerful Drama on Confusion." *San Francisco Chronicle*, 6 May 1975, 40.

Angel City

Barnes, Clive. "Unexplainable." *New York Times*, 8 March 1977, 25.

Feingold, Michael. "Sam Shepard, Part-Time Shaman." *Village Voice*, 4 April 1977, 72, 75.

Fennell, Patrick J. "Angel City." *Educational Theatre Journal* 29 (March 1977): 112–13.

Weiner, Bernard. "Sam Shepard's 'Angel City.'" *San Francisco Chronicle*, 5 July 1976, 35.

Suicide in B-Flat

Addiego, Walter V. "Portrait of the Artist as a Dead Man." *San Francisco Examiner*, 7 August 1979, 18.

Feingold, Michael. "Kleist and Shepard Flirt with Death." *Village Voice*, 15 November 1976, 113.

Gussow, Mel. "Shepard's 'Suicide in B-Flat' Presented by Yale Repertory." *New York Times*, 25 October 1976, 42.

Kerr, Walter. "A Play That Binds Us Knot by Knot." *New York Times*, 7 November 1976, sec. 2, p. 3.

Kroll, Jack. "High-Pressure Jazz." *Newsweek*, 8 November 1976, 109.

Weiner, Bernard. "Shepard's 'Suicide' Called 'A Play of Clues.'" *San Francisco Chronicle*, 27 July 1979, 56.

Inacoma

Kleb, William. "Sam Shepard's *Inacoma* at the Magic Theatre." *Theater* 9 (Fall 1977): 59–64.

Weiner, Bernard. "Sam Shepard Goes into a Trance for His New Play." *Sunday San Francisco Examiner* and *Chronicle*, 20 March 1977, 14.

Weiner, Bernard. "Stimulating Magic Theatre Piece." *San Francisco Chronicle*, 22 March 1977.

Curse of the Starving Class

Eder, Richard. "Hunger in America." *New York Times*, 3 March 1978, C4.

Fox, Terry Curtis. "Family Plot." *Village Voice*, 13 March 1978, 77.

Kauffmann, Stanley. "What Price Freedom?" *New Republic*, 8 April 1978, 24–25.

Lahr, John. "Curse of the Starving Class." *Plays and Players* (June 1977): 24–25.

Lahr, John. "A Ghost Town of the Imagination." *Village Voice*, 25 July 1977, 61.

Marowitz, Charles. "Is This Shepard or Saroyan?" *New York Times*, 15 May 1977, sec. 2, p. 3.

Seduced

Eder, Richard. "Theater: 'Seduced,' Reclusive Allegory." *New York Times*, 2 February 1979, C3.

Feingold, Michael. "Seductive." *Village Voice*, 12 February 1979, 93–94.

Gussow, Mel. "Wealthy Eccentric." *New York Times*, 28 April 1978, C3.

Kroll, Jack. "Seduced." *Newsweek*, 8 May 1978, 94.

Buried Child

Clurman, Harold. "Theatre." *Nation*, 2 December 1978, 621–22.

Eder, Richard. "Stage: Sam Shepard Offers 'Buried Child.'" *New York Times*, 7 November 1978, 61.

Eichelbaum, Stanley. "A Discordant Family Drama." *San Francisco Examiner*, 8 July 1978, 9.

Kerr, Walter. "Sam Shepard—What's the Message?" *New York Times*, 10 December 1978, sec. 2, p. 3.

Kroll, Jack. "Bucking Bronco." *Newsweek*, 30 October 1978, 106.

Oliver, Edith. "Off Broadway." *New Yorker*, 6 November 1978, 151–52.

Weiner, Bernard. "Sam Shepard's 'Buried Child'—A Major, Bitter New Play." *San Francisco Chronicle*, 6 August 1978, Datebook section, 19.

Tongues and *Savage / Love*

Blumenthal, Eileen. "Chaikin and Shepard Speak in Tongues." *Village Voice*, 26 November 1979, 103, 109.

Gussow, Mel. "Intimate Monologues That Speak to the Heart." *New York Times*, 9 December 1979, B3, 36.

Gussow, Mel. "Theater: A Shepard Joint Effort." *New York Times*, 16 November 1979, C6.

Kleb, William. "Shepard and Chaikin Speaking in *Tongues.*" *Theater* 10 (February 1977): 66–69.

Weiner, Bernard. "Squirming Permutations of Love." *San Francisco Chronicle*, 8 September 1979, 35.

Jacaranda

Dunning, Jennifer. "A Nagrin Dance to a Shepard Libretto." *New York Times*, 31 May 1979, C13.

True West

Addiego, Walter. "New Shepard Play Mines the West." *San Francisco Examiner*, 17 July 1980, E8.

Brustein, Robert. "Crossed Purposes." *New Republic*, 13 January 1981, 21–23.

Feingold, Michael. "Truthful and Consequential." *Village Voice*, 24 December 1980, 83.

Gussow, Mel. "Brothers and Rivals." *New York Times*, 18 October 1982, C18.

Kerr, Walter. "Of Shepard's Myths and Ibsen's Man." *New York Times*, 11 January 1981, sec. 2, p. 3.

Kleb, William. "Theatre in San Francisco: Sam Shepard's *True West.*" *Theater* 12 (Fall–Winter 1980): 65–71.

Sommer, Sally R. "Buried Grit." *Village Voice*, 27 August 1980, 98.

Stein, Ellin. "A Comic Treat from a Prize-Winning Dramatist." *San Francisco Chronicle*, 14 July 1980, 25.

Superstitions and *The Sad Lament of Pecos Bill*

Ahlgren, Calvin. "Shepard with Music." *San Francisco Chronicle*, 16 December 1984, 57.

Barnes, Clive. "Shepard Best Import since Orange Juice." *New York Post*, 19 September 1983.

Magnani, Peter. "Rural 'Superstitions' with Arty Overtones." *San Francisco Chronicle*, 5 July 1981, Datebook section.

Novick, Julius. "Small Tales." *Village Voice*, 27 September 1983, 95.

Winn, Steven. "'Superstitions': A Sparkling but Slight Show." *San Francisco Chronicle*, 9 July 1981, 48.

Winn, Steven. "A Wry, Soulful Double Bill of Shepard Plays." *San Francisco Chronicle*, 21 April 1984, 32.

Fool for Love

Barnes, Clive. "'Fool for Love'—Powerful Play about a Divided U.S." *New York Post*, 27 May 1983.

Barnes, Clive. "Sam Shepard's a Playwright Ahead of His Times." *New York Post*, 11 June 1983.

DeRose, David J. "Fool for Love." *Theatre Journal* 36 (March 1984): 100–101.

Feingold, Michael. "'Fool''s Gold." *Village Voice*, 7 June 1983, 81–82.

Kerr, Walter. "Where Has Sam Shepard Led His Audience?" *New York Times*, 5 June 1983.

Kleb, William. "Sam Shepard's Free-for-All: *Fool for Love* at the Magic Theatre." *Theater* 14 (Summer–Fall 1983): 77–82.

Rich, Frank. "'Fool for Love,' Sam Shepard's Western." *New York Times*, 27 May 1983, 18.

Weiner, Bernard. "Passion Fuels 'Fool for Love.'" *San Francisco Chronicle*, 11 February 1983, 64.

A Lie of the Mind

Barnes, Clive. "Sam Shepard on Tobacco Road." *New York Post*, 6 December 1985, 26, 35.

Berman, Paul. "Theater." *Nation*, 22 February 1986, 215–18.

Brustein, Robert. "The Shepard Enigma." *New Republic*, 27 January 1986, 25–28.

DeRose, David. "Slouching towards Broadway: Shepard's *A Lie of the Mind*." *Theater* 17 (Spring 1986): 69–74.

Feingold, Michael. "America Screened." *Village Voice*, 17 December 1985, 117–18.

Freedman, Samuel G. "Sam Shepard's Mythic Vision of the Family." *New York Times*, 1 December 1985, sec. 2, p. 1.

Gussow, Mel. "Sam Shepard Revisits the American Heartland." *New York Times*, 15 December 1985, H3, H7.

Rich, Frank. "Theater: 'A Lie of the Mind,' by Sam Shepard." *New York Times*, 6 December 1985, C3.

The War in Heaven

Feingold, Michael. "Angels Weeping." *Village Voice*, 2 April 1991, 85.

Weiner, Bernard. "Curtain Calls." *San Francisco Chronicle*, 19 February 1986.

States of Shock

Feingold, Michael. "Savage Tongues." *Village Voice*, 28 May 1991, 99.

Rich, Frank. "Sam Shepard Returns, on War and Machismo." *New York Times*, 17 May 1991, C1, C7.

Richard, David. "American Nightmare in a Family Restaurant." *New York Times*, 26 May 1991, H5, H20.

Index

The Author

David J. DeRose is Director of Undergraduate Theater Studies at Yale University and an assistant professor of English and Theater Studies. He holds a Ph.D. in Dramatic Art from the University of California at Berkeley. His essays on Sam Shepard have appeared in *Theater*, *American Theatre*, and *Theatre Journal*. He recently served as a literary advisor to the first Portuguese translation and production of *Fool for Love* at the Teatro Aberto in Lisbon. Professor DeRose is the author of several essays on drama from the Vietnam War era and is a contributing editor of *Vietnam Generation*. He is currently at work on a book-length study of drama from the Vietnam War era entitled *Stages in the War: American Drama and the Vietnam Generation*.

The Editor

Frank Day is a professor of English at Clemson University. He is the author of *Sir William Empson: An Annotated Bibliography* and *Arthur Koestler: A Guide to Research.* He was a Fulbright Lecturer in American Literature in Romania (1980–81) and in Bangladesh (1986–87).